Heidegger's Estrangements

Gerald L. Bruns

Heidegger's Estrangements

Language, Truth, and Poetry

in the Later Writings

YALE UNIVERSITY PRESS New Haven and London

The poems by Dan Pagis from
Points of Departure, copyright © 1981,
are used by permission of
The Jewish Publication Society of America.

Set in Baskerville type by Tseng Information Systems, Inc.
Printed in the United States of America by
Thomson-Shore, Inc., Dexter, Michigan.

Library of Congress Cataloging-in-Publication Data
Bruns, Gerald L.
    Heidegger's estrangements : language, truth, and
poetry in the later writings / Gerald L. Bruns.
        p.   cm.
        Includes index.
        ISBN 0–300–04420–8 (alk. paper)
        1. Heidegger, Martin, 1889–1976.   2. Languages—
Philosophy—History—20th   century.   3. Poetics—History
—20th century.   I. Title.
B3279.H49B75 1989
121'.68—dc 19   88–26148
                                                                    CIP

The paper in this book meets the guidelines for permanence and
durability of the Committee on Production Guidelines for Book
Longevity of the Council on Library Resources.

10 9 8 7 6 5 4 3 2 1

For Sandy Budick

To conceive what is self-evident is a task of peculiar difficulty. It is a matter of presenting what is evasive because it is constantly behind one. The behind-the-back experience of such an evasion is the source of the intrinsic uneasiness of philosophical knowledge. Evasion and nonappearance in themselves always have the greater obtrusiveness and conspicuousness, as opposed to the dependable existence of what one is accustomed to. For the philosopher, however, such an evasion has a special structure. It is a withdrawal into what is self-evident, a perplexity which is continually being renewed, which is named by one word, problem, *and which is taken over from the dialectical situation of conflict. The great fundamental questions of philosophy all have this structure: they do not allow themselves to be held at bay in a way which makes possible an unequivocal answer to them. They seem to evade the grasp of our concepts and nevertheless continue to attract in their evasiveness. To be attracted by something which retracts itself constitutes the basic movement of the philosophical interest. This attraction-retraction calls into question the conceptuality in terms of which one inquires. We can indeed say: the philosophical problem is a question which one does not know how to "raise."*

—Hans-Georg Gadamer

Contents

Abbreviations

References to Heidegger's works are cited in the text, where the first number in parentheses refers to the German text, the second to the English translation.

AD *Aus der Erfahrung des Denkens, 1910–1976* (*Gesamtausgabe*, vol. 13). Frankfurt: Klostermann, 1983. The title section, "Aus der Erfahrung des Denkens" (1947), has been translated as "The Thinker as Poet" by Albert Hofstadter, *Poetry, Language, Thought* (New York: Harper & Row, 1971), 1–14.

ED *Erläuterungen zu Hölderlins Dichtung.* Frankfurt: Klostermann, 1951 (3d ed., 1963). Contains "Hölderlin und das Wesen der Dichtung," 31–46, and "Heimkunft / An die Verwandten," 9–30. "Hölderlin and the Essence of Poetry" and "Remembrance of the Poet," trans. Douglas Scott, *Existence and Being* (Chicago: Henry Regnery, 1949), 233–91.

EM *Einführung in die Metaphysik.* Tübingen: Max Niemeyer, 1953 (3d ed., 1966). *Introduction to Metaphysics*, trans. Ralph Manheim (Garden City, N.Y.: Doubleday, 1961).

G *Gelassenheit.* Pfullingen: Günther Neske, 1959 (8th ed., 1985) *Discourse on Thinking*, trans. John M. Anderson and E. Hans Freund (New York: Harper & Row, 1966).

ID *Identität und Differenz.* Pfullingen: Günther Neske, 1957. (7th ed., 1982). *Identity and Difference*, trans. Joan Stambaugh (New York: Harper & Row, 1969).

Hw *Holzwege.* Frankfurt: Klostermann, 1950 (*Gesamtausgabe*, vol. 1). Contains the following:

> "Der Ursprung des Kunstwerkes," 7–68. "The Origin of the Work of Art," *Poetry, Language, Thought*, 15–87.

> "Nietzsches Wort, 'Gott ist tot,'" 193–247. "The Word of Nietzsche: 'God is Dead,'" trans. William Lovitt. *The Question Concerning Technology and Other Essays* (New York: Harper & Row, 1977), 53–112.

"Wozu Dichter?," 248–95. "What Are Poets For?" *Poetry, Language, Thought*, 91–142.

"Der Spruch des Anaximander," 296–343. "The Anaximander Fragment," trans. David Farrell Krell and Frank A. Capuzzi. *Early Greek Thinking* (New York: Harper & Row, 1975), 13–58.

NI   *Nietzsche I*. Pfullingen: Günther Neske, 1961. *Nietzsche*, trans. David Farrell Krell (New York: Harper & Row, 1979). Vol. 1: *The Will to Power as Art*.

SD   *Zur Sache des Denkens*. Tübingen: Max Niemeyer, 1969. Contains "Das Ende der Philosophie und die Aufgabe des Denkens," 61–80. "The End of Philosophy and the Task of Thinking," trans. Joan Stambaugh, *On Time and Being* (New York: Harper & Row, 1969), 55–73.

SZ   *Sein und Zeit*. Tübingen: Max Niemeyer, 1984 (15th ed.). *Being and Time*, trans. John Macquarrie and Edward Robinson (New York: Harper & Row, 1962).

TK   *Die Technik und die Kehre*. Pfullingen: Günther Neske, 1962. "The Turning," *The Question Concerning Technology*, 36–49.

US   *Unterwegs zur Sprache*. Pfullingen: Günther Neske, 1959 (7th ed., 1982). Contains the following:

"Die Sprache," 11–33. "Language," *Poetry, Language, Thought*, 189–210.

"Die Sprache im Gedicht," 37–82. "Language in the Poem: A Discussion on Georg Trakl's Poetic Work," trans. Peter D. Hertz, *On the Way to Language* (New York: Harper & Row, 1971), 159–98.

"Aus Einem Gespräch von der Sprache," 85–155. "A Dialogue on Language," *On the Way to Language*, 1–54.

"Das Wesen der Sprache," 159–216. "The Nature of Language," *On the Way to Language*, 57–108.

"Das Wort," 219–38. "Words," *On the Way to Language*, 139–56.

"Der Weg zur Sprache," 241–68. "The Way to Language," *On the Way to Language*, 111–36.

VA   *Vorträge und Aufsätze*. Pfullingen: Günther Neske, 1954 (4th ed., 1978). Contains the following:

"'. . . dichterisch wohnet der Mensch . . . ,'" 181–98.

"'. . . Poetically Man Dwells,'" *Poetry, Language, Thought*, 213–29.

"Die Frage nach der Technik," 9–40. "The Question Concerning Technology," *The Question Concerning Technology and Other Essays*, 3–35.

"Bauen Wohnen Denken," 139–56. "Building Dwelling Thinking," *Poetry, Language, Thought*, 145–61.

"Das Ding," 157–80. "The Thing," *Poetry, Language, Thought*, 165–86.

"Logos (Heraklit, Fragment 50)," 199–221. "Logos (Heraclitus, Fragment 50)," *Early Greek Thinking*, 59–78.

"Aletheia (Heraklit, Fragment 16)," 249–74. "Aletheia (Heraclitus, Fragment 16), *Early Greek Thinking*, 102–24.

WD *Was heisst Denken?* Tübingen: Max Niemeyer, 1961 (4th ed., 1984). *What is Called Thinking?*, trans. J. Glenn Gray (New York: Harper & Row, 1968).

Wm *Wegmarken.* Frankfurt: Klostermann, 1967 (*Gesamtausgabe*, vol. 9). Contains the following:

"Was ist Metaphysik?" 1–20. "What is Metaphysics?" trans. David Farrell Krell, *Martin Heidegger: Basic Writings*, ed. David Farrell Krell (New York: Harper & Row, 1977), 95–112.

"Vom Wesen der Wahrheit," 73–98. "The Essence of Truth," trans. John Sallis, *Basic Writings*, 117–41.

"Brief über den 'Humanismus,'" 145–94. "Letter on Humanism," trans. Frank Capuzzi and J. Glenn Gray, *Basic Writings*, 189–242.

Preface

From the Orphic
to the Hermetic
with Heidegger

*I am rather of the opinion, that the more
incommensurable, and the more
   incomprehensible
to the understanding, a poetic production is,
   so much
the better it is.*
—Goethe

. . . pushpin is as good as poetry
—Jeremy Bentham

This is a book about the relation of language and poetry in Martin Heidegger's later writings. Or, more exactly, it is about the way in which the space between poetry and language is mediated, or more accurately held open, or breached, by Heidegger's strange notion of truth as *a-lētheia*, where *a-lētheia* is no longer simply the old Greek word for unconcealment or disclosure (*alētheia*) but is also a complex pun that preserves the darkness or otherness of truth, its strangeness or reserve, its self-refusal, its "un-truth." In this book I try to follow the later Heidegger's attempt to speak about this unspeakable subject, and so the book is in part about his own darkness or strangeness— his puns, for example, which are not so funny as Joyce's but just as crucial to the impossible task of writing darkly, hermetically, say in the manner of Heraclitus or Mallarmé. This book is about the way poetry and language belong to this unspeakability, that is, it is about their archaic darkness or strangeness, their *dichten*, their resistance to discourse, their refusal of clarification and assimilation into frameworks of meaning or structural description. Of course, my subject thus puts me in the awkward position of not being able to say, exactly, what this book is about, or what its point is. A new theory of language, for example, or of poetry (or of anything at all), is not going to emerge from it. So it's a devil of a book to try to justify in advance. This is doubly so because I am compelled to write this book out of two long-standing persuasions: the first is that most (I won't say all) philosophers are so stewed in their prejudices concerning poetry that they have pretty much closed themselves off to what the later Heidegger is about—frequently they don't even have the general drift; and the second is that literary critics and theorists (I will say all) have simply exempted themselves from the study of the later Heidegger, about whom they entertain the most preposterous ideas. So it will not appear to many, if any, that I have actually written a book on Heidegger.

Let me try to address these problems with a brief narrative in which *Estrangements* appears as a sort of dialectical character.

The subtitle of the book, "Language, Truth, and Poetry in the Later Writings," contains two allusions. The more obvious one is to A. J. Ayer's great book *Language, Truth, and Logic* (1936). When I first began reading poetry—as an undergraduate at Marquette University in the fifties—this was the book against which one naturally defined oneself: the (so-called) antipoetry book—the book that said, or rather made people say (or fear) that poetry had nothing to do with knowledge, that it was empty talk charged with beautiful feelings. The pro-poetry book at that time was Jacques Maritain's *Creative Intuition in Art and Poetry* (1955), which one supplemented with readings from Eliseo Vivas, Susanne Langer, and Philip Wheelwright. This was the time when people thought the New Criticism was not just a method of close reading but an argument, or perhaps only a considerable anxiety, about the problem of poetic knowledge. A book that made you think so was one like *The Unmediated Vision* (1954) by the young tyro, Geoffrey Hartman.

The more personal allusion in my title is to a lecture given by a teacher of mine at Marquette, Victor Hamm, a Dryden scholar who did things like translate Roman Ingarden.[1] It was Ingarden who asked about the mode of existence of the literary work of art, and who said that the work makes its appearance as so many strata, the first of which is language. "But do we know what language is?" Victor Hamm would ask. Hamm was contemptuous of the "psychologism" of twentieth-century criticism and particularly about its habit of converting all questions of poetic language into talk about sensible experience. He objected even to Ingarden's reduction of language to the "sound and look" of words. From Dryden, he said, you will learn that poetry is more discourse than image. Once, inspired by sherry, he improvised a theory of Iconoclastic Criticism that would smash the Idols of the

Theatre: viz., visual immediacy, undifferentiated sensation, undissoci-
ated sensibility, verbal imagery, R. P. Blackmur, and (pace Father Ong)
"metaphor as twinned vision."[2] Poetic language is not the language
of imagery. I remember later as a Ph.D. student at Virginia reading Northrop Frye's *Anatomy of Criticism* through Hamm's eyes and
realizing that language had no reality for Frye. I mean that for Frye
words are whatever it is that comes between pictures and music. Language exists only by analogy with sounds and looks. "Literary critics
ought to know what language is," Victor Hamm would say—apropos
of, say, John Crowe Ransom's "Poetry: A Note on Ontology"—"but
they don't." All of this was before there was anything to call "structuralism." French intellectual culture meant Sartre, Marcel, Camus,
Malraux, and the *Phénoménologie de la perception*. Linguistics meant
Bloomfield and the history of English. *Syntactic Structures* had only
just been published. The name Wittgenstein still meant the theory
of pseudostatements ("Whereof we cannot speak, thereof we must
. . ."). Stanley Cavell was only now getting knocked off his horse by
J. L. Austin. *Unterwegs zur Sprache* was shortly to go to press, to the
disappointment of many Heideggerians. In many ways I am talking
about the moment in the history of literary study just prior to the dis-
covery of language, or what now gets loosely and perhaps misleadingly
called "the linguistic turn."[3]

The title of Hamm's lecture was "Language, Truth, and Poetry"
(1960).[4] It was one of the Aquinas Lectures sponsored annually by the
department of philosophy and the Marquette Aristotelian Society, and
it says something about the openness of that department that it would
invite an English professor to deliver the year's most festive philosophical talk. Neoscholasticism in those days had vitality and range.
Hamm's lecture was about how to raise the question of the truth of
poetry in an intellectual culture defined by the extremes of scientific
reasoning and "magical thinking," which was Hamm's way of summarizing the idea "that man, in virtue of his mythopoeic verbal imagination, actually *makes* the reality which he sees and feels" (23). Is there a
tertium quid between (or beyond) positivism and myth? Hamm looked
to phenomenology and Ingarden, but for me the best part of his lecture was about Cassirer's *Philosophy of Symbolic Forms*, which those of
us who scorned Aquinas (and therefore Aristotle on one side and
Maritain on the other) were passionately reading. Cassirer's construc-
tivism mediated positivism and magic for me: "Not only science, but
language, myth, art and religion as well, provide the building stones
from which the world of 'reality' is constructed for us, as well as that

of the human spirit, in sum the World-of-the-I."[5] Hamm preferred phenomenology to critical idealism, which he said was "still magic," but because of Hamm "philosophy of language" will always mean Cassirer for me, and structuralism and semiotics will always sound like a rewriting of *The Philosophy of Symbolic Forms*, one that updates its linguistics from von Humboldt to Saussure and Jakobson but which still holds fast (while pretending to have gone beyond idealism and realism) to its Kantian foundations ("How is signification, or the speaking of a language, possible?").

It was Victor Hamm who put me onto Heidegger. Not because Heidegger was anything to him; on the contrary, he referred to Heidegger as the most woebegone of "magical thinkers." (In fact Hamm had tried to visit Heidegger in 1952 but had been turned away.) Hamm mentioned to me one day (probably in 1959) *Existence and Being*, the little collection of translations that included "Hölderlin and the Essence of Poetry." For me, this essay is where Heidegger will always be found (in contrast to the elusive figure that I try to study in this book), and my misfortune was that I first studied it with *The Philosophy of Symbolic Forms* too much in my head. My thought was that here was something like what Cassirer was getting at—only whereas poetry had no particular meaning for Cassirer (it was just another "art"), Heidegger was plainly a philosopher who took it seriously (I believe now that no philosopher since Plato has taken poetry so seriously as Heidegger has). Heidegger's idea was certainly "magical" enough: the poet names all things, but such naming doesn't merely designate what is already there, rather it brings things into appearance, establishes them for the first time as being what they are. As Cassirer had got rid of the copy-theory of knowledge, so Heidegger had got rid of the copy-theory of poetry. Poetry is not about reality; it is what gives us reality. Moreover, it gives us *to* reality, situates us in it, historicizes us. It was clear that Heidegger wasn't just talking about "image-worlds" of the spirit when he talked about the Being of beings. The world isn't just what we see and feel as a project of consciousness; it is a dwelling place. Here poetry was worldmaking in its strongest sense.

The book that eventually got produced, in which I tried to answer Victor Hamm's claim on me ("But do we know what language is?"), was *Modern Poetry and the Idea of Language* (1974). Here the old division between magic and positivism survived in a distinction between two categories of poetic speech. I called the first "orphic," after the mythic singer who could summon things into his presence by the power of words; the second I called "hermetic," where poetry speaks only "in order to say nothing" (Blanchot). On the one hand there was the romantic tradition and the proliferation of worldmaking theories; on the other there were things like Flaubert's dream of writing "a book about nothing" and the formalist tradition that culminates (about where we are now) in the idea there there is nothing outside of language conceived as a vast system of differences or as text whose center is everywhere and whose circumference is inaccessible. On the one hand language is seen as an opening in which reality makes its appearance; on the other it is seen as productive of things like *Finnegans Wake* and *The Unnamable*, where the self-interfering nature of discourse implies a profound skepticism.[6] Perhaps in Blanchot one sees the workings of a dialectic (or, anyhow, reversal) that lives through (or lives out) this skepticism.[7]

In *Modern Poetry and the Idea of Language*, however, Heidegger was still mainly the "middle" Heidegger of the Hölderlin essays of the thirties and forties, where *Dichtung* as "the establishment of being by means of the word" is still characterized in terms of the *act* of the poet. Here it still makes some sense to speak of poetry in Kant's language of "constitution of the world." The bad news is that I used Heidegger's later writings only insofar as I could fit them into the poetics of establishment that gets laid out in "Hölderlin and the Essence of Poetry." In this respect I was following what was (and is still) the resolute practice of Heidegger's commentators (those few, at any rate, who actually treat of this subject).[8] And I still think that the Hölderlin essays represent one of Heidegger's deepest insights into the "worldly" nature of poetry. But if one reads the later texts closely, it becomes clear that they have less to do with poetry as the revelation or establishment of Being than with the way poetry is taken up or appropriated by the withdrawal or reserve of language, its strangeness or otherness as Saying (*Sage*), which will not let itself be put into words. I'm convinced that the later Heidegger is closer in spirit to Flaubert, Joyce, and Beckett, to Mallarmé, Kafka, and Blanchot, to Gerard Manley Hopkins and Edmond Jabès (and also to premodern writers like Rabelais and Cervantes, Swift and Sterne, and to postmodern ones like John Ashbery and Thomas Pyncheon) than to Hölderlin—or anyhow to Hölderlin as Heidegger read him in the thirties.[9]

This is not to put Hölderlin aside; rather, it is to figure him differently, taking him (for example) not simply as the primordial namer of beings and of the holy (much less as "the poet of the Germans") but now also as the poet of fragments, of the song that breaks off when language suddenly takes back its word and leaves the poet exposed to darkness and silence.[10] My thought is that we ought to begin reading Heidegger's Hölderlin-interpretation in the light of the later writings on language and poetry instead of trying to fit these later texts into the Hölderlin-interpretation. For the later Heidegger, it is no longer enough to characterize poetic speech (if that is what *Dichten* is) simply in terms of the poet's originary power of disclosure, of maintaining things in being, of the grounding, lighting, or opening up of a world; *Dichten* has now to be understood as the way of entering into the mode of being of *Gelassenheit*, the letting-go of things. As I shall show, *Dichten* is earthly as well as worldly, that is, it opens, not just a world, but paths for *Denken* (too many paths, leaving *Denken* exposed to darkness and ambiguity, wandering in forests rather than achieving breakthroughs, establishing boundaries, mastering fields, expanding horizons, planning futures, reconstructing pasts—all the philosophically legitimate projects that normally occupy and justify thinking). Moreover, it is no longer Heidegger's thought that "poetry makes language possible [*die Dichtung selbst ermöglicht erst die Sprache*]" (ED 40/EB 283), as he said in "Hölderlin and the Essence of Poetry"; rather, poetry now has to be understood in terms of the renunciation (*Verzichten*) of linguistic mastery. This means understanding poetry as the *Sichversagen* of the poet, where poetry opens itself—enters into, listens or belongs to— the mystery of language, its otherness, its nonhumanness, its density, its "danger."

My point is that there is a darker aspect of *Dichten* that is not represented in the philosophical literature on Heidegger. In fact it is not too much to say that, granting the arguable exception here and there, the subject of poetry is entirely marginal to the interest that philosophy takes in Heidegger's thinking. Philosophy in both Europe and America is still powerfully under the sway of the positivist theory of poetry as a merely "recreational" use of language, that is, as something completely out of keeping with or beneath the seriousness of philosophical inquiry.[11] The older German commentators like Gadamer and Pöggeler at least read Hölderlin, Rilke, and (above all) Paul Celan, but in the English-speaking world the situation is pathetic.[12] I will always have in my head, as a symptom of this pathos, J. Glenn Gray's remark, in an essay on poets and thinkers in Heidegger, that a relation between poetry and thinking is all very well but it would be much better all around if Heidegger had some of Plato's "distrust" of the poet.[13] Which is to say that the preoccupation with poetry remains an essential weakness in Heidegger's philosophy, and has even corrupted his language. When the subject of poetry does come up in current Heidegger studies it is treated only very schematically, without much attention to the full range of what Heidegger has to say in his later writings, and without anything like a reflective interest in the subject itself. David White's *Heidegger and the Language of Poetry* (1978) is the only study by a philosopher that appears to address the question of poetry at any length, but White's concern is to translate Heidegger into the language of consecutive argument, or what White calls "the rightness of thinking," which has no place for poetry—in fact it tries to ground itself in the customary manner on a repudiation of poetry. The idea is to turn Heidegger away from poetry back into a true philosopher, to save him from himself. Anyhow White's book is misnamed because he doesn't talk at all about the language of poetry, or about the relation of poetry and language. He reaffirms the positivist idea by reducing poetry once more to its "remedial function" in the age of technology: "if poetizing names what is out of tune in being, then being must always be out of tune in some respect in order to sustain the reality of poetizing. If being is not out of tune, then poetizing would cease to exist as a separate mode of linguistic activity."[14] As if poetry were only an accident in the history of Being.

A more typical example is Joseph Kockelmans's *On the Truth of Being: Reflections on Heidegger's Later Philosophy* (1984), which is a comprehensive exposition of the later Heidegger that devotes, however, fewer than a dozen pages (out of more than three hundred) to *Dichten*—and then (in my view) just gets Heidegger wrong. "The basic characteristic of poetizing," Kockelmans says, "consists in bringing Being into words in a truly originating manner; that constitutes the 'creative' element in poetizing, which envisions and institutes a 'new' world, i.e., a world with new options and possibilities. In this case, the human response thus tries to bring into words as carefully as possible the 'dictation' of Being itself."[15] I think that the picture of Being "dictating" to the poet is just plain silly. At all events nowhere in the later Heidegger does Being "speak." It is language that speaks (*Die Sprache spricht*), but how poetry (or thinking, for that matter) enters into this speaking is not a subject that has been taken up in any significant or interesting way. As if there were nothing there for philosophy to think about.[16]

A cautionary tale that all philosophers should bear in mind is Jorge Luis Borges's wonderful story, "Averroes' Search," where Averroes struggles with all his genius to make sense of Aristotle's *Poetics*, but can't imagine what tragedy or comedy could be, never having had the experience of such things:

> Few things more beautiful and more pathetic are recorded in history than this Arab physician's dedication to the thoughts of a man separated from him by fourteen centuries; to the intrinsic difficulties we should add that Averroes, ignorant of Syriac and Greek, was working with the translation of a translation. The night before, two doubtful words had halted him at the beginning of the *Poetics*. These words were *tragedy* and *comedy*. He had encountered them years before in the third book of the *Rhetoric*; no one in the whole world of Islam could conjecture what they meant. In vain he had exhausted the pages of Alexander of Aphrodisia, in vain he had compared the versions of the Nestorian Hunain ibn-Ishaq and of Abu-Bashar Mata. These two arcane words pullulated throughout the text of the *Poetics*; it was impossible to elude them.[17]

I read this story as a parable of the current state of Heidegger studies.

The pages that follow emphasize *Dichten* as estrangement, where poetry withdraws from *logos*, is more *phūsis* than *logos*—is, following Heraclitus, "that which loves to hide" (*phūsis krūptesthai philei* [Fr. 123]), as against that which gathers beings into a unity and acts as a foundation. Vincent Vycinas says: "With *logos* as Being and Ground, Heidegger shows again that *logos*, the ultimate language, is the ground which is given to us by poetry."[18] This seems to me to miss the whole of what the later Heidegger is after. So by contrast I emphasize Heidegger's line: "All by itself the logos does not make language" (EM 132/145). As I read the later Heidegger, what comes to matter is no longer (or not just) the relation of poet and world or of poetry and Being but rather the relation of poetry with language. So I emphasize *Dichten* as the letting-go of language, as the experience of being utterly bereft of language, as that which is exposed to the uncanny (*Unheimlich*), overwhelmed and transformed by it, as that which does not try to repress the double nature of truth as both *alētheia* and refusal or dissembling (*Versagen* and *Verstellen*) but rather brings this doubleness (where "Truth, in its nature, is un-truth" [Hw 43/54]) into the open (and, uncannily, disappears into it). It seems to me a careless misunderstanding to speak of *Sage* simply as the "Saying of Being," as if Saying belonged unproblematically to the category of revelation. *Sage* is also *Versagen*. We need to loosen up (or step back) a little and reconsider our fixation on the idea of revelation.[19] Instead of revelation, one should speak of the withdrawal of Being, the otherness of *a-lētheia*, the darkness of poetry and thinking, and one should attend to what Heidegger says about the "rift" (*Riss*) within language, its *retrait* or self-refusal, its uncontainability within any conceptual framework, its parodistic relation to the discourse of propositions, its weakness for the pun, its resistance to sense. In speaking of Saying as *Ereignis*, the so-called "event of appropriation" that appears to have turned aside the question of Being for Heidegger, one must remain open and attentive to the way in which *Ereignis* (as *Er-eignis*) is heterogeneous and dialogical, more pun than concept. As we shall see, the pun—the dark word—is crucial to Heidegger's thinking, more word than term. So far from being trivial, it is as close as we can get to language.[20]

In *Modern Poetry and the Idea of Language* I looked "Toward a Dialectic of Orphic and Hermetic Poetries." I didn't realize then how powerfully this dialectic was already at work in "Der Ursprung des Kunstwerkes" (1934–35), with its "earthly" picture of the work of art as self-standing and "cutting all ties to human beings." In chapter one I take the opportunity to correct my earlier, "orphic" reading of this essay, whose emphasis on the work's work of estrangement seems to me now the window onto the later Heidegger of *Unterwegs zur Sprache*, where the dialectic of the orphic and the hermetic is most fully at play.[21] Nor (perhaps more important) did I realize years ago what I have since learned from Gadamer, that dialectic is never ultimately constructive and progressive, never merely an *overcoming* of what exists elsewise or has gone before, but is rather an open-ended movement of thinking that plays endlessly back and forth between *aporia* and *euporia*, bewilderment and insight. It seems to me that there is a kinship here between Gadamer and Paul de Man that has never been explored.[22] At all events I had once thought it enough to say that it is not possible to develop a single coherent theory of poetry but that there must always be two theories; one is not enough for something so unpredictable and uncontainable as poetry. Orpheus must always be accompanied by Hermes. But now it seems to me that one does not simply "have" theories of poetry as if they were stable, insulated, alternative, complementary descriptions that one can pick up or put down as one pleases; rather, the two theories are nothing but trouble to one another, always undoing one another, always threatening to exchange places and roles and to leave one (as poetry itself frequently does) in the dark. I had figured Heidegger as a theorist of worldmaking, as the last romantic who says, "'Poetically Man Dwells.'" I can still figure him roughly this way, if no longer in terms of the language of foundations and "constitution of reality," that is, according to the metaphor of world-*poiēsis* (as if, as Wallace Stevens would have it, the making of the poem were the making of the world). But now one must also cope with the powerfully hermetic character of the later Heidegger, whose logic, in Otto Pöggeler's word, is a "Sigetics," and for whom the paradigmatic text is accordingly the Heraclitean fragment whose words philology no longer knows how to explicate.[23] Here Orpheus turns into a Hermes, a trickster of the between who always takes you away from yourself, the bringer of truth who is also the thief of reason.

One can accept the idea that it is not possible to construct from Heidegger's texts a systematic, self-supporting, portable, and technically applicable theory of poetry; it is unsettling to realize that a "reading" of these later texts may not be critically productive in the traditional and legitimizing sense of emancipating us from darkness and perplexity. It cannot be said of the later Heidegger that he opens a path free of mystification. "I work," Heidegger once said, quoting Cezanne, "with few results, and too far removed from what is generally intelligible."[24] "Language speaks as the peal of stillness," he says. And he adds: "The peal of stillness is not anything human" (US 30/207). What is it, then, and why doesn't Heidegger say? Is this simply the rejection of an unself-critical humanism, or is it a rejection of social reality in favor of an aestheticism without form and beauty, or a dark theology with a manipulative and evasive god, or a Gnosticism from which no traveler returns?[25] One can understand why philosophers like Paul Ricoeur "regret" and "deplore" the later Heidegger. But then one suspects that what they deplore is the darker side of philosophy where poetry is no longer marginal—no longer the peaceful woodnotes that give us welcome respite from thoughts of deep structure—but rather that which exposes philosophy to what it cannot contain within its powers of description and explanation.[26] One wonders what a nonallergic relation of poetry and philosophy would look like. Heidegger's idea seems to be that such a relation would require philosophy to follow the path —the way of *Gelassenheit*—opened up by poetry. This doesn't mean, as people like Ricoeur fear, that philosophy must turn into poetry; it is rather that philosophy must enter into what Heidegger calls the "rift" of poetry and thinking that sets both apart, "each held in its own darkness" (US 196/90). From the standpoint of poetry, the question of thinking is not *Was heisst Denken?* but *Wozu Denker?* To put it as simply as one can: poetry *exposes* thinking to language, to its strangeness or otherness, its refusal to be contained within categories and proposi-

tions, its irreducibility to sameness and identity, its resistance to sense
—in short, its denial of our efforts to speak it. Philosophy by contrast
is thinking that closes itself off to the experience with language, turns
itself over to logic, tries to protect itself by bringing language under
the control of the proposition. Poetry, of course, knows no such control; poetry is the letting-go of language.

People naturally want to be told the "cash value" of the later Heidegger for the study of literature or the doing of philosophy. What
return do we get for reading him? Literary people want to know
whether Heidegger can take us "beyond" wherever we are now. In
a world of New Historicisms and New Pragmatisms, is he competi-
tive? On this score the judgment has long since been handed down,
summarily releasing critics and theorists from the task of studying the
later Heidegger. All the smart journals of criticism and theory brush
him aside with a superior gesture.[27] Philosophers meanwhile want to
know the argument with respect to what remains philosophically at
stake (or "viable") in the later Heidegger. Where does this Heidegger
situate us with respect to the history of philosophy and its constitutive
problems? If he has abandoned this history, or claims to have ended
it, it remains true that such a claim makes sense only with respect to
what is being abandoned: the rules of philosophical argumentation,
as well as certain classical formulations of philosophical questions. On
a scale of radicality with respect to logic or metaphysics, knowledge or
belief, ethics or technology, philosophy of mind or of science, where
does Heidegger stand in comparison with his competitors in the field?
("Close thy Heidegger! Open thy Foucault!")

In view of this disciplinary momentum toward higher and more
technically advanced levels of analytical action, my approach to Heidegger is apt to seem a little too "naive," or "rhetorical," especially
since my first goal is just to discover as well as I can, under the circum-
stances, what these later texts are about, and why they are written so
strangely.[28] I'm persuaded that they have not been studied, certainly
not by people in literary criticism, who get things terribly muddled,
and who appear to believe many things about the later Heidegger
which are simply not true.[29] People seem to speak of Heidegger only
to arouse their followers against him. Indeed, when one hears, for
example (from Paul de Man, of all people), that "Heidegger himself
was very suspicious about metaphor, because his theory of language
does not allow for the play of differences and the play of misleading
elements that are involved in the pattern of metaphor. I think he sees
unmediated revelations in language"—one realizes that the misunder-

standing is global and very likely incorrigible.[30] To speak of revelation is to get the later Heidegger exactly backwards. Certainly we do not know what Heidegger's "theory of language" is (if anything). And it's doubtful that we will rest easy with his notion of poetry, since it cannot be accommodated anywhere within current critical theory, which remains housed securely in the condominium of textual analysis, even when it enlarges this analysis to the widest possible outlook (say the level of "culture studies").

On both sides, among philosophers as well as critics, the study of Heidegger seems to have been spooked by the slogan, "overcoming metaphysics." In my introduction I try to shift the question of reading Heidegger a step back from the either/or of philosophical argumentation versus critique of metaphysics, if only to allow a little space in which to let Heidegger be, strange as he is. What is entailed in the understanding of Heidegger? A good deal more, it turns out, than can be contained in simply reading him either for or against himself.

My "readings" originated as six public lectures, presented as the Ward-Phillips Lectures at the University of Notre Dame in February and March of 1987. These now have been substantially revised (with the help of critical comments from a number of people), but not so as to repress their public form or to make them appear as closet studies. My idea has always been that the reading of any text is not something that goes on inside one's head—it is not the "processing" of a text, not the "response" of a solitary subject—but that it is a social practice. I take the word "social," however, to mean something other than the "rule-governed" dispositions of an interpretive or "intersubjective" community. Making sense of a text always means making sense to other people, and this means making sense of oneself as well as clarifying what one reads. Moreover, I take this matter of clarification very seriously. I'm sensitive to the complaint (widely and endlessly repeated) against the "epigones" of Heidegger who take over his idiom and who brush the ideal of clarity aside as only so much residue of metaphysics. The form of the public lecture helped me to keep my own voice and to hold to the task of making sense—despite the fact, as I indicate repeatedly in these chapters, that the possibility of making sense is always put in question, indeed turned aside, by Heidegger's "withdrawal," not just from the norms of philosophical reasoning and argumentative language, but from the whole idea of a discourse that can be mastered or made transparent so that its message can be grasped once for all. Heidegger is nothing but trouble to the postal service; he cannot be brought under hermeneutic control.

Needless to say, I don't think of the task of making sense of the later Heidegger on the model of the production and transmission of information. I don't think of clarity as conceptual transparency and the sacrifice of nuance. On the contrary, clarity is more likely to occur in the form of the slow dawning, the glimpse, the momentary insight that darkens at once into bewilderment. I mean that clarity cannot be isolated as a steady state in which things are unearthed, brought to light, and exhibited as in a museum case of clear and distinct ideas. Nor is it a process of enlightenment or emancipation of consciousness from the limits that bind it. It is an episode in a dialectical experience where thinking is more like meditative groping, of finding and losing one's way and doubling back to start over, than it is the steady progress of inferential reasoning. Indeed, what one learns from Heidegger is that every attempt at clarification only draws one further into the darkness. One's categories (orphic or hermetic or whatever) are sure to go to pieces. So it shouldn't be held against me that what I hope to achieve in these readings of the later Heidegger is something a good deal less than the reconstruction of his "theories" of language, truth, and poetry. My readings cope with Heidegger's hermeticism but they do not cure it. Perhaps they cure us of the idea that one can justify the study of the later Heidegger only by demonstrating that he is "useful for literary criticism," or that he represents a way of doing philosophy that, however radical or eccentric, nevertheless shows how the universality of thought is still possible. For the later Heidegger is apt to leave us not knowing exactly where we are or what we are about.

In fact I think of these readings as a way of deferring the end of the story that began when I first got turned onto Heidegger. I do not think of Heidegger as being himself literary or poetic in any interesting way (the way *Finnegans Wake*, for example is just linguistically provocative and endlessly captivating as a text). It is not that the reading of Heidegger's texts requires the "methods" one brings to bear upon literature. But as with the literary text one never stops reading Heidegger once one starts, because there is no terminus, no endpoint, no saying: "Now I've got it." Philosophers brush this sort of thing aside as "unmotivated" or "recreational" (mere "rhetoric"). Philosophers are good at extracting arguments from texts but not much else, which is why texts without arguments put them to sleep. Philosophers can only read in the service of a program or project or schedule of disciplinary problems; philosophy as so many arguments about these problems is what comes *after* reading. My point, however, is that my reading of Heidegger does not just consist in the performance of an exegesis or in giving an account, as in these pages, of Heidegger's texts; rather, reading is more history than performance, that is, it consists of a history (now at least thirty years' worth, with no end in sight) carried along by reversals that need to be worked through reflectively and not brought to a premature or merely logical closure, as if understanding here could ever mean discovering once for all the point, use, method, or universal inherent in Heidegger's texts—as if these texts embodied a "theory" which one would first excavate and then evaluate or justify by putting it to use or into "practice." One reads the later Heidegger, not in order to do something to him or to get something from him, but just because the questions of language, truth, and poetry that he raises (as does no one else) remain endlessly, maddeningly, open. They evade the grasp of our concepts. What Heidegger invites us to do is to inquire into the meaning of these evasions, as if thinking were a matter of living through the breakdown, or say the historicality or finitude, of one's concepts; as if in fact it were the task or call of thinking to evade the concepts that it constructs for itself, or to escape the sense that it itself makes; as if there were always the danger, which philosophy is determined to escape, that thinking will encounter its fate as skepticism.

What happens to thinking when it is exposed to the *Dichte* in *Dichtung* (or in language)? How is it transformed? The possibility that thinking would no longer be able to recognize itself as, or in, philosophy—would no longer know what to call itself—is what incites and renews the quarrel between philosophy and poetry. The lesson from Heidegger is perhaps that this quarrel needs to be kept going, especially in an age when both philosophers and literary critics keep trying to shut it down. If you like, you can identify this age with the "epoch of metaphysics" that begins with Plato. But (as poets have always reminded us) Plato's relation to poetry was far more unstable than the histories of philosophy and criticism would have you believe; it's not clear that he was ever a Platonist. He certainly saw that poetry would always remain part of philosophy's self-definition, the other of its self-sameness, that which is denied as part of its self-assertion. He certainly understood very well the danger of exposure to the *Dichte* in *Dichtung*. But he also understood equally well how to enter into the weakness of language, that is, its darkness or reserve, its self-refusal, its genius for puns and parody, its laughter at the serious and straightforward word.[31]

I think this ancient quarrel needs to be kept going from the side of poetry as well as from the side of philosophy. The point of doing such a thing might well be much the same as keeping open the relation of Orpheus and Hermes on the idea that the thinking and poetry are caught up in the same endless movement, the ongoing give-and-take between sameness and difference, insight and perplexity, homecoming and wandering, philosophy and skepticism. Indeed, on my reading poet and thinker are both inscribed in the Heideggerian figure of the wanderer who has no settled dwelling place but belongs to the open and far from stable region between earth and sky, gods and mortals. It is this truth about itself that thinking must learn from poetry. Poetry (*Dichten*) drives thinking away from philosophy, which wants to stay in place, not so much residing as presiding, instituting, fixing, determining, clarifying, planning for the future (compare Kant's "What is Enlightenment?").[32] Poetry turns thinking away from its quests (as, for example, for the "meaning of Being"), which is why thinking doesn't reside anywhere for long but is always getting away from us. For Heidegger, homecoming is only an episode in wandering; it is not staying but only lingering. In Heidegger's lingo, whatever is stayed seeks nevertheless its own apartness, and this is true of thinking as well as of poetry. There is a rift between poetry and thinking that settles each into its own darkness (US 196/90). So now we confront the darkness into which Heidegger himself has evidently withdrawn, leaving the question of Being behind him for philosophers to formulate. Let the philosophers do their work. Meanwhile, let us try to get the sense of these questions: What is language (*Sage*)? Or truth (*A-lētheia*)? Or poetry (*Dichten*)? Why are they called by these strange, improper names? Where is Heidegger taking us?

In 1985 the John Simon Guggenheim Foundation gave me a fellowship to go to Jerusalem to study midrash. Which I did. I'm very grateful to the foundation, but I apologize for writing a book on Heidegger instead, although one could make an interesting argument, on the model perhaps of John Caputo's study of Heidegger and Meister Eckhart, that Heidegger's notion of *Gelassenheit* captures beautifully the essential wisdom of the tradition of midrash—I mean the combination of openness and strife, freedom and reverence, wordplay and refusal of single-mindedness and control, that characterizes midrashic thinking. I can never repay my debt to the Institute for Advanced Studies at the Hebrew University of Jerusalem for a fellowship and a place to live and work that quite simply altered my life. Professor Aryeh Dvoretzky, then-director of the institute, Dr. Shabtai Gairon, deputy director, Mrs. Bilha Gus and the administrative staff, made me want to stay forever. As the ancient rabbis knew, there is no greater gift than to give a scholar freedom to study—unless it is the friendship of extraordinary people. Leona and Tsvi Toker, Larry and Judy Besserman, Bill and Shirley Daleski, Elizabeth Freund, Shuli Barzilai, Harold Fisch, and especially Sandy and Emily Budick know what my year in Jerusalem meant to me. So do my colleagues (masters and friends) in the institute's research group on "Absence and Negation in Literary Theory"—Stanley Cavell, Geoffrey Hartman, Wolfgang Iser, Shlomith Rimmon-Kenan, Jon Whitman, and Shira Wolosky. I wish Dan Pagis were still alive to see what he helped me write. Jacques Derrida, whose brief stay with our group came exactly at the right moment, made me draw back from what I had written during the year by wondering (doubtfully) whether Heidegger would have been at all happy with what I was saying about him. The wisdom, patience, and good cheer of these people will always fill me with envy. My deepest debt is to Sandy Budick, director of our group, who made this *annus mirabilis* possible. This book is for him. The excitement and intensity, the joy and capacity for astonishment, that this man brings to the intellectual life, are not earthly. I was filled with the greatest pleasure and sense of well-being when I discovered that Sandy Budick is (among so much else) a Dryden scholar, and that the reader for Yale University Press of his first book was Victor Hamm.

I also want to thank Dean Michael Loux and the College of Arts and Letters at the University of Notre Dame for a summer stipend in support of my work. And I am very grateful to Edward Kline and the department of English at Notre Dame for the opportunity to present the substance of this book as the Ward-Phillips Lectures for 1987.

Parts of an earlier version of chapter six were presented at the conference on "Absence and Negation in Literary Theory" at Jerusalem in June 1986. And parts of an earlier version of the conclusion were presented at the annual meeting of the International Association for Philosophy and Literature at the University of Kansas in April 1987.

Heidegger's Estrangements

Introduction
Understanding Heidegger

---

*As I often tell my students, when you take a
word in your mouth, you must realize that you
have not taken up a tool that can be thrown
aside if it won't do the job, but are fixed in a
direction which comes from afar and stretches
beyond you.*
—Hans-Georg Gadamer, *Truth and Method*

The Quarrel Between Philosophy and Poetry

My purpose in what follows will simply be to work through Martin
Heidegger's later writings on language and poetry in order to give as
clear an account as I can of what he has to say, as well as of the way in
which his "saying" has to be enclosed in quotation marks. As Habermas says, "Communication does not belong to the basic vocabulary of
this philosophy."[1] By "work through" I mean roughly, or loosely, what
my discipline calls a close reading that lends special attention to the
language of the dark or recalcitrant text. So what follows is also about
the job of coping with Heidegger's strange language.[2] However, what
I mean by "account" is not so easy to say. What sort of account?

This question entails the large oddity of an English professor trying
to produce a commentary on the most obscure of a notorious philosopher's writings. I guess no one will misunderstand me when I say
that departments of philosophy and of language and literature work
hard to discourage this sort of thing—call it trafficking outside the
normal curriculum and its official canon. Not that anyone should care
if suddenly an English professor begins to go on about Heidegger, but
such talk is not what gets counted either as philosophy or as literary
study. So there is a problem of authority here, that is, a question of
proper discipline, or of the disciplinary norms that govern the university and make its forms of study intelligible in the sense of teachable.
Philosophy fears debasement into rhetoric; poetry fears subjection to
strange gods. One has to be careful not to arouse these fears within

the institutions of philosophy and criticism; and of course on this score Heidegger is of no help at all.

For the study of Heidegger begins with the recognition that there is something extracurricular about him, or say noncurricular. In him one encounters the limits of the school. Certainly this is true of nearly everything, including especially poetry and thinking, but with Heidegger one finds oneself turned out of school, not infrequently as a joke (the *philosophus gloriosus*), but also increasingly as someone politically or theologically sinister. The point hardly bears repeating that not all departments of philosophy make a place for the study of Heidegger. Instead Heidegger turns up as a disagreeable presence in comparative literature departments, which favor French intellectual culture and the philosopher-critics of the early Frankfurt School. For most professional philosophers Heidegger remains the best comic example of the philosophical quack. But there are others for whom the question of Heidegger is just the question of philosophy itself, I mean the question of what counts as philosophy. As we know, this was Heidegger's own self-understanding: he thought of himself as throwing philosophy into question, or getting out from under it.

What is of interest in this to people like me—nonphilosophers, non-comparatists, people who fall through the cracks—is that Heidegger's questioning eventually took shape as a reopening of the ancient quarrel between philosophy and poetry. In Heidegger's lingo it is called "the rift of poetry and thinking." I hold out some hope of understanding what this expression means, or rather where it takes or leaves us. Among normal philosophers it is usually taken, if at all, roughly as follows:

> Is the later Heidegger a thinker, a poet, or some fusion of the two? If he is exclusively or even primarily a poet, then of course his work should not be confronted with the canons of formal logic and the distinctions of classical metaphysics. Heidegger's prodigious output will then demand a critic or, doubtless, critics who are sufficiently imbued with his terminology and various interests to hazard guesses about the meaning of his works. But since the poet qua poet (and Heidegger as an exemplary of such poetry) need not pursue truth or wisdom, or at least truth controlled by standards of "right" thinking, then Heidegger's work may perhaps be justly dismissed as beautiful mystical language rather than as language engaged in the pursuit of truth which should compel assent from every right-thinking mortal lover of wisdom.[3]

On the theory given here understanding the later Heidegger means retrieving him from the poetry into which he has wandered; this means translating him back into the language of "right thinking," that is, consecutive reasoning, where he can still be counted as a philosopher, still the author of *Being and Time* (arguably Heidegger's only strictly philosophical work). Or, alternatively, it means abandoning him to rhapsodes who muck about with poets. And since "the poet qua poet need not pursue truth . . . ."

But reopening the ancient quarrel between philosophy and poetry means reopening the question of poetry's truth; that is, it means stepping back from the old idea that poetry is "beautiful mystical language" but empty talk just the same. The later Heidegger pretty much buries this old cliché about poetry; or at least (one would think) he makes it difficult for philosophers to go on living by it. But it remains unclear whether Heidegger reconnects poetry and truth in a way that we can recognize or that fits our sense of things.

Briefly, for the later Heidegger poetry's truth is no longer a function of its relation to Being or to the world. Truth is no longer any sort of relation; it is an event (*Ereignis*) into which, as I shall later put it, everything disappears: everything (the work of art, world and thing, language, even, if we let go of our usual sense or command of things, ourselves)—everything withdraws or withholds itself, shows its reserve or self-standing (its lack of logical support). Everything is released from our control; nothing is as it was, everything (even Being) is otherwise, no longer speakable (cannot be put into statements). Heidegger's own language is a letting-go that enters into this strangeness or unspeakability where objects turn into events: *Das Ding dingt, Die Sprache spricht.* Heidegger might have said it this way: As the truth of things lies in the event of their *thinging,* or of language in its *languaging,* so the truth of poetry or *Dichtung* lies in its *dichten.*[4] But what is (called *Dichten*? It is to be deeply regretted that Heidegger never gave us a lecture course on this question, but if he had he would at some point along the way have urged us to listen to the word *dichten,* and he would have asked us to hear the pun on the word for dense or impermeable (*dicht*) or thick (*dick*). Probably this would have made us a little embarrassed for him—but as for Joyce or Freud, so for Heidegger: there are no accidents in language. Or, like an old midrashist, he finds matter for thinking in every jot and tittle, every mark or wrinkle of the text. Words are more than terms. Something essential to language (and, indeed, to poetry)—something not said, perhaps not sayable—can be heard in its sounding. It is no accident that Heidegger's reflections on

Hölderlin's poetry are (if we listen) more soundings (*Erläuterungen*) than readings or exegeses (*Auslegungen*). If we ask, *Was heisst Dichten?* one answer lies in its density or impermeability, its earthliness, its resistance to penetration by analysis, its uncontainability within grammar, rhetoric, or poetics—its essential darkness, that is, its *hermetic* character: its otherness. When at the end of the second lecture on "The Nature of Language" Heidegger speaks of the "rift" (*Riss*) of poetry and thinking, he sounds the hermetic theme: "poetry and thinking [*Dichten und Denken*] are in virtue of their nature held apart by a delicate and luminous difference, each in its own darkness [in ihr eigenes Dunkel]" (US 196/90). Whatever this darkness, it belongs to truth as *a-lētheia* as much as the lighting or opening that settles us in a world. Poetry has as much to do with the shadows of *Ereignis* as with the lighting or clearing of beings—and so does thinking, which is more like wandering in the wilderness than reposing comfortably near the fireside. In fact the danger of poetry, or of language, is that it turns thinking into wandering.

Doubtless this sounds rhapsodic to a philosopher's ear. Nevertheless, this is the region in which the following readings or soundings of *Unterwegs zur Sprache* will wander.

Of course, as every schoolchild knows by now, the problem with the word "truth" (*Wahrheit*) is that it stinks of metaphysics—and so does the whole idea of reopening the quarrel of philosophy with poetry, and so does the "rhapsodic" or midrashic belief that something essential to language can be heard in its sounding, its puns or infelicities. Since the publication of Jacques Derrida's "Différance" (1968), "The Ends of Man" (1969), and "*Ousīa* and *Grammē*: Note on a Note from *Being and Time*" (1970), it has become a given among comparatists, theorists, and deconstructed logicians that understanding Heidegger means demystifying him in the other direction, that is, not by translating his "beautiful mystical language" back into the discourse of propositions, but by unmasking his language as incorrigibly metaphysical in its deep structure despite the apparent free play of its surface. Heidegger on this picture of him is a failed deconstructionist who wants to go back behind the discourse of inferential reasoning to recover a primordial "alliance of speech and Being in the unique word, in the finally proper name."[5] On this picture, the radical point would not be to reopen the quarrel between philosophy and poetry in order to resolve it or get around behind it to some primordial unity of Word and Being (the Orphic Dream); it would be to let the quarrel drop, to wonder why there ever was such a thing, to show how the distinction between philosophy and literature, or between inferential reasoning and empty talk, is a purely social and practical distinction, one of the accidents of history that we have learned to live with; and the idea is to go on living with it even though it can no longer be logically supported.⁶ Moreover, and somewhat to the same effect, it's all very well for rhapsodes to sneer back at straightforward philosophers who want to recover Heidegger for the advanced seminar, but what are we to make of Heidegger's claim (as if this were indeed the claim) that poetry and thinking have something "authentic" about them that entitles them to replace philosophy as a way of pursuing and arriving at truth? Whose truth? Understood in these terms, there is something sinister about the "jargon of authenticity."⁷ Insofar as Heidegger's step back into poetry and thinking means stepping back from critique, whether of metaphysics or of ideology or whatever, we have an obligation to protest that *Gelassenheit* or letting-go is a mask of narcissism, a return to a primitive freedom from suspicion that will allow every manner of secret fascism or theology to reimpose itself. Whatever its meaning within the superficial framework of Heidegger's later texts, the practical—that is, the social and political—meaning of *Gelassenheit* is that it is a counsel of submission that puts us at the disposal of the state, the nation, or the dominant culture. Who is being asked to let go? The meaning of "Being" is power.

It would certainly be strange if we *didn't* feel compelled to see Heidegger in this sinister light—he certainly asked for it—but the long-term effect of the hermeneutics of suspicion is to turn Heidegger into a bogey, the spook of metaphysics. In any event, the following chapters were not composed as arguments against either those who want to rationalize the later Heidegger or those who want to demystify him in order to weaken the structures of repression that he is seen to uphold. However, I think I make it pretty clear that the step back into poetry and thinking, although *not* critique in the methodological sense in which this term has been used since Kant, is nevertheless a crucial turn, that is, a movement away from the analytical culture, the technological framework, in which (for example) literary study, among other disciplines, continues to be practiced—I mean the culture into which I continue to integrate the students whom I try to teach.

I want to emphasize that I do not try to teach my students how to read a poem the way Heidegger reads Hölderlin or Trakl (if one calls that reading). People find this a little hard to believe precisely because of the technological bias of literary criticism: it is hard to imagine that an English professor would *not* study Heidegger *unless* it were to recover from him a theory of reading, a method of analysis, or a style of literary response that can compete against the theories and methods current in the field. If the chapters that follow can be said to have a lesson, however, it is that the study of the later Heidegger alienates one from the idea of the literary professor as textual analyst or methodical reader or creative respondent; that is, Heidegger undermines the whole idea of literary study as the application or response of techniques of reading to texts conceived as structures or systems, whether purely formal, linguistic, or textual systems, or whether as forms and configurations that are continuous with the social and ideological systems in which human life is framed. Heidegger takes you out of the vocabulary of theory and method, form and configuration, structure and system. So it is with a divided conscience, or a feeling of absurdity, that, in spite of Heidegger, I nevertheless continue to show my students how to perform linguistic or other sorts of analysis, recommending to them, by way of example, the technical brilliance of the essays recently collected by Mary Ann Caws and published by the Modern Language Association of America, *Textual Analysis: Some Readers Reading* (1986), which is a comprehensive showcase of the methodological options available in current literary study. One can't practice literary study in our society without mastering the techniques exhibited in this volume, which captures, one might say, the heart and soul of the critical profession. It's no accident, however, that there is, among all the astonishing array of critical positions, no *analytique heideggerienne* represented in this volume. That is simply because an *analytique heideggerienne* is like a squaring of the hermeneutical circle: there can't be such a thing, and even if there could you wouldn't want it.[8] On this line of thinking one could imagine reading Heidegger not for what he gives us but for where he takes us: imagine reading him as a way of getting out of school, that is, as a way of getting out from under the whole disciplinary operation that *Textual Analysis* enframes. Notice that this does not mean finding a substitute for analysis as the way to do literary criticism. There are no better mousetraps in Heidegger. He won't put you in the avant-garde. With or without him literary criticism, like academic philosophy, will remain methodologically unchanged. The question of whether one's relation to these familiar things remains the same is another matter.

I seem to be accumulating an inventory of reasons or motivations for reading Heidegger. One may do so (1) in order to translate his "beautiful mystical language" back into philosophy; or (2) in order to expose his language as masking this philosophy from the start; or

(3) in order to discover in his own readings, if that is what they are, a method, or model, or style of critical performance; or (4) in order to discover in him a way *out*, or perhaps only a space, or maybe only a crack—call it a "rift" or "between"—in which one is momentarily released from one's bearings, or no longer containable within one's disciplinary environment. There is something recognizably fanciful or comic in this last idea, as if one could speak of the reading of Heidegger as a *délire heideggerienne* in which one goes on reading in the same old way (there's no mystery in what it is to read), only now everything is other than usual, as if in a place where "Being" no longer *is*, where "language" is no longer something that we speak, where "poetry" is no longer the product of imagination and the subject of poetics.[9] What to make of such a place? What becomes of us there?

Hermeneutical Experience

In a passing remark Stanley Cavell once wondered "what would constitute understanding Heidegger without a conversion to his way of thinking," as if there could be no understanding of the other that did not entail becoming the other, which means becoming strange, possibly unintelligible, no longer one of us.[10]

Think of understanding Heidegger in the first place as a problem for romantic hermeneutics, where the task (as Schleiermacher says) is to understand the other first as well as, then even better than, he understood himself, if himself is the word. The problem of romantic hermeneutics, or its risk, is not that one cannot accomplish this task; rather it is that one cannot do so without being transformed, turned out of oneself and into the other in a process of estrangement from which there is no escape or return. As when it is said that the reading of Nietzsche turns one into a Nietzschean (as Nietzsche remarked somewhere, finding me is no problem, the trick is to lose me). So the idea is to read critically, that is, to emancipate oneself from the other by reflecting oneself out of the hermeneutical situation. What is questionable is whether one can say then that one understands at all. Does not understanding presuppose a fundamental openness to the truth of the other? This is the question put by philosophical hermeneutics. For Gadamer, for example, openness is not simply an open-mindedness or tolerance for another's worldview. It is more like the exposure that occurs in hermeneutical experience, where I find that the other that I seek to understand cannot be contained within the conceptual apparatus that I (or my time, place, and institution) have prepared for it. And of course this alters my own relation to this apparatus, not to mention my own self-relation or my own standing, as if the ground beneath me were suddenly giving way. This giving way of the ground is a metaphor of the essential negativity of hermeneutical experience.[11] What happens in hermeneutical experience is not necessarily that one understands anything in the sense of a positive grasping. What happens is that one experiences the limits—the finitude or historicality—of understanding itself. Only by giving ground in this way, as if entering into a place where now everything is other than usual, where things no longer answer to the usual concepts, can understanding happen. But what is there to understand?

According to Gadamer's analysis, what happens in understanding is not that I enter into the subjectivity of another, but that the other opens me, exposes me, to the subject that calls for understanding, that is, the *Sache* of thinking, the matter in question. Understanding is not a form of conceptual agreement between minds; it is not any sort of conceptualization or determination of meanings. Oh, it is all of that, if it satisfies you to think of it that way, but it is not enough to think of understanding as the recovery of another's meanings or the rethinking of an author's thoughts. It is more than Dilthey's *Nachbildung*. Understanding is always of "what is," where "what is" is not to be thought of as an objective reality but as a subject in the old rhetorical sense of *res* or thing: namely that which is in question (in the open). One studies a text for the light it throws on what is in question (and not just because one is suspicious). Doubtless the reading of Heidegger runs the risk of producing Heideggerians, but understanding Heidegger is not to be thought of simply as a product or consequence of exegesis—getting around behind the text into the mode or history of its production (getting inside or behind the back of Heidegger). Understanding goes on in frront of the text in the encounter with the *Sache* of thinking. The task of the text is to open thinking to this encounter by shaking it loose from the cozy ground of its concepts.

In Gadamer's language, what happens in the hermeneutical experience is that we are placed in the open, in the region of the question —exposed, to be sure, and ungrounded, but ungrounded in Heidegger's sense of letting-go rather than in the logical sense of being at an impasse or caught in a double bind. The hermeneutical experience in this respect is always subversive of totalization or containment. For Gadamer, this means the openness of tradition to the future, its irreducibility to the library or museum or institutions of cultural transmission, its resistance to closure, its uncontainability within finite interpretations (tradition is not an archive). For Heidegger, it means "openness to mystery" (G 24/55). On this analysis, it becomes difficult to go on characterizing understanding in terms of a philological process or as the product or goal of exegesis. Hermeneutics is not a protocol of reading or a postal service, that is, the bearing of messages from the past.[12] This is not to throw exegesis aside. One always has the job of reading a text and trying to clarify what it has to say— the job, that is, of determining what light the text sheds on its subject matter. Both philosophy and literary study draw their bearings from philology. Much of the book that follows, which stays close to the texts of *Unterwegs zur Sprache*, is, as I have said, cast in the traditional schoolroom form of a commentary concerned with the words of a text (how could it be otherwise?). But understanding is not a product of exposition. It is not reducible to the clarification of words and intentions. It is always being caught up in an experience that takes it away from itself. One might say that the hermeneutical experience is always fatal to understanding conceived simply as the expository determination of messages; insofar as it is what occurs in experience, understanding can never be fully fixed, objectified, or terminated, that is, it can never be turned into a concept or stable conceptual construction. For deconstruction, which knows thinking only in its logical form as conceptual determination, that is the end of it (the state called undecidability). But the inability to bring one's subject under conceptual control, fixing it propositionally, is not the end of thinking; on the contrary, it were better to say that the breakdown of concepts and the failure of words is an opening that takes us out of the realm where representation and calculation are all that matter to thinking. For Gadamer, this is what happens in the Socratic dialogue where the negativity in which one ends up at a loss for words is at the same time that which sets thinking free.

It has always seemed to me that deconstruction is closer to hermeneutical experience than to a theory or method of reading, say a form of linguistic analysis raised to the highest category of suspicion (Paul de Man), or maybe only another, more advanced method of "exploring the textual logic in texts called literary" (Jonathan Culler).[13] At all events it is in the spirit, or rather the space, of hermeneutical experience that the following book was written. So one ought not to be misled or distracted by my "method" of reading Heidegger, which seems to me technically too simple or old-fashioned or rhetorically primitive to count for anything as a method.

What matters is not the method but the matter of thinking, which in this case is the question of poetry, which is to say poetry and truth (the unthought matter of Heidegger studies). Heidegger reopens this question within a region where everything is other than usual—where truth, for example, is no longer a property of thought or discourse, no longer a product of representational and calculative operations, but an event in which untruth also matters, that is, where untruth is no longer derived from man and his errors or defects of consciousness (or defects of method) but belongs to the nature of truth as unconcealment or disclosure (the celebrated *alētheia*). The starting point of the following pages, what draws them out into Heidegger's later writings, is arguably Heidegger's most important text, "The Origin of the Work of Art" (1934–35), in which the *work* of the work of art, what happens with it, is explicated in terms of the *doubleness* of truth as disclosure *and* refusal or dissembling (*Versagen* and *Verstellen*). Here is where the question of poetry's truth comes back into play, but in order to get into this play one has to go through the looking glass of *délire heideggerienne* where philosophy no longer resembles itself, nor does poetry (which is no longer the art of writing verses, no longer *poiēsis* or *Poesie* but *Dichten*). In this strange region, where the concealment of beings (*Verborgenheit*), or "untruth proper," is said to be *older* than truth as disclosure, or anyhow otherwise than truth in ways we are at a loss to explain, it should not surprise us to find that poetry's truth implicates us in its darkness, its reserve or resistance to our efforts to lay bare such things as "textual logic." That is, poetry's truth emerges in the way it comports itself, not within the framework of representation and calculation, but toward the concealment of beings, or toward what Heidegger calls "mystery" (Wm 89/132–33). In "The Essence of Truth" (1934–35), this comportment is called *Seinlassen;* in the later writings (as though Being had disappeared or turned otherwise than itself) it is called *Gelassenheit*. What has poetry to teach us in this affair? This is to ask what Heidegger could be thinking of when he says (in a line that still seems not to have registered on many people), that "*Alētheia*, unconcealment thought as the opening of presence, is not yet truth" (SD 76/69). As if there were a darkness or thickness that belongs to truth the way density (*Dichte*) belongs to poetry (*Dichten*): "Does this happen by chance? Does it happen only as a consequence of the carelessness of human thinking [or say the logical weakness characteristic of puns and poetry and other 'infelicities' of speech]? Or does it happen because self-concealing, concealment, *lēthē* belongs to *a-lētheia*, not just as an addition, not as shadow to light, but rather as the heart of *alētheia*?" (SD 78/71). I think a careful reading of *Unterwegs zur Sprache* is what is needed in order to get into the sense or spirit of this question.

To put it in a slightly different way, I understand the later Heidegger as opening us up to the ancient and discredited tradition that figures poetry in terms of the darkness of speech, that is, the *ainigma* or dark saying that reduces us to bewilderment and wonder and exposes us to the uncontrollable. The *ainigma* is not a riddle; it is that saying whose light is inaccessible, or perhaps unbearable (cannot be borne or borne away). One cannot dispel the darkness of enigmas. One can only enter into it as into a mystery. I call this a discredited tradition because, of course, it was always the whole task of philosophical reflection to banish darkness in behalf of plain speaking and the purity of concepts. No philosophy, in short, without demystification.[14] The ancient quarrel between philosophy and poetry of which Plato speaks is a quarrel of light and darkness, that is, a quarrel between the plain and the obscure, between the discourse of the one and that of the indeterminate two, between the word inscribed in the mind of one who knows and the inscrutable unresponding text, between logos and mythos, between the concept and the pun, the proposition and the metaphor, the tethered and the ambiguous word. Heidegger reopens the place between these regions of discourse. Or (better) he enters this "between" where (as with Heraclitus the Obscure and his inscrutable texts) the relation of poetry and thinking is no longer a determinate difference and a mere quarrel but a "rift" in which the two are exposed or at risk, not so much with respect to each other as to what Heidegger calls language. Naturally in the place of the later Heidegger language is called by a strange name (*Sage*), and so is everything else. It is by no means clear, of course, that Heidegger would have wanted things expressed quite this way. He always regarded the question of poetry, important as it is, as subordinate to the question of thinking. So in behalf of the question of poetry one is compelled to push Heidegger a little further into this "rift" than he himself thought it necessary to go. Hence the third place in my subtitle, where perhaps "Thinking" ought to go, is reserved for "Poetry."

1933/34—and After

I want to emphasize that my appeal to the negativity of hermeneutical experience is not meant to brush aside the problem of romantic hermeneutics, that is, the problem of turning into Heidegger. When Cavell wonders what it would be to understand Heidegger without a conversion to his way of thinking, I imagine he is not talking about becoming the kind of phenomenologist whose professional occupation is to write articles and books about Heidegger or Heideggerian themes. Suppose one were to take Cavell as wondering what it would be to understand Heidegger independently of a transformation into not just the strange but the monstrous. This is evidently different from asking what it would be to become a follower, that is, a disciple of Heidegger's—a station to which no one, to my knowledge, not even phenomenologists who get called "epigones" of the master, has ever aspired. Think of Aristodemus following Socrates both everywhere and also to the point of going barefoot; and of other young Athenians who made themselves querulous and unsatisfiable in imitation merely of what they could see and hear (that is, of Socratic method); and of Alcibiades, who, speaking drunkenly in the *Symposium*, drew up the true indictment against Socrates, I mean the indictment brought by the friends of Socrates, those whom Socrates had filled with "this philosophical frenzy, this sacred rage" (218b), and who had found that this madness, or beauty, could not be contained within the inherited forms of life—could not even be brought under the category of the human; could not even be recognized as human, as if to follow the way of Socrates or philosophy required the abandonment of the human, even its repudiation. For the human one could substitute Cavell's word, ordinary, namely that which calls for acknowledgment. The paradox of Socrates is his loving repudiation of the human. It is a paradox the more because who is more ordinary, or human, than Socrates, with his fat face and silly talk? Yet open him up, as Alcibiades claims to have done, and nothing is more passing strange, nor less human. This paradox is part of what Martha Nussbaum calls "the fragility of goodness."[15]

What happens when you try to follow Heidegger up or down one of his paths of thinking, studying him, trying out his moves, finding yourself caught up in him? One thing that happens is that you begin to appreciate why people are careful to confine themselves to forms of mental activity that have no history—have, for all the world, nothing to do with history—I mean purely analytical programs like formal logic, philosophy of language, linguistics, semiotics, most forms of literary criticism, perhaps most of what gets taught in school: programs you can get into and out of quickly and cleanly without the burden of having done anything more blameworthy than test, or apply, a certain method, skill, technique, or training. Unfortunately one cannot for a minute take up Heidegger for study without at the same time taking up his history and confronting it as one's own, and this means confronting Fascism, National Socialism, Anti-Semitism, and the Holocaust: the history that catches us all, in Cavell's language, somewhere between acknowledgment and avoidance: the history that reduces our institutions—the State, the Church, the School—to bureaucratic offices declaring their eternal blindness, ignorance, or narrow responsibilities. (Even now dissertations are being written on the nonoccurrence of the Holocaust.) The fact is that Heidegger's work, as Fred Dallmayr has said in a perfect metaphor, is "encumbered by a heavy political mortgage," namely the years 1933/34, when Heidegger, as rector of the University of Freiburg, pledged his allegiance, and his university, not to mention the institution of philosophy, to Hitler.[16]

For interesting reasons that need not be developed here, Marxist critics have a special feeling for this topic. Here, for example, is Terry Eagleton on Heidegger's "philosophy":

> What is central to Heidegger's thought . . . is not the individual subject but Being itself. The mistake of the Western metaphysical tradition has been to see Being as some kind of objective entity, and to separate it sharply from the subject; Heidegger seeks rather to return to pre-Socratic thought, before the dualism between subject and object opened up, and to regard Being as somehow encompassing both. The result of this suggestive thought, in his later work particularly, is an astonishing cringing before the mystery of Being. Enlightenment rationality, with its ruthlessly dominative, instrumental attitude towards Nature, must be rejected for a humble listening to the stars, skies, and forests, a listening which in the acid words of one English commentator bears all the marks of a "stupefied peasant." Man must "make way" for Being by making himself wholly over to it: he must turn to the earth, the inexhaustible mother who is the primary fount of all meaning. Heidegger, the Black Forest philosopher, is yet another Romantic exponent of the "organic society," though in his case the results of this doctrine were to be more sinister than in the case of [F. R.] Leavis. The exaltation of the peasant, the downgrading of reason for spontaneous "pre-understanding," the celebration of wise-passivity—all of these, combined with Heidegger's

belief in an "authentic" existence-towards-death superior to the life of the faceless masses, led him in 1933 into explicit support of Hitler. The support was short-lived; but it was implicit for all that in the elements of his philosophy.[17]

This passage is worth quoting because it summarizes very well a dominant view of Heidegger, particularly among theorists and comparatists, which is that Heidegger's texts are intelligible only to the extent that his political crimes have inscribed themselves in them.[18] Heidegger's way of thinking leads to fascism, or to the kind of voluntarism on which fascism feeds—*is*, for all of that, fascism in its nascent or dormant state, whence it follows that any "convert" to this way of thinking, or indeed anyone who adverts to it, or studies it, with anything less than Eagleton's superficiality and donnish contempt for German stupidity, ought to be called out as ideologically sinister.

Eagleton's superficiality, coupled with the lesson of Marxism itself, which is that there is no such thing as an uncontaminated idea, makes it tempting to brush Heidegger's fascism aside with a weary gesture. After all, philosophy is what matters, not politics. Only it won't do, not if one takes seriously the hermeneutical insistence on the historicality of understanding, its embeddedness in concrete situations. For it is not just Heidegger's work but also one's study of it that is politically mortgaged, and the note is unpayable. It is not that one cannot argue —as Dallmayr, among others, argues—that the idea of a geometrical (much less organic) connection between Heidegger's early fundamental ontology and his endorsement of Hitler is insupportable; it is just that one cannot distance oneself in one's study of Heidegger from the judgment that condemns Heidegger for his political action; indeed, one cannot distance oneself from the action itself and (much worse) from Heidegger's subsequent refusal to acknowledge the history to which it belonged. The historicist Dilthey liked to speak of the connectedness or hanging-together (*Zusammenhang*) of life. Connectedness makes understanding possible, but it also implicates understanding in what it studies. The case of Heidegger compels us to take this idea in its strongest possible sense, which is that one belongs to what one studies in ways that cannot be conceptualized in terms of the neutral workings of inferential reason or the melodrama of ideological analysis. We have learned from Hannah Arendt, as if we could not learn it from historical experience, that a human action is not an isolatable event, an atom of behavior, but is boundless and uncontrollable in its effects. So we must imagine Heidegger's action spreading across the text of philosophy like a deep stain; and not only across the text but also across the hands that take it up for study.[19]

What one cannot get out of one's mind, or off one's hands, is never reducible to the concept of ideology; one needs to recover more ancient or mythical concepts like that of ruinous memory. To what category of knowledge does one's knowledge of a crime belong, say the evil deed of one's father or son? Students of Ezra Pound's poetry know the meaning of such knowledge intimately, know the living of it. The spirit in which one studies is not a free-floating, Cartesian ego but is absorbed by the historicality of its texts. Here historicality means more than intertextuality. It could be that no word can adequately serve this surplus meaning of historicality except *miasma,* the Greek word for defilement. One's life of study is always in question because one's texts for study can never be demystified, that is, can never be handled or dismantled in a purely analytical way as so many logical, textual, or ideological objects. In a book about our vulnerability to texts, called *Saving the Text,* Geoffrey Hartman tries to recuperate the old idea that words can cure or wound as well as mean.[20] Not a very philosophical (in the sense of analytical) approach to words, but Heidegger would have understood Hartman very well. Words are more than terms. The point is that words do not just echo or resonate with their historicality, that is, they are not just expressive or reflective of their contexts in the forms laid out by the various historicisms old and new. Rather it is that words situate you in their historicality in the sense of exposing you to it, placing you under its claims and also under the claims against it. Imagine being inserted into another's history. This is part of what Gadamer means in the line that I have used as an epigraph for this introduction—"when you take a word in your mouth you must realize that you have not taken up a tool that can be thrown aside if it won't do the job, but are fixed in a direction which comes from afar and stretches beyond you."[21] Only we must not construe this directionality in a purely formal way as a logic that catches you up or as the working out of some philosophical history, that is, neither as internal necessity nor as a line of customary usage, nor even as a context that unfolds in every direction because of hidden intentions or the play of signifiers.

No, the point is that the word you take in your mouth could turn out to be lethal. Here it is not enough to say that words are embedded in history; it is better to say that they *are* history, that is, that they constitute its linguisticality—are the reason, for example, why history moves simultaneously and dangerously in two directions. Things recede into the past in the familiar way, filling us with pathos and nostalgia or relieving us, so we would have it, of the evil of our ancestors; but they also come down to us from the past, bear upon us and carry us away, projecting us onto a future we hadn't counted on, taking the future out of our hands and exposing us to it. Hence history's tragic potential. To understand history in this double sense is to capture something of what Gadamer means by linguisticality or the historicality of belonging to tradition. Here what needs to be contextualized is not just tradition, say the text of philosophy; what needs to be contextualized is one's belongingness, that is, one's own situation with respect to all that comes down to us from the past. And this is very difficult. As Gadamer says, "illumination of this situation—effective-historical reflection [*die wirkungsgeschichtliche Reflexion*]—can never be completely achieved" (TM 269). We cannot objectify (and therefore emancipate ourselves from) our own historicality.

I wrote this book on Heidegger in a small, comfortable office at the Institute for Advanced Studies at the Hebrew University of Jerusalem. In the office next to mine worked a shy, infinitely gentle man who had, because of some bureaucratic mistake, survived one of Hitler's death camps. His name was Dan Pagis, the Israeli poet, one of whose poems is about the moment of his survival:

THE ROLL CALL

He stands, stamps a little in his boots,
rubs his hands. He's cold in the morning breeze:
a diligent angel, who worked hard for his promotions.
Suddenly he thinks he's made a mistake: all eyes,
he counts again in the open notebook
all the bodies waiting for him in the square,
camp within camp: only I
am not there, am not there, am a mistake,
turn off my eyes, quickly, erase my shadow.
I shall not want. The sum will be all right
without me: here forever.[22]

Another of his poems is called "Written in Pencil in the Sealed Railway-Car":

here in this carload
i am eve
if you see my other son

cain son of man
tell him that i   [PD 23]

Elsewhere Pagis writes: "Too many tongues are mixed in my mouth" (PD 33). Attempts at conversation made Dan Pagis very uncomfortable, but occasionally, with special patience, he would show me how to resolve some of Heidegger's puns. He also brought it home that philology of this sort proceeds not in a space of its own but inside a moral tangle that no one knows how to resolve. He did not know how to resolve it for me. He simply remained himself unreconciled to Heidegger's texts, which he nevertheless knew. But how is it possible to remain unreconciled to a text that one studies? One takes the thing in one's hands, but one does not appropriate it. But how not, if understanding is to occur? In Cavell's language, what would it be to understand without conversion, that is, without reconciliation or transformation into the irreconcilable? One says that one is unreconciled—Heidegger's political action has left its mark on his text, a mark of Cain—yet one takes the thing in one's hands and cares for it, and for a while, not just for a while but metaphysically, nothing is more important or more perfect than this text. So one is borne away, reconciled after all. "Too many tongues are mixed in my mouth."

Adorno in his *Aesthetic Theory*, in a section called "'Culpability,'" speaks of the way works of art (one could say works of philosophy just as well) help to "reinforce the existence of a separate domain of the spirit and culture whose practical impotence and complicity with the principle of unmitigated disaster are painfully evident." Within this space such things as the Holocaust have no bearing; such things do not happen, are unthinkable, one can erase them with dissertations. There is no bearing witness in such space. Neither art nor philosophy can come into being except within this space that each helps to set aside, and so by definition, Adorno says, each is "socially culpable," reconciled to "the principle of unmitigated disaster." Adorno wants to say, however, that the "authentic" work possesses an "irreconcilable component." It refuses to be contained, entirely contained, within the aesthetic or analytic space that holds it in thrall, under a spell, blind to catastrophes of history, able to attend serenely to its business. So its culpability is "culpability" within quotation marks: it is not quite, but not not, culpable.[23] What a delicate thread Adorno holds out and which the study of Heidegger tries to take hold of with its clumsy fist! For this study goes on within or in virtue of "a separate domain of the spirit and culture" that itself continues on its way as if nothing had happened, as if it had no history or nothing to do with history. This is why it is important to disrupt this space with what Dan Pagis has written:

> Too many tongues are mixed in my mouth. But
> at the crossing of these winds,
> very diligent, I immerse myself
> in the laws of heavenly grammar: I am learning
> the declensions and ascensions of
> silence.

> *Who has given you the right to jest?*
> *What is above you you already know.*
> *You meant to ask what is within you.*
> *what is abysmally through you.*
> *How is it that you did not see?*　　　　[PD 33]

In an essay on *King Lear*, "The Avoidance of Love," Cavell says that the difference between understanding a lyric poem and seeing the point of a tragic action is that in the one case we experience something like the joy of recognition, whereas in the other we suffer the brutal exposure or unmasking of our own willful blindness.[24] This insight is part of Cavell's ongoing reflection on acknowledgment as moral knowledge whose opposite is not just vincible ignorance but rather deliberate avoidance, a refusal to acknowledge the existence, or say the suffering or even the annihilation of the other. The study of Heidegger needs to be placed within the context of this reflection. Moral knowledge as Cavell understands it cannot be contained within the separate domain of spirit and culture; rather it belongs to what Levinas calls "the relationship in which the other is a neighbor, and in which before being an individuation of the genus *man*, a *rational animal*, a *free will*, or any essence whatever [that is, a conceptual entity], he is the persecuted one for whom I am responsible to the point of being a hostage for him, and in which my responsibility, instead of disclosing me in my 'essence' as a transcendental ego, divests me without stop of all that can be common to me and another man, who would thus be capable of replacing me. I am then called upon in my uniqueness as someone for whom no one else can substitute himself."[25]

Here is a line of thinking that helps us to cope with Heidegger's political action in a way that is different from the usual ideological analysis. The judgment according to ideology, in which Heidegger's action or text is simply part of the sinister superstructure of German social reality, doesn't have much in it. It simply assimilates Heidegger into the general category of bourgeois political failure in the face of fascism, that is, bourgeois willingness to embrace fascism as a way of securing its own interests; so bourgeois philosophy, in the heat of its own ideological needs, fails to see fascism for what it is. However, Cavell and Levinas give us a language in which to account for Heidegger's political action, as well as his own response to his action (his own judgment of it), as a failure, even a refusal, of moral thinking. Here failure or refusal is not confined to the period of Heidegger's rectorship in 1933/34. If this were all that mattered, then one could say, as Hannah Arendt does, that "Heidegger himself corrected his own 'error' more quickly and more radically than many of those who later sat in judgment over him—he took considerably greater risks than were usual in German literary and university life during that period."[26] Heidegger, on this interpretation, "corrected his course" —followed, if none too quickly, the rule of Socrates, which enjoins the thinker to choose between politics and philosophy as if it were a choice between the love of power and the claims of justice; enjoins the thinker, in other words, to withdraw from the public realm into a separate domain of the spirit and culture in which reflection can occur without an evil conscience. For people like Karsten Harries, Heidegger's thinking after *Being and Time* amounts to a repudiation, in philosophy's name, of social and political reality, that is, a radical isolation of philosophy from the historicality, or from the claims, of everyday life.[27] By contrast, Fred Dallmayr, in an important essay on "The Ontology of Freedom: Heidegger and Political Philosophy," takes Heidegger—chiefly "the middle Heidegger" of the 1936 lectures on Schelling's *Essence of Human Freedom*, but also of course Heidegger as the critic of technology—to be "a philosopher of human 'solidarity'" (PP 107).

However this question is decided, there remains for me good reason to take Heidegger as the very model of the moral failure of philosophy —the model of the philosopher who can perhaps awaken to his own subjective venality, his own error or naiveté or misspent language, but who can never wake up, even long after the fact, to the tragedy of his own history. Of course, a great deal remains to be learned about Heidegger. We are still many years from a comprehensive view of his life and work, not to mention his times. For all we know the worst still lies hidden in some corner of the unpublished archive. But it is hard not to read the work of Stanley Cavell with Heidegger in mind and not feel compelled to take Heidegger as the philosopher of avoidance who addresses history mainly in order to exculpate himself, or (worse) who sanitizes history by refusing every awareness of what occurred in it. I mean that the worst thing about Heidegger is the way he sealed himself off from the other in an act of knowing and inexcusable disregard. He looked at the Holocaust and shrugged his shoulders. The following from Cavell's remarkable essay on tragedy and the question of acknowledgment seems to me to speak directly to the question of Heidegger, especially the Heidegger of the *Der Spiegel* interviews who seems neurotically disengaged from the history in which he took part:

> What we forgot, when we deified reason, was not that reason is incompatible with feeling, but that knowledge requires acknowledgment. (The withdrawals and approaches of God can be looked upon as tracing the history of our attempts to overtake and absorb acknowledgment by knowledge; God would be the name of that impossibility.) Either you have to be *very* careful about what you know—keep it superficial or keep it away from the self and one's society and history and away from art and from heaven—or else in order not to acknowledge what you have learned you will have to stifle or baffle feeling, stunt the self. This is why, in the visions of Marx and Kierkegaard, reason and philosophy must be made to end. [MWM 347]

Talking, Listening, Keeping Silent

This question of acknowledgment raises a problem about Heidegger's notion of language, which I would like to formulate in the following preliminary way.

The first temptation in addressing what Heidegger has to say about language is to look for foundations in sections thirty-four and thirty-five of *Being and Time*, "Being-There and Discourse. Language" and "Idle Talk." These are certainly valuable texts, not the least because they insist upon the ontological as against epistemological character of language—or, more plainly, its social as against its strictly logical character. "The existential-ontological foundation of language," Heidegger says, "is discourse or talk [*Rede*]" (SZ 161/203). For Heidegger, at least at this period, what matters is not how language connects up with reality, not how it depicts things, but rather how it exists in the world, how it occurs and what happens with it. And here he clearly anticipates J. L. Austin and the later Wittgenstein. The mode of being of language is talk among human beings. It is constitutive of being-with-one-another, that is, constitutive of human sociality. Language in this sense is not anything that can be comprehended by way of grammar, rhetoric, logic, or the forms of cognitive science. It is not anything about which one could have a theory; rather, it is an entirely untheorizable practice, irreducible to the description of rules.[28] "Our Being-with-one-another," Heidegger says, "is discursive as assenting or refusing, as demanding or warning, as pronouncing, consulting, or interceding, as 'making assertions,' and as talking in the way of 'giving a talk'" (SZ 161/204). It is not for nothing that Heidegger puts the expression "making assertions" inside quotation marks. Talk is not predication, although it is predicative in the sense that it is always "talk about something" (SZ 161/204); but what it is about always presupposes or depends on its pragmatic power of binding people together, constituting them as Being-with-one-another in the world. This means that what matters is not the propositional content of discourse but rather its dialogical character; and for the same reason what matters is not the speaking subject, the monological ego, but the mode of being called "being-with." "Communication," Heidegger says, "is never anything like a conveying of experiences, such as opinions or wishes, from the interior of one subject to the interior of another" (SZ 162/205). So scratch the expressive-theory of discourse. Talk is not expressive of subjectivity, therefore is not expressive of intersubjectivity; think of it rather as productive of solidarity.

In order to grasp the essence of language, if "grasping" is the word, one does not need a theory of meaning or truth. We should, Heidegger says, "dispense with the 'philosophy of language'" (SZ 166/209). Better to reflect upon the phenomenon of hearing or listening, about which it would never occur to anyone to frame a theory. "Hearing [*das Hören*]," Heidegger says, "is constitutive for discourse" (SZ 163/206). As we shall see, the priority of hearing over speaking is one of the constants in Heidegger's thinking with respect to language, perhaps the only constant. And hearing—listening, hearkening, attending to what is said (or unsaid)—is preeminently social, whereas speaking always has the structure of soliloquy. Listening presupposes the worldly condition of being-with-others. Speaking obscures this condition. Indeed, to approach language from the standpoint of speaking is already to have constructed the theoretical framework of the monological subject with its rules and performatives, whereas to approach language from the standpoint of listening—well, it is not clear that there is anything to be approached in this event, not clear that language can be objectified (and therefore approached, much less grasped) on the basis of listening. Listening seems to dissipate the entity called Language. Listening leads not to language as such, whatever that is, but to the being of language, which occurs in talk. And there is more to talk than speaking.

There is, for example, keeping silent (*das Schweigen*). "*Keeping silent,*" Heidegger says, "is another possibility of discourse, and it has the same existential foundation," namely talk (SZ 164/208). Moreover, there is more to keeping silent than to speaking. Understanding, taken in Heidegger's sense of understanding as an *existentiale* or mode of being of *Dasein*, follows from listening rather than from speaking.[29] "Speaking at length [*Viel-sprechen*] about something," Heidegger says, "does not offer the slightest guarantee that thereby understanding is advanced. On the contrary, talking extensively about something covers it up and brings what is understood [say the being of *Dasein*] to a sham clarity —the unintelligibility of the trivial. But to keep silent does not mean to be dumb" (SZ 164–65/208). Keeping silent is the mode of being (listening) in which understanding occurs. It is not just keeping one's mouth shut; it is being attentive to what is said. "He who never says anything [that is, who just keeps his mouth shut] cannot keep silent at any given moment. Keeping silent authentically is possible only in genuine discoursing. To be able to keep silent, *Dasein* must have something to say" (SZ 168/212).

Here, however, things get complicated, especially for human solidarity or the condition of "Being-with-one-another." For what is it to have something to say? What is it for discourse to be genuine or authentic—and how well does discourse stand up under the strain of human sociality, which frequently, as Heidegger goes on to say, follows "the route of *gossiping* and *passing the word along* [auf dem Wege des *Weiter-* und *Nachredens*]" (SZ 168/212)? In a memorable passage Heidegger writes:

> Idle talk is constituted by just such gossiping and passing the word along—a process by which its initial lack of grounds to stand on [*Bodenständigkeit*] becomes aggravated to complete groundlessness [*Bodenlosigkeit*]. And indeed this idle talk is not confined to vocal gossip, but even spreads to what we write, where it takes the form of "scribbling" [*das "Geschreibe"*]. In this latter case the gossip is not based so much on hearsay. It feeds upon superficial reading [*dem Angelesenen*]. The average understanding of the reader will *never be able* to decide what has been drawn from primordial

sources with a struggle and how much is just gossip. The average understanding, moreover, will not want any such distinction, and does not need it, because, of course, it understands everything. [SZ 168–69/212]

Heidegger begins the section on idle talk by saying that "The expression 'idle talk' [*Gerede*] is not to be used here in a 'disparaging' signification" (SZ 167/211), but it is hard to know what he could mean by this in view of the terrible things he has to say about such talk. Yet this puzzle opens onto something more complicated still: what is this talk about "drawn from primordial sources with a struggle"? This does not sound like an event of the everyday but rather like something out of romance, or say out of philosophy. It suddenly sounds like language is to have a double foundation. We are told that the "existential-ontological foundation of language is discourse or talk," but talk in order to be foundational for language must itself be grounded upon something "drawn from primordial sources with a struggle." And it is hard to say what that something is. The problem with talk about foundations, of course, is that it always comes to this, I mean it always runs us around as if in endless circumlocutions about something we know not what. The later Heidegger will have done with talk about foundations.

Actually, however, there's not much mystery here, not much metaphysics. The point is not to be misled by the way Heidegger situates listening in the context of Being-with-one-another and talking, because what he wants to say is that in listening we do not (just) listen to other people, nor indeed do we listen to talk as such, that is, to the discursiveness of assenting or refusing, demanding or warning, as if the point were to respond to speech acts. Rather the task of listening is hermeneutical. It is to pick up on what is said *and make it one's own.* "Idle talk," Heidegger says, "is the possibility of understanding everything without previously making the thing one's own. If this were done [making the thing one's own], idle talk would founder," that is, it would cease to be idle. As if idle talk could be thought of as having the determination to stay the way it is, guarding against the danger of being turned into authentic discourse by being taken up or appropriated as the ownmost possibility of *Dasein.* The problem is, according to Heidegger, that we do take up idle talk just in this way, preserving its idleness, and our own. "Idle talk is something which anyone can take up; it not only releases one from the task of genuine understanding, but develops an undifferentiated kind of intelligibility, for which nothing is closed off any longer" but is just turned into so much gossip (SZ 169/213). So between idle talk and hermeneutics one has to choose.

The distinction in *Being and Time* between authentic discourse and idle talk will turn up in the later Heidegger as a distinction between words [*Worte*] and terms [*Wörter*] and again between poetry and everyday discourse (or between poetry and thinking on the one hand and customary usage on the other). It seems crucial to understand that the distinction here is not a formal or analytical distinction between categories or genres of speaking—for example, it is not comparable to the traditional distinction between ordinary and literary or philosophical language. Thus the distinction between idle talk and authentic discourse is not a distinction between empty and full, frivolous and serious, superficial and deep, light and heavy. It is not like the philosophers' distinction between their own grounded or tightly woven arguments and what is otherwise (in the mouths of the rest of us) "just talk." Similarly, poetry as the later Heidegger understands it—namely, as *Dichten*—cannot be assimilated into a category of style. Much less is it a category of consciousness or the expression of a specially endowed subject, someone set off from the "they" [*das Man*] of *Being and Time* by virtue of some special power of insight or knowledge. Rather, poetry is closer to listening than to speaking, that is, it is less a form of linguistic competence or a *poiēsis* than a hermeneutical condition of openness to what is said, or more accurately to what is unsaid: openness, perhaps, to the unsayable, or to what cannot be put into words —as language, for example, cannot be put into words. Rather we will need to think of poetry as openness to the *otherness* of language. This is the direction in which the later Heidegger aims to take us.

Certainly poetry on this line of thinking is not (or cannot be contained by) a kind of writing. In *What is Called Thinking?* Heidegger says that *Dichten* is not *Dichtung*, nor is *Dichtung* the same as *Literatur:*

> For us, poesy [*Dichtung*] has long since been a part of literature, and thinking [*Denken*] likewise. We find it fitting that poesy and its history are dealt with in literary history. It would be foolish to find fault with this situation, which has reasons of long standing, or even to attempt changing it over night. And yet—Homer, Sappho, Pindar, Sophocles, are they literature? No! But that is the way they appear to us, and the only way, even when we are engaged in demonstrating by means of literary history that these works

of poetry really are not literature [but belong to what is spoken rather than to what is written].

Literature is what has been literally written down, and copied, with the intent that it become available to a reading public. In that way, literature becomes the object of widely diverging interests, which in turn are once more stimulated by means of literature —through literary criticism and promotion. Now and then, an individual may find his way out of the literature industry, and find his way reflectively and even edifyingly to a poetic work; but that is not enough to secure for poesy [*Dichtung*] the freedom of its natural habitat [*Wesenort*]. Besides, poesy must first itself determine and reach that habitat [*Ort*]. [WD 154–55/134]

Of course, in our current critical situation ("the literature industry") it is hard to think of poetry as anything but a kind of writing—in fact our whole intellectual orientation is against the possibility (makes it inconceivable) that poetry might be a *listening* to the otherness of language, that is, to its strangeness or nonhumanness, its indifference to our linguistic competence, its uncontainability within the structures of communicability, its resistance to sense. However, what if it were so that the difference between the authentic and the idle, or between poetry (as *Dichten*) and everyday speech—or, for that matter, between poetry and literature (or, for all of that, between thinking and phi-losophy)—were not a difference in how language is used, or in how something is made, but a difference of *place*, say a difference between the familiar world around us in which everything is in its customary place, and a place where everything is otherwise (where poetry is not literature, where thinking is not philosophy, where language is not for speaking)? Getting to, or near, this place, if there is such a place (perhaps it is only a place enclosed in quotation marks), means at the very least finding our way "out of the literature industry," where much of the later Heidegger remains unthinkable, even laughable, anyhow resistant to sense, as if Heidegger were the other of criticism. The readings that follow can be taken as an attempt in this direction.

The question that will remain is where the notion of listening to the otherness of language leaves us with respect to one another, that is, with respect to the solidarity established by discourse or talk. Does openness to the otherness of language (whatever else it means) mean closing off solidarity or being-with (being open to) other people? This is a question about the social dimension and ethical character of the later Heidegger's notions of language and poetry. The unsettling thing about the later Heidegger's thinking—as opposed to the middle Heidegger of the Hölderlin essays, where poetry appears foundational for human solidarity—is that there seem to be no people in it. Possibly this is a false impression that a close reading will dispel, but there is no doubt that the topology of the later writings is dominated by the nonhumanness of language. How it is with us with respect to this non-humanness is one of the regulating questions of this book. Does the hermetic nature of the later Heidegger's thinking, both in the strangeness of its language and in its subject matter, entail a rejection of social reality and a repudiation of the human? Or is it simply that we cannot recognize ourselves in Heidegger's thinking? I'm not sure that I can settle these questions satisfactorily, much less once for all; but perhaps a careful reading of the later Heidegger will put us in a better position to cope with them.

Chapter One
The Aesthetics
of Estrangement
Heidegger on the Work
of Art

It is more salutary for thinking to wander into the strange than to establish itself in the understandable.
—"Logos (Heraclitus, Fragment B50)"

The Otherness of Truth

If the first temptation in taking up Heidegger's notion of language is to read *Being and Time* as a foundational text, the second is to leap immediately from *Being and Time* to the essays in *Unterwegs zur Sprache* in which Heidegger at last brings the question of language up for reflection. But if we want to understand the relation of language and poetry in Heidegger's thinking, we need to start differently.[1]

For me the crucial text for the study of the later Heidegger is "The Origin of the Work of Art," in which language is hardly mentioned. This is the essay—actually, a series of three lectures—in which Heidegger studies a painting by Van Gogh, which he then puts aside for a building, a Greek temple, as a model or instance of the work of art. It is also the text in which he introduces for the first time the mysterious notions, if "notions" is the right word, of earth and world. Heidegger says: "The temple-work, standing there, opens up a world and at the same time sets this world back again on earth, which itself only thus emerges as native [*heimatliche*] ground" (Hw 32/42). The rest of "The Origin of the Work of Art" is, in a sense, Heidegger's elaborate and sometimes baffling reflection on this sentence.

What is crucial about "The Origin of the Work of Art" is that each of Heidegger's later meditations on language and poetry presupposes the strange and untheorizable relationship of earth and world. What are these things, exactly? One doesn't know what to call them; they belong to the domain of quotation marks, where they are no longer earth and world in any usual sense. With them Heidegger begins to lay out something like a semantic field in which his thinking with respect to language will go on, but language does not itself inhabit this field. Moreover, there's no mapping this field, no giving a comprehensive picture of it ("field" is a wayward metaphor). As Derrida says in perhaps the most important essay so far on Heidegger's language, "The *Retrait* of Metaphor" (1978), there is a serious problem about the translatability of this semantic "field," that is, a problem about whether we can actually make our way in it—whether, for example, we can translate ourselves into it the way we would insert ourselves into a strange tongue.[2] In fact there is a major sense in which Heidegger's strange talk is not a tongue, that is, not a language in which anyone, perhaps not even Heidegger, could grow competent (and so make sense); it is not anything one becomes a speaker (much less a master) of. One is always outside this language, or rather this language is always outside one's own. Perhaps we should imagine ourselves in the position of the native whose speech is being parodied by another. Indeed, much of the later Heidegger's language seems to have the bearing of parody upon customary (everyday as well as philosophical) discourse. He does not introduce a new lexicon or philosophical diction; rather he loosens the grip we have on the words we have in hand, allowing them to get away from us. My hope, however, is that if we proceed slowly, we can come to some sense of these words, some sense of how to respond to them even though they leave us hesitating or groping in the dark.

"Upon the earth and in it," Heidegger says, "historical man grounds his dwelling in the world" (Hw 35/46). This "grounding" is the *work* of the work of art. The world is the human world which comes into the open or into its own in virtue of the work of art, which establishes a clearing in which we can enter into time and being. The earth, by contrast, is that which withholds itself from this work. The earth is characterized by reserve and refusal. It resists every effort we make to break into it and bring it under control or make it work for us. As Heidegger says, the earth is "that which is by nature undisclosable [*unerschliessbare*], that which shrinks from every disclosure and constantly keeps itself closed up [*sich verschlossen hält*: reserved, incommunicative, withdrawn]" (Hw 36/47). The earth, however, nevertheless goes into the work of art and belongs to the essence of its "createdness [*das Geschaffensein*]"; but it is too early to say what this means.

"The world," Heidegger says, "is not the mere collection of the countable and uncountable, familiar or unfamiliar objects that are there." The world is not anything we can represent to ourselves; it is not picturable, not a spectator's world. "World is never an object that stands before us and can be seen" (Hw 33/44); rather, as we have already learned from *Being and Time*, what counts is the environmental character of the world (SZ, sect. 15–18): the world is the "wherein" wherein we live and which involves us in everyday practical ways. Only now, in "The Origin of the Work of Art," the world is there with something else or something other (the other of the world), namely the earth. By contrast with ourselves in the world, Heidegger says, "A stone is worldless. Plant and animal likewise have no world; but they belong to the covert throng of a surrounding into which they are linked" (Hw 33–34/45). Stone, plant, and animal are of the earth. "A stone presses downward and manifests its heaviness. But while this heaviness exerts an opposing pressure upon us it denies any penetration into it. If we attempt such penetration by breaking open the rock, it still does not display in its fragments anything inward that has been disclosed. The stone has instantly withdrawn [*zurückgezogen*] again into the same dull pressure and bulk of its fragments" (Hw 35/46–47).

The key word here is *zurückziehen*: to withdraw. What is this withdrawal? In French it is *retrait*, Derrida's complex pun. Much of our understanding of the later Heidegger will depend on the sense this notion comes to have for us.

Here withdrawal is basic to the opposition of earth and world. "Earth," Heidegger says, "shatters every attempt to break into it." And again: "The earth is essentially self-secluding [*Sichverschliessende*]" (Hw 36/47), whereas the world is self-disclosing—Heidegger calls it "the self-disclosing openness of the broad paths and essential decisions in the destiny [*Geschick*] of an historical people" (Hw 37/48). So earth sounds the note of estrangement, whereas world means solidarity, homeland, and nationhood.

Earth and world are unalterably opposed to one another, striving against one another. Heidegger attaches supreme importance to this strife, as in the following passage—where, however, strife is not quite its usual self:

> The opposition of earth and world is a striving [*Streit*]. But we would surely all too easily falsify its nature if we were to confound striving and discord and dispute, and thus see it only as disorder and destruction. In essential striving, rather, the opponents raise each other into the self-assertion [*Selbstbehauptung*] of

their natures. . . . In the struggle, each opponent carries the other beyond itself. Thus the striving becomes ever more intense as striving, and more authentically what it is. The more the struggle overdoes itself on its own part, the more inflexibly do the opponents let themselves go into the intimacy of simple belonging to one another [*umso unnachgiebiger lassen sich die Streitenden in die Innigkeit des einfachen Sichgehörens los*]. The earth cannot dispense with the Open of the world if it is itself to appear as earth in the liberated surge of its self-seclusion [*Sichverschliessens*]. The world, again, cannot soar out of the earth's sight if, as the governing breadth and path of all essential destiny, it is to ground itself on a resolute foundation. [Hw 37–38/49]

Attention normally falls upon the last sentence of this passage in which the world grounds itself on a "resolute foundation [*sich auf ein Entschiedenes gründen*]." In the later writings Heidegger drops talk of foundations. Thinking entails the letting-go of (or from) such things. More to the point of the later Heidegger is the following, "The more the struggle overdoes itself on its own part, the more inflexibly do the opponents let themselves go into the intimacy of simple belonging to one another."

As a way of glossing this line, one might recall the question that concluded Heidegger's inaugural lecture, "What is Metaphysics?" (1929): "Why are there any beings at all, and why not rather nothing?" (Wm 19/112). Part of the answer seems to lie in this "intimacy of simple belonging together" of earth and world. Left to itself, the earth would simply fold in upon itself like a black hole; emancipated from the earth, the world would dissipate like a cloud of dust expanding in every direction. "World and earth," Heidegger says, "are always intrinsically and essentially in conflict, belligerent by nature" (Hw 44/55). However—and here Heidegger introduces his strange notion of rift (*der Riss*: rent, tear, but also sketch, design, or plan)—"The conflict," he says, "is not a rift as a mere cleft is ripped open; rather, it is the intimacy with which opponents belong to each other. This rift carries the opponents into the source of their common ground [*Dieser Riss reisst die Gegenwendigen in die Herkunft inhrer Einheit aus dem einigen Grunde zusammen*]. It is a basic design [*Grundriss*]. It is an outline sketch [*Auf-riss*] that draws the basic features of the rise of the lighting of beings [*der die Grundzüge des Aufgehens der Lichtung des Seienden zeichnet*]. This rift does not let opponents break apart; it brings the opposition of measure and boundary into their common outline" (Hw 51/63).

The rift will turn up at crucial moments in each of Heidegger's major texts on language. There is no way to make sense of the term once for all—it is a radically heterogeneous notion, a singular word, best understood as a parody of the concept of deep or basic structure. The main thing is that one has to be careful when trying to figure out the rift not to idealize it by converting it into a hidden unifying principle, as if beneath earth and world there were a transcendental ground or ultimate foundation (*Letztbegrundung*) that upholds the two in eternal oneness. It is true that Heidegger speaks of earth and world as sharing—or at all events as having—a common ground (*aus dem einigen Grunde zusammen*), but, as Gadamer points out in an essay on "The Hermeneutics of Suspicion," common ground is incomparably different from the *Letztbegrundung* of formal philosophy (Gadamer recalls: "I remember very well how Heidegger said one day to me, '*Letztbegrundung*—what a strange idea!'").[3] Common ground is rather a common boundary where rift is not a shared region but a binding difference (or dif-ference: *Unter-Schied*). What is it to share, not an identity, but a difference? It appears that *der Riss*, as it emerges in "The Origin of the Work of Art," is Heidegger's first attempt to get away from talk about foundations. Perhaps one could say that "rift" is a way of letting-go of the ground.

The point for now is that it is in the context of the rift of earth and world that Heidegger introduces the notion of truth. One might say, should say, that what matters with respect to the work of art is not beauty but truth, only truth is not what we think. Already in *Being and Time*, of course, Heidegger had opposed truth as *alētheia*, the Greek unforgetting, to the logical conceptions of correspondence and noncontradiction (sect. 44). *Alētheia* is disclosedness or unconcealment (*Entdecktheit* or *Unverborgenheit*). In "The Origin of the Work of Art," Heidegger adds a new turn: truth is not *alētheia* purely and simply, because *alētheia* is always bound to concealment. For example, Heidegger writes: "In the midst of beings as a whole an open place occurs. There is a clearing, a lighting [*eine Lichtung*: one word in the German text is given two translations]. Thought of in reference to what is, to beings, this clearing *is* in a greater degree than are beings. This open center [*Mitte*: middle, midst] is therefore not surrounded by what is; rather, the lighting center [*die lichtende Mitte*] itself encircles all that is, like the Nothing that we scarcely know" (Hw 41/53).

Like the Nothing we scarcely know (wie das Nichts, das wir kaum ken-nen): the allusion here is to "What is Metaphysics?" whose theme is the Nothing disclosed in anxiety or the slipping away of beings. Here is an important passage from "What is Metaphysics?" where the Nothing has to do less with mere negation than with otherness and estrange-ment:

> Nihilation [*das Nichten*] is not some fortuitious incident. Rather, as the repelling gesture toward the retreating whole of beings, it discloses these beings in their full but heretofore concealed strangeness as what is radically other—with respect to the Noth-ing [*verborgenen Befremdlichkeit als das schlechthin Anderer—gegen-über dem Nichts*].
>
> In the clear night of the Nothing of anxiety the original open-ness of beings as such arises: that they are beings—and not noth-ing. But this "and not nothing" we add in our talk is not some kind of appended clarification. Rather it makes possible in advance the revelation of beings in general [*der Offenbarkeit von Seiendem überhaupt*]. The essence of the originally nihilating Nothing [*des ursprünglich nichtenden Nichts*] lies in this, that it brings *Dasein* for the first time before beings as such. [Wm 11–12/105]

Des ursprünglich nichtenden Nichts: this splendid negativity would later be appropriated by the French—by Sartre and with even more in-triguing results by Maurice Blanchot, and in comic fashion by Samuel Beckett.[4] In "The Origin of the Work of Art," however, this meta-physical lexicon of *being* and *nothingness* disappears into the semantic space of *Unverborgenheit* and *Entziehung*. What is, is, only in virtue of its emergence into the open, the clearing or lighting; but this emer-gence is not anything like the creation, constitution, or objectification of beings as merely present entities, because what is, is, only in virtue of withdrawal or concealment. "Every being we encounter and which encounters us," Heidegger says, "keeps to this curious opposition of presence and absence [*Anwesens*] in that it always withholds itself at the same time in a concealedness [*indem es sich zugleich immer in eine Verbor-genheit zurückhält*]. The clearing in which beings stand is at the same time a concealment [*Verbergung*]" (Hw 42/53). As if the light were also a darkness.

Concealment, Heidegger says, can be twofold. It "can be refusal [*Versagen*] or merely a dissembling [*Verstellen*]" (Hw 42/54); that is, it can be self-seclusion or withdrawal on the one hand, and masking, disguise, or figure on the other, where something appears only by concealing itself as something other or as what it is not. In any event, Heidegger says, "the open place in the midst of beings, the clearing, is never a rigid stage with a permanently raised curtain on which the play of beings runs its course" (Hw 42/54). It is not presentation or representation as a steadfast object of a spectator's gaze. "The un-concealedness of beings—this is never a merely existent state, but a happening [*ein Geschehnis*]. Unconcealedness is neither an attribute of factual things in the sense of beings, nor one of propositions" (Hw 42/54). It is not anything that can be predicated of anything (predicated, for example, of knowledge or of assertions as to states of affairs); or for all of that it is not anything that can be put into words. Perhaps we should imagine truth being put into quotation marks.

The thing to say is that truth is an event of estrangement; but before saying this I think we need to study carefully the following passage about the nature of truth:

> We believe we are at home in the immediate circle of beings. That which is, is familiar, reliable, ordinary [*vertraut, verlässlich, geheuer*]. Nevertheless, the clearing is pervaded by a constant concealment in the double form of refusal and dissembling [*in der Doppelgestalt des Versagens und des Verstellens*]. At bottom, the ordinary is not ordinary; it is extraordinary, uncanny [*Das Geheuer ist im Grunde nicht geheuer; es ist un-geheuer*]. The nature of truth, that is, of unconcealedness, is dominated throughout by a denial [*von der Verweigerung*]. Yet this denial is not a defect or a fault, as though truth were an unalloyed unconcealedness that has rid itself of everything concealed. If truth could accomplish this, it would no longer be itself. This denial, in the form of a double concealment, belongs to the nature of truth as unconcealedness. Truth, in its nature, is untruth [*Die Wahrheit ist in ihrem Wesen Un-wahrheit*]. [Hw 43/54]

Scholia: In "The Essence of Truth" (1930) Heidegger had characterized truth as freedom, or letting beings *be*, which is what we seldom do. "Man clings to what is readily available and controllable even where ultimate matters [*das Erste und Letzte*] are concerned" (Wm 90/134). And again: "Certainly among readily familiar things there are also some that are puzzling, unexplained, undecided, questionable. But these self-certain questions are merely transitional, intermediate points in our movement within the readily familiar and thus not essential. Wherever the concealment of beings as a whole is conceded only as a limit that occasionally announces itself, concealing as a fundamental occurence has sunk into forgetfulness" (Wm 90/134). It is part of the work of the work of art, that is, its truth, not to allow this forgetfulness of concealment, of the truth of un-truth, to occur. This is because concealment belongs to the truth of the work as to truth itself.

Of course, the statement that "Truth, in its nature, is untruth," is certainly outrageous and obviously false, but this (I mean, as a *statement*) is plainly not how the line is to be taken: it is not a proposition after all. Heidegger says that he puts "the matter this way in order to serve notice . . . that denial in the manner of concealment belongs to unconcealedness as clearing. The proposition, 'the nature of truth is untruth,' is not, however, intended to state that truth is at bottom falsehood. Nor does it mean that truth is never itself but, viewed dialectically, is always also its opposite" (Hw 43/54–55). Truth is not linked dialectically to its opposite—dialectic for Heidegger would perhaps be a form of what he calls "errancy" (*die Irre*: see "The Essence of Truth," where Heidegger says that "Man's flight from the mystery toward what is readily available, onward from one current thing to the next, passing the mystery by—this is *erring*" [Wm 92/135]). Rather, truth is always there with its *other*, not its opposite. The otherness of truth is not merely an accidental divergence from essence, an error or mistake or falsehood. It is rather that truth itself is inscribed by a rift that splits it, so to say, lengthwise, joining the familiar and the strange, openness and refusal, clearing and dissembling, unconcealedness and withdrawal, darkness and light. Clearly, truth here is no longer that which takes up its residence in knowledge and the discourse of propositions. "Truth occurs as such," Heidegger says, "in the opposition of clearing and double concealing. Truth is the primal conflict in which, always in some particular way, the Open is won within which everything stands and from which everything withholds itself that shows itself and withdraws itself as a being [*Die Wahrheit ist der Urstreit, in dem je in einer Weise das Offene erstritten wird, in das alles hereinsteht und aus dem alles sich zurückhält, was als Seiendes sich zeigt und erstellt*]" (Hw 49/60–61). Truth is not a transcendental logos but is always self-divided, earthly as well as worldly. It is "the opposition of clearing and concealing": "truth does not exist in itself beforehand, somewhere among the stars, only later to descend elsewhere among human beings" (Hw 49–50/61). So it does not belong to the usual category of revelation. As Heidegger will later put it, "*Alētheia*, unconcealment as the opening of presence, is not yet truth" (SD 76/68). Truth is always historical; it is always an event.

However, what this means is still very far from clear. It is easy to say that truth is not correspondence between mind and world or word and object; truth is not a logical picture of the world nor any sort of representation of states of affairs that consciousness might frame for itself. Nor is it how things hang together in a conceptual scheme. Truth is unconcealedness, and also concealment—but how exactly is this formulation to be understood? Heidegger's earliest understanding is formulated in terms of the work of art and *its* otherness or strangeness, its openness to mystery and withdrawal from the readily available: which is to say perhaps *its* truth, which is never reducible to unalloyed unconcealment. Perhaps one can say that the work of art discloses the otherness of truth.[5]

Opening: The Work of Art in Its Orphic Character

"The Origin of the Work of Art" is a bewildering essay, partly because its long first section on "Thing and Work" (which is frequently the only section anyone reads) is, as Heidegger says, a "detour" designed to take us out of the long-standing prejudice of aestheticism that the work of art is an object that we can take into our possession and subjugate to our experience (Hw 28/39). The point is perhaps to get away from van Gogh's painting, that is, away from the mode of the subjecting subject, whether as artist or as observer. We need to get into the mode (or rather the truth) of the work.

There is a difference for Heidegger between thing and equipment and again between thing and work. We can take up equipment and put it to use—even use it up—but we ought to let things be: things are not for our use, even though it is part of our modernist frame of mind that things exist as objects in subjection to subjectivity. An important notion, perhaps *the* important notion, in Heidegger's later thinking is *Gelassenheit*, letting-go, which begins to take on a life of its own for the first time in "The Origin of the Work of Art." I will come back to *Gelassenheit* again and again, but for now it is only necessary to understand this difference between thing (understood in its usual sense, which will shortly change) and work: the work is not any sort of object, it is an event. It has about it, to be sure, thingly and equipmental features: it is a sort of being and we can do all sorts of things with it (it can teach us things). But the work of art does not really come into its own until it *works*. The reality of the work (say its truth) lies in what occurs when it comes into its own. This coming-into-its-own means, among other things, that the museum is no place for works of art.

Museums imply spectator-theories of art against which the whole of "The Origin of the Work of Art" pitches itself. Similarly, the library, possibly also the book, is no place for *Antigone*.

"Where does the work belong?" Heidegger asks. "The work belongs, as work, uniquely within the realm opened up by itself. For the work-being of the work is present in, and only in, such opening up" (Hw 30/41).[6] This question of belonging is easier to clarify with respect to a Greek temple, which never just exhibits itself or lends itself to display, than with the example of a van Gogh painting, which after all does empirically belong to a museum. In order to clarify the work of opening-up, Heidegger speaks of the temple as follows:

> Standing there, the building rests upon rocky ground. This resting of the work draws up out of the rock the mystery [*das Dunkel*] of that rock's clumsy yet spontaneous support. Standing there, the building holds its ground against the storm raging above it and so first makes the storm itself manifest in its violence [*und zeigt so erst den Sturm selbst in seiner Gewalt*]. The luster and gleam of the stone, though itself apparently glowing only by the grace of the sun, yet first brings to light the light of the day, the breadth of the sky, the darkness [*die Finsternis*] of the night. The temple's firm towering makes visible the visible space of air. The steadfastness of the work contrasts with the surge of the surf, and its own repose brings out the raging of the sea. Tree and grass, eagle and bull, snake and cricket first enter into their distinctive shapes [*Gestalt*] and thus come to appear as what they are. The Greeks early called this emerging and rising in itself and in all things *phūsis*. It clears and illuminates, also, that on which and in which man bases his dwelling. We call this ground the *earth*. What this word says is not to be associated with the idea of a mass of matter deposited somewhere, or with the merely astronomical idea of a planet. Earth is that whence the arising brings back and shelters everything that arises without violation. In the things that arise, earth is present as the sheltering agent. [Hw 31/42]

Here the phenomenon of opening is vividly sketched out: the Greek temple is not any sort of representation—it "portrays nothing," Heidegger says (Hw 30/41)—rather its work is to bring things into the open, drawing the rock up out of darkness, making the storm manifest, bringing the light of day to light and the night of night to darkness—summoning all things into their being as if by some great orphic calling. The world is brought into the open within the shelter of the earth. "The temple-work, standing there, opens up a world and at the same time sets this world back again on earth, which itself only thus emerges as native ground" (Hw 32/42).

Naturally we want to know *how* the temple does it, and probably no argument exists that could finally persuade us that this is not the question to ask—the question of *how the temple works*. This question is part of the errancy of the modern age, the age of structuralism, of analytical and calculative reason, which has no other interest in things except in how they work or what strategies they employ. The question of how the work works is a question concerning technology. It belongs to what Heidegger will call the *Ge-Stell* or Enframing of our time. This is by no means a bad question in itself. We belong to our own time and cannot expatriate ourselves to other worlds. Not to be analytical or structurally-minded–not to understand the importance of how works of art are made and how their rules of operation are to be described—is not to have grasped the emergence of art in the age of technology.

Nevertheless, the whole point of "The Origin of the Work of Art" is to estrange us from the analytical or instrumental interest in the work of art that makes the work intelligible and valuable within the aesthetic and structuralist (now poststructuralist) condominium. And certainly nothing is more strange than Heidegger's account of the temple-work as it "sets up a world" (Hw 34/45). Who would not want to experience the temple-work as it goes about its originating "function"? However, Heidegger's account of the temple-work cannot be translated into anything we could recognize as aesthetic experience. Indeed, as Gadamer points out in the introduction to his edition of *Der Ursprung des Kunstwerkes*, the concepts of Heidegger's work after *Being and Time* cannot be justified according to normal philosophical procedures, including the appeal to experience or to empirical evidence or to analytical results.[7] This is Gadamer's way of putting Derrida's question about the translatability of Heidegger's language; it is a question, not just about the accessibility of Heidegger's thinking, but about the closure of our own—the way our own thinking has sealed off from whatever is not itself (from the horror of unreason).

In *Modern Poetry and the Idea of Language* I tried to normalize Heidegger's conception of the work of art by assimilating it into a distinction between orphic and hermetic conceptions of poetic language. In the hermetic view language is a system that depends on nothing external for its intelligibility. Likewise a poem is a system of relations whose principle of intelligibility is formal rather than semantic, as in

Flaubert's dream of "a book about nothing," or in Valéry's poetics, or in Foucault's idea of the "radical intransitivity" of literary language, where poetry or literature becomes, as Foucault says, "a manifestation of a language which has no other law than that of affirming—in opposition to all other forms of discourse—its own precipitous existence; and so there is nothing for it to do but to curve back in a perpetual return upon itself, as if discourse could have no other content than the expression of its own form."[8] By contrast, the orphic view is given in the whole tradition of romantic poetics, where poetry is not just the construction of works in the sense of formal objects; it is also, and foundationally, the making of worlds. From von Humboldt to Cassirer, from Coleridge to Wallace Stevens, and from Hölderlin to Heidegger, one can see the reconceptualization of the ancient myth of Orpheus, who could summon things into being by the sheer power of his language. Heidegger's great essay, "Hölderlin and the Essence of Poetry," which belongs to the same period as "The Origin of the Work of Art," is perhaps the most perfect recuperation of this myth. "The poet," Heidegger says, "names the gods and names all things in that which they are. This naming does not consist in something already known being supplied with a name; it is rather that when the poet speaks the essential word, the being is by this naming nominated as what it is. So it becomes known as being. Poetry is the establishing of being by means of the word [*Dichtung ist worthafte Stiftung des Seins*]" (ED 41/281). Moreover, poetry is foundational not only for the world but for language as well. One imagines, Heidegger says, that "the essence [*Wesen*] of poetry must be understood through the essence of language. [But] poetry is the inaugural naming of being and of the essence of all things—not just any speech, but that particular kind which for the first time brings into the open all that which we then discuss and deal with in everyday language. Hence poetry never takes language as a raw material ready to hand, rather it is poetry which first makes language possible. Poetry is the primitive language of a historical people. Therefore, in just the reverse manner, the essence of language must be understood through the essence of poetry" (ED 43/283–84).

I still think that I've got it right about the orphic character of Heidegger's Hölderlin-interpretation and about its difference from the hermetic theory, but I think now that the writings on Hölderlin do not provide the threshold to the later Heidegger in quite the way that "The Origin of the Work of Art" does. And I think that the difference lies in the concept of estrangement, that is, in the question of the otherness of truth and the otherness of the work of art as that which closes itself up, conceals itself, withholds itself and breaks the will-to-power. In the later Heidegger poetry can no longer be characterized unproblematically as originary and foundational; on the contrary, it appears instead that the essence of poetry is to be found in its renunciation of the power of the word.

Closing: The Work of Art in Its Hermetic Character

Readers familiar with "The Origin of the Work of Art" will have seen that I am coming round to this essay by the back door and have been reading it, well, not backwards exactly, but also not as if it were a piece of consecutive thinking, for it is not. Heidegger says: "Art then is the becoming and happening of truth" (Hw 59/71). This means, in part, that the work of the work of art is to set up a world according, say, to the orphic thesis. Heidegger says, "The work holds open the Open of the world" (Hw 34/45). But we have seen that the notion of truth as disclosure or unconcealedness has been redeployed by Heidegger within the "semantic field" of the rift of earth and world. This means that the truth of the work of art cannot simply be a feature that makes it reminiscent of the myth of Orpheus. There is in fact another feature of the work of art, I mean another feature of the working of its work, and that is precisely its earthly character. What does this mean? Well, it means that you can't simply assimilate Heidegger's aesthetics into a poetics of worldmaking.

According to Heidegger, the rift of earth and world manifests itself in the work of art, and it does so first of all in the createdness of the work, since the work is itself an emergence into the Open—but *it is an emergence out of earthly materials*. "When a work," Heidegger says, "is created, brought forth out of this or that work-material—stone, wood, metal, color, language, tone—we say also that it is made, set forth out of it" (Hw 34/45). The work opens up a world, sets it up if you want to use the foundationalist metaphor, but the earthly material out of which it is made is not therefore used up. As Valéry says, speaking from the history of Mallarméan experience (with its critical encounter with *le Néant*, which breaks the hold that meaning has on language), the difference between ordinary speech and poetic creation is that in poetry language is not annihilated by the production of meaning or the understanding of what is said. Rather language, by which Valéry means the materiality of language, reserves the poem to itself and will not allow it to be used up in the process of signification.[9] This is also Heidegger's point: The work opens up a world, but the thrust of the work is always to return to earth, that is, to withdraw (in the strong Heideggerian sense of this word) from the Open into the stone, wood, metal, language, or tone whence it emerged into its createdness. Its createdness means that it abides in the Open *as* this withdrawal.

Imagine, for example, a poem struggling to withdraw from the world it opens up, I mean draw back (*zurückziehen*) into language. Imagine a poem trying to hide in its words, where words are not signs or signifiers in a system but, as Gerard Manley Hopkins always took them to be, something belonging to the same region as elements of the physical universe, bodies subject to gravity and the laws of energy.[10] Hopkins never thought of words just in terms of meaning (one cannot imagine any poet thinking just in these terms); rather, he recuperated the ancient philological imagination on which the tradition of allegory is based, which is that words are shining or dark, luminous or enigmatic, and that the task of exegesis is not to eliminate darkness or enigma but to enter into it and abide with it, because illumination always occurs *within* darkness, not in opposition to it. Darkness is the other, not the opposite, of light. This is something that Hopkins's friend, Coventry Patmore, could never understand. He wanted Hopkins to write immediately intelligible poetry, and Hopkins resisted, arguing that the darkness of poetry is not a defect of its language but the essence of it.[11]

Think of the opposition between poetry and the idea of a philosophical language, that is, between the dark saying or dissembling figure and the lucidity of the self-justifying or self-evident proposition, the statement that can be taken just as it stands, which never requires interpretation because it can never be taken differently. Heidegger, like Hopkins before him, plants his feet squarely against this ideal of transparent expression. "Tree and grass, eagle and bull, snake and cricket first enter into their distinctive shapes and thus come to be what they are. The Greeks early called this emerging and rising in itself and in all things *phūsis*" (Hw 31/42). But Heidegger knows the dark saying of Heraclitus, which is that "Phūsis loves to hide [*phūsis krūptesthai philei*]" (Fr. 123). Heidegger discusses this saying in "Alētheia (Heraclitus, Fragment B16)" (Wm 263–64/133). The work of art is *phūsis* in this double sense of disclosure in which all things come to appear as what they are and self-withdrawal (*Sichzurückziehung*) or self-concealment in which the work closes in upon itself, refuses to give itself up to our penetrating gaze.

Certainly it is clear that truth, as Heidegger understands it, is not to be thought of as the *product* of the work of art. It is never any sort of meaning, idea, or knowledge—never, in short, anything that can be put into words. Rather, truth occurs *in* the work *as* the conflict of earth and world. This conflict is characterized by Heidegger as a rift (*Riss*), where rift carries the double meaning of tear, rip, and also design or sketch. As always with Heidegger, one is never compelled to choose among alternative senses of a word; on the contrary, one is actually forbidden to make such a choice. Heidegger's way is to let words be (the way one lets puns pun): one should not try to compel them in this or that direction or confine them to a fixed construction. One should never try to make words a mouthpiece for saying this or that, because their work is not this sort of saying: it is not the expression of meanings, not, at any rate, in the usual sense of the differentiation of senses. Words are not to be thought of as meanings at all, never mind that we find it impossible to think of them, or speak of them, or with them, in any other way. We cannot speak of words and language without constant reference to the concept of meaning, especially if our language is English or French. Heidegger means to cure us of this addiction to theories of meaning and signification, but it is still too early for him to succeed.

Truth occurs *in* the work as the rift of earth and world, where rift carries the double meaning of tear and sketch—rift-design (*Auf-Riss*). How does this rift show itself in the work? Heidegger's answer is: in the *createdness* of the work, which manifests itself in the work's desire to withdraw into its earthly materials. But there is more. The rift-design, Heidegger says, shows itself in the *Gestalt* of the work—fixes itself in the work as its *Gestalt* (Hw 52/64). Heidegger uses the word *Gestalt* differently from its use in the psychoaesthetic tradition; with Heidegger the word entails a pun on *Ge-Stell* or Enframing (and on a good deal else besides, given the prestige of the root -*stell* in the German philosophical tradition). Here the point is that truth occurs in the work as both disclosure or unconcealedness (*Unverborgenheit*) *and* "denial in the double form [*Doppelgestalt*] of refusal and dissembling" (Hw 43/54), that is, denial in the sense of not saying or in not appearing to be what it is. It is difficult to resist a temptation here to improvise a Heideggerian theory of metaphor on the basis of this conception of *Gestalt* or *Doppelgestalt* as refusal and figurality in which something manifests itself—enters into the open—as something other than itself or other than usual. Metaphor conceived in a Heideggerian spirit would thus emphasize otherness, difference, strangeness, disguise, allegory. In fact, at the outset of "The Origin of the Work of Art," Heidegger offers a preliminary characterization of the work of art precisely in the traditional language of rhetoric and grammar: "The work of art," he says, "is, to be sure, a thing that is made, but it says something other than the mere thing itself is, *allo agoreuei*. The work makes public something other than itself; it is an allegory. In the work of art something other is brought together with the thing that is made. To bring together is, in Greek, *sumballein*. The work is a symbol" (Hw 9/19–20).

It turns out, however, that the whole purpose of "The Origin of the Work of Art" is to emancipate us from the traditional language of figurality. A theory of metaphor is precisely what we no longer need in order to reflect on the otherness of the work of art. This is why so much of "The Origin of the Work of Art" is given over to the *createdness* of the work, where createdness, however, is less a condition of the work as a product of the artist's hand than it is the condition of the work's earthliness—a condition which is not subject to or brought about by the artist but is prior to all handiwork and which craftsmanship or *poiēsis* presupposes. In fact, "The Origin of the Work of Art" has very little to say about the artist. "The emergence of createdness from the work," Heidegger says, "does not mean that the work is to give the impression of having been made by a great artist" (Hw 53/65). A theory of the artist—a theory of genius, for example, or of imagination —is as superfluous to the work of art as a theory of metaphor.[12]

For Heidegger, the createdness of the work is the mark of its radical otherness, its reserve, its self-refusal, its *Sichzurückziehung*. "The event [*Ereignis*] of its being created does not simply reverberate through the work," Heidegger says; "rather, the work casts before itself the eventful fact [*Ereignishafte*] that the work *is* as this work, and it has constantly this fact about itself. The more essentially the work opens itself, the more luminous becomes the uniqueness of the fact that it is rather than is not. The more essentially this thrust comes into the Open, the stronger and more solitary the work becomes" (Hw 53–54/ 65–66). The work is not anything that anyone can be in possession of: we cannot appropriate it or make it our own because the work, in coming into its own (*eigen*), belongs to nothing but itself. This is the meaning of the event (*Ereignis*) of its createdness. The work is never an artist's or a connoisseur's delight or a critic's reconstruction. Indeed, it cannot be placed in the false predicament in which current criticism finds itself when it tries to choose between authorial intention and readerly response as the source or ground of the work's intelligibility.

The work is entirely solitary; it stands on its own and does not require to be grounded in anything that is not itself. But we should not mistake this for a theory of the autonomy of the work of art. Heidegger takes the hermetic character of the work of art beyond formalism, or anyhow elsewhere, in a different direction.

Poetry as Estrangement

I arrive now at what appears to be the critical moment, perhaps one could say the theoretical center, of Heidegger's essay. Heidegger at any rate signals this effect: "this view of the nature of the work's createdness," he says, "now enables us to take the step toward which everything thus far tends" (Hw 54/66). The following passage shows the way:

> The more solitary the work, fixed in the figure [Gestalt], stands on its own and the more cleanly it seems to cut all ties to human beings, the more simply does the thrust come into the Open that such a work *is*, and the more essentially is the extraordinary [Ungeheuere] thrust to the surface and the long-familiar [bislang geheuer] thrust down. But this multiple thrusting [vielfältige Stossen] is nothing violent, for the more purely the work is itself transported into the openness of beings—an openness opened by itself —the more simply does it transport us out of the realm of the ordinary [or out of the customary: aus dem Gewöhnlichen heraus]. To submit to this displacement means: to transform our accustomed ties to world and to earth and henceforth to restrain all usual doing and prizing, knowing and looking, in order to stay within the truth that is happening in the work. Only the restraint of this staying lets what is created be the work that it is [Die Verhaltenheit dieses Verweilens lässt das Geschaffene erst das Werk sein, das es ist]. This letting the work be a work [das Werk ein Werk sein lassen] we call the preserving [Bewahrung] of the work. [Hw 54/66]

In trying to understand the later Heidegger, everything depends on restraint, letting-be [Gelassenheit], and staying within the truth that occurs in the work. It is certain that what Heidegger calls "the preserving of the work" is something radically different from any of the ways our culture teaches us to comport ourselves with respect to art. It is certainly very different from curatorship, connoisseurship, criticism, or acts of interpretation that try to protect the work of art from its historicality. On the contrary, it is perhaps the historicality of the work that we need most carefully to understand.[13]

What Heidegger asks us to consider, however, is the fact that the work of art "seems to cut all ties to human beings." How is this otherness to be understood? For it is the case that the truth which occurs in the work cannot be characterized simply as the setting up of the world that we find already at hand; it is at the same time a work of *estrangement*—the work abolishes the familiar and transports us "out of the realm of the customary." Recall the passage quoted earlier in which Heidegger first laid open the double character of truth: "We believe we are at home in the immediate circle of beings. That which is, is familiar, reliable, ordinary." Here is the situation in which the work of art makes its appearance. The createdness of the work, its earthly character, also means its historicality, its situatedness. The work does not occur in an aboriginal void or in the papertime of literary or art history. The work is an event that occurs in the history of a people, and it is always like the breaking-in or intervention of an outsider, of something refractory and uncontainable, even though the otherness of the work of art does not mean that it originates elsewhere in some otherworldly place or alien context and only subsequently visits human history. As we have seen, "truth does not exist in itself beforehand, somewhere among the stars" (Hw 49–50/61). "Does truth, then," Heidegger asks, "arise out of nothing? It does indeed if by nothing is meant the mere *not* of that which is, and if we here think of that which is as an object present in the ordinary way, which thereafter comes to light and is challenged by the existence of the work as only presumptively true being. Truth is never gathered from objects that are present and ordinary" (Hw 59/71). The occurrence of truth always means estrangement from what is merely present and familiar. However, this does *not* mean the romantic coloration of the commonplace with the air of the supernatural; it does not mean the breaking-in of transcendence or the eternal return of the same. It is rather as if "the immediate circle of beings" in which we feel ourselves so comfortably disposed were not a world after all but a closure which it then becomes the task of art to break open and perhaps even to bring crashing down. The truth of the work cannot be appropriated. The work resists appropriation. It refuses to be allegorized; it is the undoing of allegory.

We must be careful, however, not to deform the work of estrangement into something like a doctrine of emancipation from convention or habituated response. Heidegger's thinking leads elsewhere. The work of estrangement occurs when the work comes so radically into its own—becomes so powerful and solitary—that "it seems to cut all ties to human beings." It is so wholly other that we can see nothing in it; it mirrors nothing we can recognize. (One cannot help thinking here of the Mallarméan poem or a text like *Finnegans Wake*).[14] Its otherness means that we can make no place for it within any framework that makes the world an intelligible object for us. The work won't be an object for our subjective gaze, nor will it produce or reproduce any such object. Its work of estrangement is completely different from formalist or structuralist defamiliarization in which the familiar is re-experienced with a new innocence or a new awakening of the senses or with the sort of enlightened consciousness that is made possible by the breaking-down of conventions and the overturning of tradition. The work of estrangement in Heidegger's aesthetics is not the break-up of the forms and habits of mind, perception, or experience in which we encounter anything; it is not any sort of critique of consciousness. It is not a crisis in the history of art.

Heidegger calls this work of estrangement poetry. He says: "All art, as the letting happen of the advent of the truth of what is, is, as such, *essentially poetry* [*im Wesen Dichtung*]." Yet it is the following line that I want to emphasize: "It is due to art's poetic nature [*dem dichtenden Wesen*] that, in the midst of what is, art breaks open an open place, in whose openness everything is other than usual."[15] Moreover, it is not just that things *look* different from before; rather, "everything ordinary and hitherto existing becomes an unbeing [*Unseienden*]" (Hw 59/72). Poetry is not *poiēsis* and it is not any sort of worldmaking; it is not just a change in the look of things. We must shake the idea that it is anything productive. Think of it rather as a sort of annihilation of whatever is present.

A sort of annihilation, but of what sort? Naturally we imagine an empirical vanishing or a logical negation or a metaphysical yawning of the abyss, but the un-becoming (or, say, un-coming) of things is not simply their return to a primordial state of nonbeing. The phenomenon in question here is related to the "slipping away of beings" that Heidegger talks about in "What is Metaphysics?":

> In anxiety occurs a shrinking back before [*Zurückweichen vor*] . . . which is surely not any sort of flight but rather a kind of bewildered calm. This "back before" takes its departure from the Nothing [*vom Nichts*]. The Nothing itself does not attract; it is essentially repelling. But this repulsion is itself such a parting ges-

ture toward beings that are submerging [*das versinkende Seiende*] as a whole. This wholly repelling gesture toward beings that are in retreat [*abweisende Verweisung auf das entgleitende Seiende*] as a whole, which is the action of the Nothing that oppresses *Dasein* in anxiety, is the essence of the Nothing: nihilation [*die Nichtung*].

It is neither an annihilation of beings nor does it spring from a negation. Nihilation will not submit to calculation in terms of annihilation and negation. The Nothing itself nihilates [*Das Nichts selbst nichtet*]. [Wm 11/105]

Perhaps Heidegger is thinking back to this analysis when he says that in the work (or truth) of the work of art "everything ordinary and hitherto existing becomes an unbeing [*Unseienden*]." But the essay "What is Metaphysics?" still belongs to the region of *Being and Time*, with its preeminence of *Dasein*. It still casts everything (although with a different cast) within the Kantian framework of the subject. And so there is a counterpart in experience for the slipping away of beings, namely, anxiety. But in the aesthetics of "The Origin of the Work of Art" there is nothing for us to experience. Our relation to the work of art and its work is not that of experiencing subjects.

So estrangement in "The Origin of the Work of Art" is neither a structuralist nor an existentialist concept. It is neither defamiliarization nor alienation. Put aside for awhile the idea of emancipation from mental bondage. For it is not *we* who are disconnected from beings that slip away in "the clear night of Nothing"; rather, art disconnects beings from the hold that *we* have on *them*. If art emancipates anything, it is not consciousness or subjectivity but rather the world. Art overturns the will-to-power: it takes the world out of our hands and allows it to come into its own. Admittedly, it is hard for us to imagine a world taken away from us as something not or our doing, or which cannot be laid out in a narrative of crisis or rupture or loss, but *that* is precisely what the otherness of the work of art comes to. So forget about quoting Wallace Stevens on the withdrawal of imagination in winter and other tales of decreation. Indeed, Heidegger makes a special point of rejecting romantic poetics as an illustration of the matter of his thinking: it is "questionable," he says, "whether the nature of poetry . . . can be adequately thought of in terms of the power of imagination" (Hw 60/72–73). Here's a line that literary criticism ought to think seriously about, although it's not a thought we're ready for, since it would mean taking the whole history of criticism from Kant to Lacan as a fantastic error.[16] Perhaps this helps to explain why literary critics and theorists keep themselves in such cheerful ignorance of Heidegger's aesthetics, which emancipates work and world from the claims of experience and the categories of idealism. After all, as Heidegger says, thinking perhaps of Hegel, "perhaps experience is the element in which art dies. The dying occurs so slowly that it takes a few centuries" (Hw 66/79). So much, one might say, for aesthetics. Or literary criticism.[17]

Letting Go

In the essay on "The End of Philosophy and the Task of Thinking" (1964), Heidegger says that "philosophy is ending in the present age." This does not mean that philosophy now stops, only that it has become all that we have ever asked it to be. Or, say, that it has arrived. "It has found its place," Heidegger says, "in the scientific attitude of socially active humanity. But the fundamental characteristic of this scientific attitude is its cybernetic, that is, technological character. The need to ask about modern technology is presumably dying out to the same extent that technology more definitely characterizes and regulates the appearance of the totality of the world and the position of man in it" (SD 64/58). Technology, after all, is nothing strange or frightening; it is what is familiar, ordinary, reliable. It is not the giant machine; it is the compact system. We do not ask about it because there is nothing questionable about it. We can neither imagine nor desire ourselves to be without it.

Heidegger is thus not being ironic when he says that there is nothing wrong with technology. It is the case, however, that technology constrains us to think and act only in ways that *it* can understand. Thus human practice now means "rule-governed behavior," the function of "performatives," and the management of "programs"; it implies the construction, maintenance, or analysis of self-regulating systems—cultural systems, kinship structures, ideologies, conceptual schemes, interpretive communities, genetic codes, deep structures, behavior patterns, and so on. As for theory: "'Theory,'" Heidegger says, "means now: supposition of the categories which are allowed only a cybernetical function but denied any ontological meaning. The operational and model character of representational-calculative thinking becomes dominant" (SD 65/58–59). The task of such thinking in this event would be, for example, to construct a perfect picture of the world, or of the work of art—to show us "how it works," and how it can be made to function or produce effects more efficiently. At the end of philosophy, philosophy does not stop. "The end of philosophy," Heidegger says, "proves to be the triumph of the manipulable arrangement of a scientific-technological world and of the social order proper to this world" (SD 65/59). The Newton of this social order would probably be Max Weber, who produced the first principia of bureaucratic culture, withits concern for effective management, operational guidelines, program implementation, career development, and technical innovation. If you want to know how the work of art fits into this order of things—the *Ge-Stell* or Enframing (VA 23/302)—you need only look to the university study of literature, with its commitment to technical virtuosity in the analysis of texts, its preoccupation with concepts of method, system, rule, and function, and its genius for constructing totalist schemes in which every formal and thematic property of the literary work can be accounted for (Northrop Frye). The task of criticism is to make literature intelligible according to the norms of representational-calculative thinking, so that it becomes the "function" of literature within the *Ge-Stell* either to give us back an image of man, say the "human form divine," or to disclose in its systematic workings the mastercode of Western culture in any of its several symbolic, semiotic, ideological, logocentric or textual forms.

Now "The Origin of the Work of Art" does not propose a new task for criticism, say a new nontechnical (therefore impressionistic or subjective) approach to the work of art. Heidegger's aesthetics is not translatable into the aggressive language of approach, attack, strategy, struggle, overcoming, breakdown, penetration, subversion, dismantling, mastery, and grasp. Instead, Heidegger likes to think in terms of "belonging-together," which confounds the whole notion of approach. In "The Principle of Identity" (1957), for example, Heidegger says:

> We do not yet enter into the domain of *belonging* together [Zusammen*gehören*]. How can such an entry come about? By our moving away from the attitude of representational thinking. This move is a leap in the sense of a spring [*eines Sprunges*]. The spring leaps away, away from the habitual idea of man as the rational animal who in modern times has become a subject for his objects. Simultaneously, the spring always leaps away from Being [*Der Absprung springt zugleich weg vom Sein*]. But Being, since the beginning of Western thought, has been interpreted as the ground in which every being as such is grounded.
>
> Where does the spring go that springs away from the ground?

Into an abyss? Yes, as long as we only represent the spring in the horizon of metaphysical thinking. No, insofar as we spring and let go [*loslassen*]. [ID 20/32]

What is it to "let go"—to "spring and let go"? And where does such leaping from the ground take us?

Heidegger's earliest answer lies in the original spring of the work of art. Specifically, it lies in the character of poetry as this is taken up at the end of "The Origin of the Work of Art," where "All art is essentially poetry," that is, where, "in the midst of what is, art breaks open an open place, in whose openness everything is other than usual." Poetry in this sense is very far from the attitude of representational thinking, and similarly it is inaccessible to the analytical and performative attitudes of the various structuralist criticisms. In an essay on "The Thing" (1950), Heidegger distinguishes between the thing as being and the thing as object: the one stands on its own, self-possessed and solitary in the manner of the work of art, the thing as thing characterized by its otherness (its *thinging*), its difference from the usual, its reserve or resistance to any approach that seeks to take hold of it as an object.[18] The thing as object, however, is not self-assertive or self-supporting but is upheld by the conceptual apparatus that allows us to hold it before us as a logical entity that can be represented categorically in the form of assertions (VA 160–61/168–69). Poetry belongs with things, not with objects. Poetry lets things go and comes into its own in this event of letting-go. It nihilates what is merely present before us or set over against us in the form of representations; it breaks the hold we have on things and allows them to come into their own as beings.

What Heidegger gives us in "The Origin of the Work of Art" is a notion of poetry that might properly be characterized as revolutionary, in the sense of emancipatory, but not romantic. It is not romantic because it is entirely outside the subject-object relationship that is the main axle of romantic poetics. Poetry is neither worldmaking nor liberation of the human spirit from the constraints of nature, culture or historicality. It is revolutionary, however, because of the way it erupts (springs up) within what is. "The truth that discloses itself in the work," Heidegger says, "can never be proved or derived from what went before. What went before is refuted in its exclusive reality by the work. What art founds can therefore never be compensated and made up for by what is already present and available" (Hw 62/75). Poetry "breaks open" a space in which everything is other than usual, in which things can come into their own for the first time as things in all their radical singularity; it lays open a clearing in which things are what they are in all the strangeness of their self-possession, that is, in their resistance to our conceptual scheming, our positing of things as objects and our control over them according to the strategies of instrumental reason.[19] "Poetic projection comes from Nothing in this respect," Heidegger says, "that it never takes its gift from the ordinary and the traditional" (Hw 63/76).

And what Heidegger wants to say is that what thinking must learn from poetry is precisely this ability to "spring and let go," that is, to let things be by "moving away from the attitude of representational thinking." However, what this means exactly remains to be seen.

Naturally, of course, being creatures of the *Ge-Stell* that we are, we want to know not what this means but how it works—how poetry does it, as if what thinking had to learn was a new method of getting on, a new program of performances, strategies, moves, revolts or disruptions. This is what the American appropriation of deconstruction wants to know.[20] Estrangement, however, is not a poetic performance or poetic effect that thinking can pick up on; it is not a style that thinking can imitate, not a sound or look that it can appropriate. We will have missed the whole point if we think of estrangement as something to be methodologically produced.

And what of language? By poetry (*Dichtung*) Heidegger does not mean the art of making verses (*Poesie*), but he does say that "the linguistic work, the poem in the narrower sense, has a privileged position in the domain of the arts." This is so, because the poem is made out of, or rather comes out of, language. Language is the earth out of which poetry emerges and into which it withdraws; but it is more. We need, Heidegger says, "the right concept of language [*des rechten Begriffes von der Spraches*]" (Hw 60/73). For language is not simply earthly material like color or stone. Heidegger wants to link language up with truth as *alētheia*, that is, he wants to recuperate Orpheus: "language alone brings what is, as something that is, into the Open for the first time. Where there is no language, as in the being of stone, plant, and animal, there is also no openness of what is, and consequently no openness either of that which is not and of the empty [*des Nichtseienden und das Leeren*]" (Hw 60/73).

It is at this point, at the very end of "The Origin of the Work of Art," that Heidegger introduces, I think for the first time, his notion of language as Saying (*Sage*): "Language, by naming beings for the first time, first brings beings to word and to appearance. Only this naming nominates beings *to* their being and *from out of* their being. Such Saying [*Sagen*] is a projecting of the clearing, in which announcement is made of what it is that beings come into the Open *as*" (Hw 60–61/ 73). This passage opens two paths. One is to the Hölderlin essays and to the theory of the poet as the orphic figure of inauguration or origi-nal naming who names the gods and names all things, who names the holy and whose task is remembrance in the epoch of forgetfulness.[21] But there is more to language and poetry than can be found along this path, because, as "The Origin of the Work of Art" shows, there is more to truth than *alētheia*; *lēthē* belongs to *alētheia*. The second path (the breach or pun in *a-lētheia*) opens onto the question of poetry and language (as Saying) as this turns up in *Unterwegs zur Sprache*, where poetry opens thinking to the withdrawal of language—holds open the possibility of a "thinking experience with language." The point of this book is to see where this path takes us—where it turns us loose.

Chapter Two
The Step Back
Heidegger's Uncanny Hermeneutics

All by itself the logos does not make language.
—Introduction to Metaphysics

The Weakness of the Logos

In Plato's *Euthyphro* (11b–e) Socrates compares words to the statues of Daedalus, which were said to be so lifelike that they had to be restrained like slaves, because they kept trying to escape. Untethered words wander around aimlessly, whence we get our concept of ambiguity or the waywardness of discourse. However, the tying down of one's words is not easy. In fact, sometimes Socrates makes it sound like the question is all that can be justifiably put into words. For the rest one should keep silent, or speak only in the most guarded fashion, darkly, and then perhaps only of things of no consequence. Or perhaps one should speak and say nothing. Anyhow, one should never make claims for the truth of what one says, as indeed Socrates never does, except once, in the *Apology*, where he claims to tell the truth about himself; but the truth, he says, is that he himself is really of no consequence. This must be why Plato was willing to put Socrates into words. In the *Seventh Letter* Plato warns against putting anything that matters into language. It is part of the "weakness of the logos" (342e: *tōn logon asthenes*) for whatever we say to get away from us. Only a fool would commit what he knows to language; much less would he put what he has learned into a form which is unrevisable and which can fall into the wrong hands, namely the form of a written text. In any event, Plato says, he has never permitted any of his teachings to be written down. He has only, in the spirit of play, written about a youthful Socrates, who for his part made a special point of saying that he was never the sort who had anything to say.

Behind this way of thinking about language and discourse (what the later Heidegger tries to appropriate) is the antique tradition of the secret and the mystery, that is, the tradition of the unspeakability of wisdom and the necessity of the dark saying, or saying without speaking, as when one whispers or talks in riddles or figures or places a finger gently against the side of one's cheek.[1] According to this tradition, on things that matter it is always necessary to withdraw from speech—to keep silence (*sigen eschein*), or, in more colorful language, to make silence (*sigen poiēisthai*), which makes one wonder what silence looks like, or how it happens. (It is not just the absence of sound.) Perhaps the worst thing would be to put what matters into the form of a public lecture. The main difference between philosophy and rhetoric is that in the one you conceal your thoughts, in the other your selves.

The modernist response to the weakness of language has been to follow dreams of an ideal language, as in Enlightenment projects for a Philosophical Character in which systems of exact denotation would for the first time make possible the undistorted expression, or rather depiction, of things. The dream was (perhaps still is) of a logically perfect language in which at last everything could be put, not into words exactly, but into a transparent form of signification.[2] One thinks of Gottlob Frege, father of analytic philosophy of language, who made no attempt to conceal his contempt for "natural language," or whatever the unsystematic thing is that we speak. On Frege's view, the main problem of language is not only that it is incoherent, or cannot be coherently systematized, but that it is opaque. Hence the need to invent a formalized language whose syntax lies "open to view."[3] This desire for a language "open to view" has its counterpart in what Jean-François Lyotard calls "the ideology of communicational 'transparency,' which goes hand in hand with the commercialization of knowledge."[4] What matters in discourse on this model is efficiency in the formulation and quick retrieval of information. Everything must be "open to view." Nothing is to be left unsaid (except what is merely excessive). Nothing is to require interpretation. To interpret is to remain uninformed. This ideology has generated a number of flourishing industries, among them the textbook industry, the speed-reading course, the expository writing program, and now a new cultural development summarized by the phrase, "computer literacy." What happens to language within the framework of such an ideology? The answer is, as we know already from the Enlightenment and its unsatisfiable desire for emancipation from language, that language just as it stands is the enemy of reason. The problem with poetry is that it throws in with language, thickens it instead of refining it to transparency (hence the etymology of *Dichten*). It is certainly the case that much of what we understand as poetry or literature cannot be accommodated within the doctrine of transparency. One has only to think here of the inscrutability of Mallarmé or the monumental example of *Finnegans Wake*, which one could take as a synecdoche for the history of poetry. (But one could go all the way back to the Hebrew Bible, before a word for poetry was ever needed, and which contains many words we have no idea how to translate.) So far as I know, Heidegger is the only philosopher ever to take up the question of language outside of, one might say explicitly against, the ideology of transparency that comes down to us from the Enlightenment. And this is because he takes up the question of language by linking it with poetry as the darkness of saying.

In his "Dialogue on Language Between a Japanese and an Inquirer" (1954), Heidegger says that he withheld his lecture on "Language" (1950) from publication for many years, not so much because the transcript distorted the message of the lecture as because the lecture itself was of such a problematical, perhaps misdirected, character. What sort of speaking was it? It was not, Heidegger says, "speaking *about* language" (US 147/49). This statement puzzles his Japanese interlocutor, but Heidegger is reluctant to clarify himself. Forgive me for being so guarded, he says.

I. What prompts my reserve [*Zurückhaltung*] is the growing insight into the untouchable [*Unantastbare*] which is veiled from us by the mystery of Saying [*das Geheimnis der Sage*]. A mere clarification of the difference between saying and speaking [*Sagen und Sprechen*] would gain us little.

J. We Japanese have—I think I may say so—an innate understanding for your kind of reserve. A mystery is a mystery only when it does not even come out *that* mystery is at work.

I. To those who are superficial and in a hurry, no less than to those who are deliberate and reflective, it must look as though there were no mystery anywhere.

J. But we are surrounded by the danger, not just of talking too loudly about the mystery, but of missing its working.

I. To guard the purity of the mystery's wellspring seems to me hardest of all.

J. But does that give us the right simply to shun the trouble and risk of speaking about language?

I. Indeed not. We must incessantly strive for such speaking. What is so spoken cannot, of course, take the form of a scientific dissertation. . . .

J. . . . because the movement of questioning that is called for here might too easily congeal.

I. That would be the smallest loss. Something else is more weighty, and that is whether there ever is such a thing as speaking about language. [US 148–49/50]

One could say simply that the point of this dialogue is to raise the question of *metalanguage,* that is, the question of the medium for reflection on language—except that basic to Heidegger's thinking is the way language resists subsumption into a *metalanguage*: it won't let itself be turned into words. It has the character of self-refusal (*Sichversagen*). Heidegger's dialogue recurs more than once to the question of how language turns up, is talked about, in different languages, that is, in different tongues. Already in *Being and Time* Heidegger had remarked that the Greeks had no word for language (SZ 165/209), and neither, it appears, do the Japanese (US 114/23). So far from being a deficiency in these languages, however, this empty semantic space, just to call it that, is for Heidegger an indication of how close or near Greek and Japanese are to language—in contrast to modern European languages, not excluding German, which seem on this point to have wandered off. Perhaps our languages have been too overburdened with speaking and have tried to escape. An odd thing to say, perhaps, but think of the great line from E. M. Forster's *Passage to India*: "A perfectly adjusted organism would be silent" (Chap. 14).

The lecture on "Language" is in good measure about the difficulty of addressing the subject of language. How can one talk about it without turning it into something else, something it is not (as if it were something in the first place)? The essence of the weakness of the logos, just to call it that, is contained in this question (which haunts all that we say on any subject). Heidegger says: "to talk about language is presumably worse than to write about silence. We do not wish to assault language in order to force it into the grip of ideas already fixed beforehand. We do not wish to reduce the nature of language [*das Wesen der Sprache*] to a concept" (US 12/190). This refusal to conceptualize is where the later Heidegger is to be found. It is what calls for his strange idiom. It is why the word "communication" is not in his vocabulary.

In order to avoid speaking about language (conceptualizing it), and also in order *not* to avoid speaking about it ("We must incessantly strive to do so"), however impossible such speaking or not-speaking may prove to be, Heidegger appropriates the discursive secrecy proper to ancient theories of wisdom, where it is said that one can only speak of the highest (of anything) by not speaking, that is, by speaking strangely or in strange tongues or by exploiting in radical and even shocking ways the "weakness of the logos."[5] Accordingly, Heidegger abandons from the start anything that we would recognize or accept as a proper or authoritative language for talking about language. In place of a philosophical language or language of the schools—grammar, rhetoric, logic, philosophy of language, linguistics, semiotics, various literary criticisms—Heidegger takes up the idiom of "The Origin of the Work of Art." "To discuss language," he says, "to place it, means to bring to its place of being not so much language as ourselves: our own gathering into the appropriation [*Die Sprache erörten heisst, nicht so sehr sie, sondern uns an den Ort ihres Wesens bringen: Versammlung in das Ereignis*]" (US 12/190). It would be premature to try to say what this means just now, but we can get some sense of it by marking the word *erörten*, to discuss, which is also a pun on the word for place (*Ort*), and which puts into play the connection between speaking (about), that is, speaking categorically, and placing, or fixing in the sense of determining the sense or conceptual status of a thing. It is clear that the pun (weakest logos of them all, the pun is always out of place) is basic to Heidegger's refusal of conceptualization—his negative discourse.

Of course, to discuss anything is not to fix it conceptually but to go back and forth with respect to it without arriving at a final determination. Discussion is not assertion. Back-and-forth is the mode of dialogue as well as of the pun. Heidegger speaks of bringing ourselves to the "place of being" of language, its essential place, but this it turns out is not so much a place as an event, called *Versammlung in das Ereignis*. The metaphor of the gathering event, if it is a metaphor, belongs to Heidegger's reflections on the logos of the Pre-Socratics, who understood logos in its primordial sense of gathering as letting-lie-together, and who also stressed, as Heidegger reads them, the *strength* of the logos, its *deinon*, which is to say its power, strangeness, uncanniness. The key texts here are Heidegger's commentary on the first chorus in *Antigone* of Sophocles (*Introduction to Metaphysics* [EM 119–32/131–45]) and the essay "Logos (Heraclitus, Fragment B50)" (VA 212/70).

However, it is in terms of *Ereignis*, the event of coming into one's own—of appropriation or of being appropriated in such a way that one stands on one's own, apart or unsubsumed—that Heidegger will eventually want to talk about language; but before this can occur the word "language" will have to be converted from its familiar sense or what we take it to mean into something that belongs with the decorum of Heidegger's way of speaking. Of course, we are still quite some way from understanding what this propriety calls for, but here it is enough to say that there can be no question of situating language, placing it in any scheme of things; it cannot be made the subject of any predication or conceptual determination. As if there could be a decorum of not fitting in. This is in part because it is not any sort of being or entity. In a weak moment, Heidegger once referred to language as "the house of being" (*Letter on Humanism*), but, like truth, language is not anything that can be fitted into a metaphor but is rather an event (*Ereignis*)— but, of course, to say this may also be to speak metaphorically, or anyhow opaquely. Or, again, language is not a domain or region exactly, but it does have a proximity or neighborhood into which we can enter, perhaps into which we can wander even without knowing it. It might not be too much to say that language for the later Heidegger is more forest than house. Certainly the difference between event and region in the later Heidegger is not easy to determine.

The first step is clearly to break the hold that customary (*gewöhnlich*) ways of speaking about language have on us. The first step is always the classic Heideggerian "step back"—a retreat (*retrait*) from or letting-go of previously held ground. (The point of this chapter, however, is to lend a number of senses to the "step back.") If we ask, as Heidegger does, "What about language itself? . . . In what way does it occur as language?" (US 12/190), the answer is that it occurs in speaking. But Heidegger's way of putting this is to say that "Language speaks [*Die Sprache spricht*]" (US 12/190). That is to say, not man, but language does it. "To reflect on language," Heidegger says, "demands that we enter into the speaking of language in order to take up our stay [*Aufenthalt*] with language, i. e. within *its* speaking, not within our own. Only in that way do we arrive at the region within which it may happen —or also may fail to happen—that language will call to us from there and grant us its nature [*dass aus ihm die Sprache uns ihr Wesen zuspricht*]. We leave the speaking to language. We do not wish to ground language in something else that is not language itself, nor do we wish to explain other things by means of language" (US 12–13/190–91).

However, it is in the nature of language (isn't it?) to make sense of something in terms of something else. This was Plato's idea, as Gadamer has shown in his essays on Plato's dialectic. Plato's way of coping with the "weakness of the logos," Gadamer says, was to show that nothing can be determined purely in itself or by itself alone. The One must always be there with the indeterminate Two, the plastic *dyad* that Aristotle refers to in his account in the *Metaphysics* (I.6) of Plato's unwritten teachings. The understanding of anything is always a dialectical process, an endless back-and-forth or give-and-take between the One and the Many, determinacy and indeterminacy, perplexity and insight.[6] Accordingly, on this view, making sense of language would mean linking it up with something other or different from itself—but this, Heidegger says, is not the way of language, however much it must remain ours. On the question of language we must not try to overcome the weakness of the logos by any dialectical process or intertwining of language with what it is not; rather, the task of thinking is to enter into this weakness, even at the risk of saying little or nothing. Elsewhere, in "Language in the Poem: A Discussion [*Erörterung*] of Georg Trakl's Poetic Work" (1953), Heidegger will call this entering into a dialogue with poetry, where thinking is exposed to the darkness or essential ambiguity of the poetic work, its strangeness or apartness.

"We do not wish to ground language in something else that is not language." This sentence is the cue for the following quotation from a famous letter that Johann Georg Hamann wrote to Herder in 1784:

> If I were as eloquent as Demosthenes I would yet have to do nothing more than repeat a single word three times: reason is language, logos [*Vernunft ist Sprache, logos*]. I gnaw at this marrowbone and will gnaw myself to death over it. There still remains a darkness, always, over this depth for me; I am still waiting for the apocalyptic angel with a key to this abyss [*Abgrund*]. [US 13/191]

"Reason is language": here is the *locus classicus* of linking language up with something else. Yet Heidegger is interested not so much in the traditional motto as in the darkness that surrounds it, the "abyss" which opens beneath it the more one repeats it: "We speak of an abyss," Heidegger says, "where the ground falls away and a ground is lacking to us, where we seek the ground and set out to arrive at a ground, to get to the bottom of something" (US 13/191). However, what would it be *not* to seek a ground but to give up ground, that is, to abandon ourselves to the *Abgrund*? As if the step back were off a precipice. In this event, instead of saying, "Reason is language, logos," or words to that effect, we should say, following Heidegger off his deep end, "Language is language." Which, of course, says nothing. "This statement," Heidegger says, "does not lead us to something else in which language is grounded. Nor does it say anything about whether language itself may be a ground for something else. The sentence, 'Language is language,' leaves us to hover over an abyss as long as we endure in what it says" (US 13/191).

"Language is language" is a purely formal, or rather comically empty predication ("Rose is a rose is a . . ."), but it is so only if we try to take it as a proposition, as belonging to the realm of assertions (where "Rose is a rose is a rose" is a parody of an assertion). Heidegger's sentence, after all, makes no attempt to ground language logically; it is not "speaking about language." Logically, it is just a silly statement. But Heidegger takes it differently—it is still empty talk, to be sure, but empty with a strange and buoyant kind of emptiness that doubles as something else. "Language is—language. Language speaks [*Die Sprache spricht*]. If we let ourselves fall into the abyss denoted by this sentence, we do not go tumbling into an emptiness. We fall upward, to a height [*Wir fallen in die Höhe*]. Its loftiness opens up a depth [*eine Tiefe*]. The two span a realm [*eine Ortschafte*] in which we would like to become at home, so as to find a residence, a dwelling-place for the life [*Wesen*: being, essence, nature] of man" (US 13/191–92).

Here is another vivid characterization of letting-go (*Gelassenheit*). Letting go of the ground means floating free, untethered. Here one might think back to Heidegger's essay on "The Essence of Truth," where freedom means "letting things be." Suppose one lets go of speaking and allows language to go its own way, not taken up in something higher but now out of reach, inaccessibly other, singularly itself? Instead of making statements about language in an attempt to master or fathom it, place or subsume it, we let language speak, silly as it may sound. In fact, it sounds pretty silly. Language speaks—and what do we get? Nothing less than a dream-fantasy of falling upward (*Wir fallen in die Höhe*). Giving up ground, letting go into the *Abgrund*, becomes a flight into the empyrean! The abyss turns into an opening between the high and the deep, a realm that in turn opens up a place, or a prospect of a place, say a dwelling place, a homeland we always wanted. This metaphorical abandonment, if that is what it is, effectively displaces the philosophical figure of grounding or foundation that is otherwise the indispensable portion of serious philosophical talk—say of weighty as against flighty talk. Left to itself, it appears, language is flighty, frivolous: language speaks and, losing all clarity and definition and going every which way like an untethered slave, it shows its weakness. And that, Heidegger wants to say, is its strength.

Actually, of course, this is not quite right. After all, it remains Heidegger who talks so loosely about falling upward into the open. He loosens his talk, untethers it, in order to let it go into the idiom of "The Origin of the Work of Art," with its talk of earth and world, the ordinary and the uncanny, the untruth of truth. "To reflect on language," Heidegger says, "means—to reach the speaking of language [*das Sprechen der Sprache*] in such a way that this speaking takes place [*ereignet*] as that which grants an abode for the being of mortals" (US 14/192). I shall show in a moment where this talk of homecoming comes from, and where it leads us. One wants to say that, if the theme of "The Origin of the Work of Art" is estrangement, the theme of the lecture on "Language" is homecoming: except that, strange as it may sound, it is by no means clear that the difference between homecoming and estrangement, dwelling and wandering, can be maintained.

From Linguistics to Hermeneutics

If language is an event (*Ereignis*), how does it happen? How does it occur as language and not as something else (for example, as logos, or as meaning or truth—in the usual senses of truth)? The answer is: it occurs in speaking—but this is still no answer. Heidegger wants to know, "What does it mean to speak? [*Was heisst sprechen?* What is called speaking?]" (US 14/192). It is, of course, incorrect to say that "Language speaks." This expression is meaningless, or at least highly allegorical, the more so when placed against the background of the formal study of language as this comes down to us in grammar, rhetoric, logic, and more recently in linguistics, semiotics, and philosophy of language. In this tradition, the question of what it is to speak is not very interesting except insofar as it asks for an explanation as to how language works, how speaking comes about, how speakers can produce infinite sentences by finite means. In our time this is a question about *parole*, usage, pragmatics of language, and—underlying all of this as a formal condition of its possibility—*langue*: language as the chain, play, place, system, or ensemble of signifiers. If language (as *langue*) shows itself in speaking, it is not itself intelligible as speech. *Parole* is nothing if not opaque. *Langue* meanwhile is a purely formal construction which we can describe according to any number of current models. It is a generative-transformational system (Chomsky); it is an "absent cause," a "total system immanent in its effects" (Althusser); it is a Symbolic Order which inscribes itself ideologically (not in but) as human consciousness, and so makes possible not only discourse but the totality of human culture (Lacan). And so on through all the possible theories of deep structure.[7]

However, Heidegger's concern is not what lies behind or beneath speaking as a condition of its possibility but with what lies *in front of it*. This is part of what it means to give up ground, that is, to give up the attempt to uncover foundations or logical priorities. Heidegger's concern with speaking is hermeneutical rather than analytical. Instead of asking Kant's question about how speaking (or meaning or knowledge) is possible, he asks: Where does it occur? "Language speaks," he says. "What about its speaking? Where do we encounter such speaking? [*Wo finden wir solches?*]" (US 16/193–94). This last turns out to be a way of asking a basic hermeneutical question: Where do we stand with respect to language?

The answer to this, as Heidegger works it out, involves the reading of poetry—if "reading" is the right word. Heidegger says that we find language speaking only in "What is spoken purely [*ein rein Gesprochenes*]," in contrast to what is spoken "indiscriminately" any old way [*nur beliebig Gesprochenes wahllos*]" (US 16/194). This sounds at first like a familiar distinction, say between poetic and everyday discourse. But what is to be made of the relationship between "speaking" and "what is spoken," whether purely or randomly? This does not appear to be anything like the usual distinction between utterance and meaning. What is spoken purely is not any sort of content or message; rather, it is just the poem: "Rein Gesprochenes ist das Gedicht" (US 16/194). What does this mean?

It is characteristic of Heidegger that precisely at the moment when he is most baffling—he refuses to explain himself. "What is spoken purely," he says, "is the poem. For the moment we must let this statement stand as a bare assertion" (US 16/194). In place of an explanation Heidegger provides a poem, "Ein Winterabend," by Georg Trakl. All that Heidegger says is that there is a bond "between what we think and what we are told by language when we hear what is spoken purely in the poem" (US 16/194). Here is the poem:

EIN WINTERABEND

Wenn der Schnee ans Fenster fällt
Lang die Abendglocke läutet
Vielen ist der Tisch bereitet
Und das Haus ist wohlbestellt.

Mancher auf der Wanderschaft
Kommt ans Tor auf dunklen Pfaden
Golden blüht der Baum der Gnaden
Aus der Erde kühlem Saft.

Wanderer tritt still herein;
Schmerz versteinerte die Schwelle.
Da erglänzt in reiner Helle
Auf dem Tische Brot und Wein.

To which Heidegger appends these lines from an earlier version of
the poem:

Seine Wunde voller Gnaden
Pflegt der Liebe sanfte Kraft.

O! des Menschen blosse Pein.
Der mit Engeln stumm gerungen,
Langt, von heiligem Schmerz bezwungen,
Still nach Gottes Brot und Wein.

[US 17/194–95]

A WINTER EVENING

Window with falling snow is arrayed,
Long tolls the vesper bell,
The house is provided well,
The table is for many laid.

Wandering ones, more than a few,
Come to the door on darksome courses.
Golden blooms the tree of graces
Drawing up the earth's cool dew.

Wanderer quietly steps within;
Pain has turned the threshold to stone.
There lie, in limpid brightness shown,
Upon the table bread and wine.

*

Love's tender power, full of graces,
Binds up his wounds anew.

O! man's naked hurt condign [worthy].
Wrestler with angels mutely held,

Craves, by holy pain compelled,
Silently God's bread and wine.

Where are we to stand with respect to this poem? This seems to be very much the same as asking how we stand with respect to language. Remember that in "The Origin of the Work of Art" Heidegger accorded the poem "a privileged position in the domain of the arts" (Hw 60/73) because it is linguistic: it comes out of and bears the marks of language.

So how do we deal with the poem? Naturally our first impulse is the impulse of the school, which is to speak about the poem in a way that will be consistent with the demands of the classroom. Heidegger in fact engages in a little of this—for example, he gives us the name of the poem's author, saying mysteriously, however, that it is in the nature of any successful poem "to deny [*verleugnen*: also, to disown] the poet's person and name" (US 18/195). Without pausing to explain what this might mean, Heidegger also summarizes briefly what the poem is about—not surprisingly, it is a homecoming poem. "The poem's content," Heidegger says, "is comprehensible. There is not a single word which, taken by itself, would be unfamiliar or unclear" (US 18/195). Truth to tell, it is not a very prepossessing poem. Which makes one wonder what was the point of all that talk in "The Origin of the Work of Art" about the withdrawal of the work into the earth, its self-refusal, its resistance to the analytical gaze? I said, "Imagine a poem hiding itself in its words." None of that here. Trakl's poem seems hardly to put up a fight. It lays itself bare for our inspection.

Yet Heidegger does not quote the poem in order to perform any sort of exegesis upon it or to demonstrate its transparency. On the contrary, his point is that any normal reading of the poem—any reading consistent with the various rules of philology, for example—will presuppose and reinforce ready-made doctrines about language and poetry. Heidegger's example of such a doctrine is the romantic idea that "language is expression, produced by men, of their feelings and the world view that guides them." Language is subjective performance. Then Heidegger wonders: "Can the spell this idea has cast over language be broken?" (US 19/196).

But what's wrong with this idea? Nothing is more venerable, after all, or seems more consistent with empirical evidence, or reading experience, than the expressive theory of poetry and art. It is this theory which authorizes exegesis—the reading-out of what has been put into words. It is the linchpin of romantic hermeneutics. Of course, one might prefer, more than thirty-five years after Heidegger's lecture on "Language," a more up-to-date or upscale theory, say the idea that poetry is expressive not of the poet but of language itself, a *reine Sprache*, in Paul de Man's words, "a pure language which does not exist except as a permanent disjunction which inhabits all language as such, including and especially one's own."[8] Such a pure language is never translatable as a meaning, but its formal operations can be laid bare by philology, even when these operations are radically different from what philosophy of language makes them out to be—even when these operations exhibit, as they do for Paul de Man, "the madness of words."[9] What remains constant throughout the transition from romantic theory to semiotics and the new rhetoric, or from philosophy of language to certain appropriations of deconstruction, is the posture of analytic rigor with respect to the text, whether the text is a logical proposition or a poem.[10] What is constant throughout the substitution of one method of reading for another is method itself, whose task remains as always to lay language "open to view."

Heidegger, however, doesn't have a method. This is the main reason why his readings of poems by Hölderlin and Rilke, for example, are such notorious scandals (for Paul de Man as well as for Else Buddeberg and Beda Alleman).[11] Nothing he says about a poem can be confirmed by analysis. Nothing he says can be duplicated by anyone else's experience or reading (duplicated in the sense of following a program to the same end). He seems to be saying the opposite of what Hölderlin says (yet not in the sense of reading Hölderlin against himself). His approach to poetry is not philological in either a humanist or a Nietzschean sense. But Heidegger would say that he does not have an "approach" to poetry. The poem is not anything to be approached. It is not anything objective. It is a speaking, and one does not approach speaking, rather one is pulled up short and one listens, as if to a pure speaking in which nothing is expressed.

An account of Heidegger's hermeneutics is possible only so long as one remembers that hermeneutics is not a method of treating texts but is rather a tradition of reflection, say upon a family of questions having to do with what happens when anything occurs in language (or at all). So the question of Heidegger's hermeneutics is not a question of how he does something, how he reads a poem, for example. It would be more accurate to say that it is a question of what he does *not* do. Heidegger's hermeneutics is a renunciation of exegesis.[12] And in his hermeneutics lies the key to all that he wants to say about our relation (whether as poets or thinkers) with language.

In "The Onto-Theo-Logical Constitution of Metaphysics" (1957), Heidegger speaks of beginning "a conversation with Hegel" (ID 31/ 42). Thinking, Heidegger says, must never exclude the history of philosophy (neither, he implies, must it exclude what is in excess of this history). This is what we learn from Hegel, who was the first thinker, Heidegger says, to think "in the context of a conversation with the previous history of thinking" (ID 33/43). In Hegel we see that thinking is always hermeneutical in the sense that it is always open to and involved with the thinking of another, not in the sense that it tries to master another's thought, but rather that it opens itself to the other with respect to the matter in question (*Sache*). In this it is in stark contrast to the solitary progress of Descartes, who repudiates previous thinking, thought and unthought—who repudiates everything except his own subjective experience, and who sets out on his own according to the rule of method. However, as Heidegger says, thinking must always try "to elucidate the otherness of the historical at the same time as [it tries to] elucidate the otherness of the matter of thinking [*der Verschiedenheit der Sache des Denkens zugleich die Verschiedenheit des Geschichtlichen . . . ans Licht zu heben*]" (ID 36/46). For Hegel, this meant "to enter into the force and sphere of what has been thought by earlier thinkers" (ID 37/47). This is the task of romantic hermeneutics: to enter into the spirit of the other and to understand it first as well as and then even better than it understands itself. For us, Heidegger says, it is the same as with Hegel, but with this difference: "We do not seek that force in what has already been thought: we seek it in something that has not been thought [*Ungedachten*]" (ID 38/48). The task of thinking is not to overcome the subjectivity of another; still less is it to give a philological account or exegesis of it. For Heidegger, otherness is not subjective. It is "der Verschiedenheit der Sache": it is the other of the subject as the matter of thinking.

"For Hegel," Heidegger says, "the conversation with the earlier history of philosophy has the character of *Aufhebung*, that is, of the mediating concept in the sense of absolute foundation" (ID 39/59). *Aufhebung* means overcoming the other, not so as to be rid of it, but rather to preserve what is thought by taking it up—elevating it—to higher ground: not cancellation or abolition pure and simple, but also fulfillment. *Aufhebung* is the method of subsumptive thinking. However, Heidegger says that it is not our wish to go beyond Hegel. He is not an obstacle to our future, nor is it with hindsight that we can see where he went astray and so find what he was after and build the mousetrap that eluded him. He does not suffer from obsolescence. We do not need to break with him and his conceptual scheme. Hegel opens up a path for us to follow, but this does not mean that we follow in his footsteps or along a path of antagonism and repudiation, reading Hegel against himself. "For us," Heidegger says, "the conversation with the history of thinking is no longer *Aufhebung,* but the step back [*der Schritt zurück*]" (UD 39/59).[13]

The "step back" does not mean a return to previous positions or the recuperation of lost ground. It is *not* nostalgia for a lost language. It does not mean becoming Pre-Socratic. The "step back" is related to letting-go and listening, as in a conversation, where one's task is to listen to the other, not in order subsequently to reproduce another's meaning, as if one were simply eavesdropping or keeping the minutes of the conversation without entering into it. What is it to take part in a conversation? One must listen in order to pick up on what is said and enter into it, perhaps to take off in unforeseen directions and without the warrant of what the other meant. The point is always to keep the conversation going and not to get in the way of the matter (*Sache*) in question. Picking up on what is said does not mean simply joining another's monologue, picking up where it left off, and for the same reason it cannot mean trying to control the conversation by coercing the other to say only what you are prepared to hear or only what can be logically justified or made consistent with experience. A conversation is a good example of ungrounded talk. It has a movement, a back-and-forth, of its own; one gets caught up in it and carried away by it so that one is no longer fully in control of what one says. What one says seems to come out of its own accord or as if in response to what is called for by the changes rung on the matter in question. In conversation one is apt to be pulled up short by one's own words and to experience forcefully the weakness (or is it the strength, say the self-possession?) of language.

Hence the truism that the conversation itself, and not anyone in it, is the author of all that is said in it. What is said can never be traced back to an individual subject. What one says is never simply one's own expression; it comes out of the otherness of the conversation and not out of one's own subjective processes. True invention means that you find what you say lying in front of you, not inside of you. What is said in a conversation presupposes all that has just been spoken, just as all that was previously said depends for its sense upon what comes later. Picking up on what is said and giving it a different turn means that what is said cannot be isolated as either an original intention or a secondary elaboration. A conversation cannot be objectified in this way and treated as a text that one could open up by way of philological analysis. Picking up on what is said is always an event within the conversation, not a reflection from the outside. Picking up on what is said is always an attempt to bring out what is left unspoken, hearing the pun in another's concept. Heidegger would say that the unspoken is the true source of what is said. Perhaps this is why transcripts and tape recordings of conversations are always banal. They show only idle talk—confusion, bad grammar, hemming and hawing, double-talk, joking, everyone talking at once carelessly and frequently at cross-purposes. What they show is that a conversation cannot be understood from the outside but only in the way of belonging and appropriation. Conversations are impossible to study because they cannot be objectified. Even dreams can be textualized, but conversations are like the dance. One cannot get command of them without destroying them.

All of this would need to be worked out in greater detail in something like a "hermeneutics of the conversation," but perhaps enough has been said to suggest how it stands with Heidegger and a given poem. His relationship to a poem is like a relationship to the other in a conversation. The elucidation of the other is like picking up on the words in play rather than like giving an interpretation of what someone means or laying bare the structure or madness of another's discourse.

Here one should study Heidegger's *Erläuterungen zu Hölderlins Dichtung* (1936–44), which are what one should call *soundings* rather than *readings* of Hölderlin's texts, ringing the changes rather than plumbing the depths. It cannot be said that Heidegger ever "reads" a poem by Hölderlin in any sense that can be fitted into any philological conception of construction, not even in its upside-down or inside-out sense of deconstruction. Certainly *die Erläuterung* is never *die Auslegung*. Rather we should compare Heidegger's relation to the poets with his "conversation with early thinking" as this occurs in his lectures on the Pre-Socratic texts—as in "The Anaximander Fragment" (1946), which is about the inaccessibility of the Anaximander text to historical and philological reconstruction (Hw 343/57). "Only in a thoughtful dialogue with what it says can this fragment of thinking be translated [*Der Spruch des Denkens lässt sich nur in der Zwiesprache des Denkens mit seinem Gesprochenen übersetzen*]," Heidegger says (Hw 302–03/19).[14] Similarly, in the essay, "Logos (Heraclitus, Fragment 50)," Heidegger says of the words of Heraclitus that "We do not know their content, in the sense of being able to revive Heraclitus' own way of representing things" (VA 211/69). What Heidegger calls "the fundamental words of early thinking"—*phūsis, lōgos, moira, eris, alētheia, hen*—will always be closed to us except perhaps as we are able to linger in their company, or their neighborhood, and pick up on their resonances.[15] We need to situate ourselves dialogically *with* the text rather than analytically against it, in the mode of listening rather than reading. Of course, this disregard of the analytic attitude is outrageous from the standpoint of the basic standards of scholarship, but Heidegger makes no pretense to scholarship. For him the text is never a formal object of historical and analytical scrutiny. It is not made of statements or coded messages, and perhaps it would be true to say that it is not made of words, either, anyhow not what we usually think of as words, namely elements in a signifying system, whether internally coherent or otherwise. The text is certainly not the repository or trace of an intention. In a later chapter I shall show that for Heidegger poetic language is language that has been let go in the sense that the poet's relationship to her words is renunciative rather than enunciatory. It is not a sort of speaking; it does not belong to the category of subjective performance or predicative operation. It is a listening, which is one's mode of belonging to a conversation. But listening in what sense, and for what?

Heidegger says that he has introduced Trakl's poem into the discussion (*Gespräch*) of language "because, in a way not further explicable, it demonstrates a peculiar fitness [*die Eignung*] to provide some fruitful hints [*einige fruchtbare Winke*] for our attempt to discuss language" (US 20/198). Suppose one were to say that the basic unit of the poem is not the word or the signifier but *der Wink*—the hint which is there for you to take up or to ignore? To take the hint means to go where (perhaps vaguely) it motions you to go, no knowing whereto in advance: not even the poem knows where you will end up if you take one of its hints. To the ear of literary criticism this sounds silly, but perhaps one could raise the hint into something like a hermeneutical concept by saying, for example, that the elucidation (*die Erläuterung*) of a poem is more the poem's work than it is ours. One could borrow a metaphor from Gerard Hopkins and say that the *Erläuterung* of the poem is the spark the poem throws off when struck. It would be the light that it sheds on a matter of concern to us, not the light we shed on its inner sanctum in our reading of it. *Die Erläuterung* would be different therefore from philological clarification. It would be different from the purification of texts that occurs when we try to remove textual corruptions and restore documents to their original pristine state. Texts are not documents for Heidegger. They are more earthly than worldly. You cannot get around behind them or inside them to an originating intention or ground of signification. Thus *die Erläuterung* in Heidegger's sense more nearly resembles the allegorization of a text than the analysis of it. Allegory is the appropriation of dark texts; that is, it means taking a text differently from its literal sense because there is no taking the text literally—its literal sense is no sense at all: nothing can be made of it. Like the Pre-Socratic fragment, it is all dark, an unmitigatable strangeness. Allegory is a taking-off from the text rather than an exegesis that extracts something from the text in order to hold it up to the light. The dark text surrenders nothing of itself. Moreover, Heidegger would want to say that *die Erläuterung* has more to do with sound than sight, ear than eye—that is, it may not be quite right to translate it as "elucidation," throwing light on a text. Take *die Erläuterung* as a pun rather than as a philological term of art.

The thesis here is that for Heidegger the poetic text is like a Heraclitean fragment: it is a dark saying, an *ainigma*—not a riddle or conundrum or a logical puzzle that we could eventually work out or whose answer we might guess, but a saying shrouded forever in darkness. The saying may now and again seem to have a plain sense, as indeed Trakl's poem does, but Heidegger's counsel is that we should never trust our perception of plainness, just as we should always be suspicious of standard translations and long-standing authorized readings that cover over the uncanny with what fits our customary usage. Transparency is always misleading, maybe always an illusion. In any case the main point about an enigma for Heidegger is that it is not to be penetrated or laid open to view; there is no way of shedding light on what it means in the sense of a content or message that can be conceptually retrieved. It resists philology of every sort, ancient, modern, or postmodern. It won't be purified of its earthly character. As Heidegger says, the proper response to a Heraclitean fragment is to "step back" as before a riddle (VA 217/75: *vor dem Rätsel zurückzutreten*). Better for thinking, he says, "to wander into the strange [*Befremdlichen*] than to establish itself in the understandable [*Verständlichen*]" (VA 218/76). The poem, like the dark saying, is a text of hints. How do we go about finding the meaning of a hint? Here the hermeneutical metaphor of "taking" the text in a certain way, now this way, now that, leads *away* from the text. What is it to take a hint? (It is, more often than not, to get lost.)

Calling

Whereas in our current intellectual situation we are all trying to get "beyond hermeneutics," Heidegger seems to be headed in the opposite direction. Toward what end? What's Heidegger up to? Unfortunately, there's no translating Heidegger into the language of progress and achievement. His is a wayward or wandering hermeneutics, or a hermeneutics "without why." He does not think in order to be followed. Thinking is hard to follow; its sociality does not consist (pace Habermas) in its communicability.

Instead of proceeding, therefore, we need to back up (or to stand back and see where we are). Remember that the question before us is this: What is it to speak? That is, what is speaking called when it is not just anyone speaking—indeed, when it is not anyone at all, neither God nor man, but only language? "Language speaks." Heidegger says, without explaining what he means, that we can hear, or should listen for, the speaking of language in the poem by Trakl—

> Window with falling snow is arrayed,
> Long tolls the vesper bell.

"This speaking," Heidegger says, "names [*nennt*] the snow that soundlessly strikes the window late in the waning day, while the vesper bell rings" (US 20/198). And so it does: this *is* what the poem literally says —the window is flaked with snow, and vesper bells are sounding. But Heidegger doesn't pursue any sense of what the poem is *about;* rather, he takes his "step back" from the poem and asks, not about the poem's content, but about the naming that occurs when the speaking in the poem "names the winter evening time" (US 20/198).

"What is this naming?" (US 20/198). The poem is not about this naming (it is not secretly a poem about language). Instead, the poem appears to give Heidegger something like a language for talking about language—not a metalanguage, exactly, because the poem can't be said to supply a vocabulary, and anyhow the poem remains opaque, that is, quite apart from its lucid imagery of homecoming it remains for Heidegger a dark saying which he picks up on without explicating anything that can be attributed to the text. Rather, Heidegger draws his language for talking about language from what the language of the poem gives off in the way of hints—hints, for example, as to what we otherwise, in the language of signs, would call "naming."

As to the naming: the main point about it is that it is very far from designation or signifying, very far from being a performative in the language of signs. "This naming," Heidegger says, "does not hand out titles. It does not apply terms, but it calls into the word. The naming calls" (US 21/198). This isn't Adam's sort of proper naming. Nothing is conferred in such naming; no signs are assigned, no identities are determined, nothing is conceptualized as a present object. Naming as determination is renounced in the strong sense of renunciation that Heidegger will develop in his lecture on "Das Wort" (US 222/142). Here the point is that the speaking of language is not any sort of grammatical, logical, or linguistic operation (it is not a performative). As Heidegger says in the essay on "What are Poets For?" ["*Wozu Dichter?*"] (1946), "The nature of language does not exhaust itself in signifying" (Hw 286/132). As if there were more to speaking than meaning; or, more exactly, not something *more* but something *else* or something other.

"The naming calls" (US 21/198). The German text here reads: "Das Nennen *ruft*"—not *heissen* (as in *Was heisst Denken?*), but *rufen*, as if naming were more like shouting than like identifying or knowing what something is called.

In *Being and Time* Heidegger had characterized conscience as a call (*Ruf*). "Calling," he said, "is a mode of discourse" (SZ 296/315). Moreover, it is a mode of discourse like listening and keeping silent rather than like the making of assertions. In fact it would not be too much to say that calling is headed in the opposite direction from asserting. It is not progressive utterance. What is important about calling is that it cannot be traced back to a caller. What matters is what comes to lie in front of the call, not in what lies behind it. (In this respect it is like the hint.) Heidegger says: "The caller maintains itself in conspicuous indefiniteness. If the caller is asked about its name, status, origin, or repute, it not only refuses to answer, but does not even leave the slightest possibility of one's making it into something with which one can be familiar when one's understanding of Dasein has a 'worldly' orientation" (SZ 274/319). The keynote of the call is strangeness. The caller is always inaccesibly Other. "The caller," Heidegger says, "is unfamiliar to the everyday they-self [*dem alltäglichen Man-selbst*]; it is something like an alien voice" (SZ 277/331). The call is uncanny discourse, because it is a voice out of nowhere. Imagine hearing disembodied voices. This is your basic definition of madness. For Heidegger, however, there is no getting behind the call, just as there is no getting behind or to the bottom of madness. The dream of psychoanalysis, of course, is to get behind such voices and to break the hold they have on us; it is a program of demystification designed to cure us of a bad conscience.

Heidegger would say that psychoanalysis is a technique of familiarization designed to emancipate us from the uncanny and insert us back
into the everyday, or to give us back our "everyday they-self" or to
enable us to function among such folk. By contrast Heidegger's sense
of the call is all otherness and mystification.

Sidenote: It hardly needs to be added that Heidegger is very far
from the culture that designates madness as a disorder in the chemis-
try of the brain, or something to be brought under control by recipes.
In "The Anaximander Fragment" he revives the antique connection
between the madman and the seer: "in what," he asks, "does the
essence of madness [*das Wesen der Raserei*] consist? A madman is beside
himself, outside of himself: he is away" (Hw 320/36), as in the madwoman of the wilderness. The madwoman is the figure of the other or
the strange. Madness is not anything mental; it is not a problem inside
one's head. It is just that madfolk wander in other regions than the one
in which we do business. Likewise, to be a seer does not mean to possess a special kind of mental power—visionary imagination, prophetic
insight, transcendental transport. It means belonging to a place different from the one that lies before us as objective, accessible, familiar,
ordinary, reliable, normal, sane—different, in short, from the rational
universe that lies open to view and responsive to explanation (answerable to our concepts). It means belonging to a place where everything
is other than usual, where the *gewöhnlich* has been displaced but not
replaced by anything determinate that, given time, we could become
familiar with—not replaced, in short, by something new or advanced.

Similarly, the call has to do with regions rather than with minds or
with callers who have something in mind. "The call," Heidegger says,
"does not report events; it calls without uttering anything. The call
discourses in the uncanny mode of keeping silent" (SZ 277/322). This
is the line of thinking, minus the subjectivist talk about conscience
and *Dasein*, that Heidegger picks up again in the present context of
the lecture on "Language" and its question of what happens when
language speaks. The speaking of language is uncanny discourse. Language speaks only by naming, but this is naming in the uncanny mode
of calling in which nothing gets said (nothing gets intended or expressed), and in which one loses sense or control of what words mean:
hence perhaps the proximity of madness. What if language were the
way to madness? (Talk of the "madness of words"!) Or if madness
were the way to language? Naming as calling in any event is dark or
uncanny saying in the manner of the archaic word or fragment, the

enigma, and the poem in its earthly character of withdrawal, reserve, dissembling, *dichte,* opacity—poetry as the other of predication and the determination of meaning. Imagine a naming that leaves things nameless or unsignified, lets them go as if off on their own, otherwise than being. In the "Letter on Humanism," which is about being homeless in an utterly familiar place, Heidegger says: "if man is to find his way once again in nearness of Being he must first learn to exist in the nameless" (Wm 150/199).

What region is this?

Chapter Three
The Abandonment of Philosophical Language

---

*I can provide no credentials for what I have
said—which, indeed, you do not ask of me—
that would permit a convenient check in each
case whether what I say agrees with "reality."*
—Letter to a Young Student

Nearness of the Fourfold

The question remains, or continues to draw us out: What is it to speak?
That is, what is it for speaking to occur when no one speaks but only
language? "Language speaks [*Die Sprache spricht*]." We are very far
from understanding what this can mean. All we can say is that Heidegger encourages us, allows us, to think of speaking in terms of calling
rather than as signifying. But where does this leave us?

In the last chapter I tried to show that what matters is what comes
to stand in front of the call, not what lies behind it, nor what gets
determined as such as a product of the call. It is pointless to ask, of
the call, "Who's there?" or "What do you want?" No one called, because no one is there. The call has to do with regions rather than with
expressions of the subject and determinations of the object. Indeed, it
has to do with indeterminate regions that Heidegger calls "the remote
and the near [*die Ferne und die Nähe*]" (indeterminate because you can't
tell where one leaves off and the other begins). In the essay on "Language" Heidegger says: "The calling here calls into a nearness [*Das
Herrufen ruft in eine Nähe*]. But even so the call does not wrest what
it calls from the remoteness, in which it is kept by the calling there.
The calling calls into itself and therefore always here and there—here
into presence, there into absence" (US 21/198–99). When language
speaks, it summons what is called from the remote into the near, but
what is called never fully abandons its remoteness, say its strangeness
or uncanniness. It comes near, but no further. It always holds itself
back, that is, withholds itself from the presence into which it draws.

Presence and absence are like near and far, the one trailing endlessly into the other. Neither is definable or containable.

Of course, it's unsettling—logically destabilizing—to have adverbs doing the work of nouns. The indefiniteness of here and there, near and remote, presence and absence, belongs to the decorum of "The Origin of the Work of Art," whose talk of the open, of world and earth and the rift, left us hanging. One doesn't know what to call these things, since they aren't things. Call them "phenomena." At least "phenomenon" is a philosophical term. One can't be serious, feel serious, unless one can attach a philosophical term to what one is talking about. But earth and world and rift aren't phenomena. We can call them that, but they won't answer to our conceptions.

By now, however, we should have gathered that our hermeneutical task with respect to Heidegger is not to master or overcome his language—not to translate it into a language of conceptual definitions and analytical distinctions, as if he were simply treating familiar philosophical problems in a strange or, say, poetic-like idiom. Nor is it to read Heidegger against himself, as if there were a will to his text that needed breaking. Perhaps we should just say after all that our recourse in reading is to the model of the hint, whence our task with respect to Heidegger's language would be to see where it takes or leaves us. At all events the production of a glossary will get us nowhere.

One way to think of Heidegger's language is by way of the second part of *What is Called Thinking?* (1954), where Heidegger speaks of attending to the word as *word* as against the word as *term* (*Worte* v. *Wörter*). It is too early to clarify this distinction, but we should mark it. "To speak a language," Heidegger says, "is totally different from employing a language [*eine Sprache benützen*]. Common speech [*gewöhnliche Sprechen*] merely employs language. This relation to language is just what constitutes its commonness [*Gewöhnlichkeit*]. But because thinking and, in a different way, poetry do not employ terms but speak words [*nicht Wörter benützen, sondern die Worte sagen*], therefore we are compelled, as soon as we set upon a way of thinking, to give specific attention to what a word says [*eigens auf das Sagen des Wortes zu achten*]" (WD 87–88/128). Again, we should leave open the question of what Heidegger means by *Gewöhnlichkeit*, translated here as commonness. It would be premature to say that he simply means everyday as against poetic or philosophical usage. *Gewöhnlichkeit* does not obviously exclude the philosophical. The word "term," after all, belongs to logic. Whereas to attend to the word as word, Heidegger says, is to step back from grammar and logic; it is to venture into what he calls "the gambling game of language [*das Spiel der Sprache*]" (WD 87/128), where the meanings of words remain unsettled (open to chance?). The game of language is where the pun, for example, comes into play.

Possibly it is easier to play this game in some languages than in others. For example, English is, to be sure, still the language of Locke, Hume, the Royal Society, John Stuart Mill, Bertrand Russell, Michael Dummett—that is, the indefatigable tradition of logical empiricism from which the English-speaking world draws its norms of rationality and its picture of what philosophy of language is. But English is as much Shakespeare's language as it is Mill's or Russell's. It is the language of people like Emerson and William James, Walt Whitman and William Carlos Williams, who believed that a poem can be made out of anything, even newspaper clippings. It is the language of the prairie and the outpost, of drifters and exiles and deported convicts. And of course it is the language of James Joyce and Samuel Beckett. English is heteroglot; it takes a struggle to make it something in which to philosophize. In Bakhtin's words, English turns more easily into a "dialogized heteroglossia" than into a "unitary language," which is to say that it is a multiplicity of tongues competing for the same lexicon, and it is easier to let it go than to try to control it.[1] It is not so easy to say this about French. French is a philosophical language; it inhabits chiefly the region opened up by the French Enlightenment. Its *genius loci* is Descartes; its Shakespeare is Racine. Its poets—Poe, Mallarmé, Valéry—are eminent rationalists, or else they are self-consciously, polemically mad like Rimbaud and Artaud. In French punning requires a method called deconstruction. When Derrida says, in "The *Retrait* of Metaphor," that "There is always more than one language in language," he is being provocative.[2] The nightmare of the French is to open a French dictionary and find it filled with English words. In a book that I mention in the introduction, *Philosophy Through the Looking-Glass*, Jean-Jacques Lecercle has tried to map out a theoretical region of discourse called *délire*. *Délire* is the space between "the dictionary and the scream" (PLG 44). Language enters into this space when it tries to escape its own logic or shows itself to be uncontainable within the ensemble of signifiers and differential relations that constitute *langue* as a total system whose function it is to control discourse and to bring it under the governance of unitary language or a cultural monologue. *Délire*, like deconstruction, means disruption of the system, as when language grows aware of its own materiality, that is, its body and also its libidinality. In the end, however, language holds itself together,

keeps its wits; it does not turn into something else. *Délire*, like deconstruction, never doubts that language is a system.

I want to say that Heidegger's *délire*, his gambling game, is very
different from this, because with Heidegger language turns into something else, we cannot say what. But none of this will make any sense
to us, of course, unless we get into Heidegger's game, or into *das Spiel
der Sprache*.

Near the end of chapter one I mentioned Heidegger's distinction
between thing and object. A thing stands on its own, is self-standing,
unsubsumable, in contrast to the object, which is always held in place
before a subject in a structure of representation or conceptual framework. The object is not a thing but a product of representation. In
"What Are Poets For?" for example, Heidegger says that the "sphere
of the objectivity of objects remains inside consciousness" (Hw 281/
127). Whereas the thing belongs to the indeterminate regions of the
near and the remote.

Indeed, the essay on "The Thing" (1950) is marked by repeated ask-
ings of the question, "What is nearness?" (VA 163/171).[3] The question
is not meant to be answered but to carry us along, as if the point were
not to settle anything. What we learn chiefly about nearness is that it
is not another word for the everyday in which we find everything in
its customary (*gewöhnlich*) place in good or not so good working order.
Nearness is not a region of unalloyed presence in which everything is
objectified and determinate, unmistakably and verifiably there before
us, subject to our control, answerable to our conceptions. Heidegger
wants to say that it is the region opened up by the speaking of language when language calls into what is absent. What is summoned
when language calls, say the thing, may or may not respond, but in
any case it never becomes present as such but always remains turned
this way or that toward what is absent. So we can never get a good
picture of it. The thing resists consciousness or the power of framing
representations; it resists transformation into an object, that is, into a
conceptual entity capable of being put into a statement. "Object" is a
philosophical term, but one doesn't know what to call a thing. Obviously from the standpoint of objects it is doubtful that things exist.[4]

Put it simply that the thing resists integration into the *Ge-stell* or
Enframing of technology where objective knowledge, and therefore
philosophy, is possible; rather, the thing belongs to *das Geviert,* which is
Heidegger's word for the fourfold or gathering-together of earth and
sky, gods and mortals.[5] However, the *Geviert* is not exactly opposed
to the *Ge-stell* (they are not polar opposites), because the *Geviert* is

not a sort of primitive alternative to technology—it is not a counter-scheme or utopian substitute for reality; it is not meant as a more adequate version of how things are or should be. The fourfold is that other world which by comparison with ours is strange, uncanny—and, one wants to say, surely imaginary. Call it a poetic realm got up by Heidegger from the fragments of Hölderlin's poetry, with its longing for vanished mythologies. Philologically speaking, this is in fact where Heidegger's talk of the fourfold comes from, but it won't help to use Hölderlin as a gloss for what Heidegger has to say here. The point to cling to is that the fourfold does not represent another world besides our own; rather, in ways we can't explain, it *is* our own. We haven't got a world, no more than a stone does, unless it is this one, and it says something about us that we are bound to find this a preposterous statement. But it is only with respect to the preposterous fourfold that we can arrive at any sense of what it is for language to speak.

Let me simply read the paragraphs from the essay on "The Thing" in which (I gather for the first time) Heidegger unfolds the fourfold. The first half of the essay is something like a phenomenological description of a jug, which is neither a Latin *res* nor a medieval *ens* nor a Kantian *object* but is just a thing in the Old High German sense of *thing* and *dinc,* that is, the etymological sense (according to Heidegger) of "gathering" (VA 167/174). For Heidegger, it would be more fruitful to say, not that the jug *is* a thing (*res, ens,* or object), but that it *things* (*es dingt,* meaning, according to Heidegger's risky etymology, "it gathers"). The thing *things* the way the rain *rains.* Only notice that you normally wouldn't say "the rain rains"; rather, you say "it rains," or "it is raining," where the pronoun *it,* however, doesn't have any referent. You can't ask what it is that rains, because *it* isn't anything at all, that is, it is not an object of which raining can be predicated. *It* is a phantom subject of the predicate *rains:* the subject has, in effect, withdrawn into the predicate. Withdrawal is the keyword: the *it* cannot be conceptualized.[6] So also with the thing in Heidegger's nonphilosophical sense of the word: "the thing *things*" is a locution from which the subject of the predicate withdraws itself, refuses itself as a conceptual or objective entity—conceals itself in the *thinging.* And the thinging of the thing is, Heidegger says, the gathering (or fouring) of the fourfold:

> Earth and sky, divinities and mortals—being at one with one another of their own accord—belong [*gehören*] together by way of the simpleness of the united fourfold [*aus der Einfalt des einigen Gevierts zusammen*]. Each of the four mirrors in its own way the

presence of the others. Each therewith reflects [*spiegelt*: mirrors] itself in its own way into its own [*in sein Eigenes*], within the simpleness of the four. This mirroring does not portray a likeness [*Dieses Spiegeln ist kein Darstellen eines Abbildes*]. The mirroring, lightening each of the four, appropriates [*ereignet*] their own presencing into simple belonging to one another. Mirroring in this appropriating-lightening [*ereignend-lichtenden*] way, each of the four plays [*spielt*] to each of the others. The appropriative mirroring [*Das ereignende Spiegeln*] sets each of the four free into its own [*in sein Eigenes frei*], but it binds these free ones into a simplicity of their essential being toward one another [*wesenhaften Zueinander*].

The mirroring that binds into freedom is the play that betroths [*zutraut*] each of the four to each through the enfolding clasp of their mutual appropriation [*aus dem faltenden Halt der Vereignung*]. None of the four insists on its own separate particularity. Rather, each is expropriated [*enteignet*], within their mutual appropriation [*Vereignung*], into its own being [or simply "into its own": *zu einem Eigene*]. This expropriative appropriating is the mirror-play of the fourfold [*Dieses enteignende Vereignen ist das Spiegel-Spiel des Gevierts*]. Out of the fourfold, the simple onefold of the four is ventured [*getraut*]. [VA172/179]

This onefold *ventured* (*getraut*) by the mirror-play of the fourfold is what Heidegger calls the world. "World" here is to be taken in *almost* the same sense in which it occurs in "The Origin of the Work of Art," except that now world is not opposed to earth but occurs as the gathering—the mutual belonging, appropriating, or dwelling-together—of earth and sky, gods and mortals. Perhaps the key word here, however, is a pun: *trauen*, to marry, *sich trauen*, to venture or to risk, *zutrauen*, to credit or to trust, which Hofstadter translates as "betrothe." This venturing of the world out of the fourfold is a setting-forth or sallying-forth, but also a risking or a gambling or trusting-to-chance that is very much in the spirit of the letting-go or *Gelassenheit* of language that allows these remarkable paragraphs to unfold.

In the mirror-play, dwelling-together, or expropriative-appropriating of the four—the world occurs. Heidegger calls this occurrence (*Ereignis*) the *worlding* of the world, where world is de-objectified (what other word is there for it?) by the same play or throw of words that turned the thing from an object into an event (*Ereignis*) called *thinging*. The event of the world is not an episode of worldmaking in either Ernst Cassirer's or Nelson Goodman's sense, nor even in the sense given by Wallace Stevens in "The Idea of Order at Key West," where there never was a world for the woman who sings by the sea except the one she, singing, made.[7] The mirror-play of the fourfold is not a mirroring in the sense of a representation that objectifies the world. It is not a productive process of which we could construct a model whose workings we could then explain and manipulate or abort. If we try to imagine the mirror-play we will come up with a blank. Perhaps ironically, there is nothing picturable here.

All that can be said is that the mirror-play of the fourfold lets the world *world*:

> The world presences by worlding [*Welt west, indem sie weltet*]. That means: the world's worlding cannot be explained by any-thing else nor can it be fathomed through anything else. This impossibility does not lie in the inability of our human thinking to explain and fathom in this way. Rather, the inexplicable and unfathomable character of the world's worlding lies in this, that causes and grounds remain unsuitable for the world's worlding. As soon as human cognition here calls for an explanation, it fails to transcend the world's nature [*das Wesen der Welt*], and falls short of it. The human will to explain just does not reach the simpleness of the simple onefold of worlding. The united four are already strangled in their essential nature when we think of them only as separate realities, which are to be grounded in and explained by one another (VA 172/179–80).

Sidenote: Recall "Hölderlin and the Essence of Poetry," where the "poet names the gods and names all things in that which they are . . . Poetry is the establishing of being by means of the word. . . . [When] the gods are named originally and the essence of things receives a name, so that things for the first time shine out, human existence is brought into a firm relation and given a basis. The speech of the poet is establishment not only in the sense of the free act of giving, but at the same time in the sense of the firm basing of human exis-tence on its foundation." Hence the famous quotation from Hölderlin: "'. . . poetically, dwells / Man on this earth'" (ED 41–42/281–82). But in "The Thing" all talk of Being and beings has been withdrawn in favor of the thinging of things and worlding of the world. Poetry is no longer brought in as an *explanation* for the appearance of the world— no longer an orphic explanation of the earth. The event of the four-fold is "inexplicable and unfathomable," and this means specifically that the event can no longer be rendered in the philosophical language of "causes and grounds," of establishment and foundations. Poetry is no longer foundational for the world. The world as the event of the fourfold, as the thinging of things—as worlding—is without ground (without why).

The main point to understand about the fourfold, however, is that we are already in it insofar as we are in a world at all. This is so even though we do not conceive the world in these terms, as obviously we do not: the fourfold is not conformable to any intelligible world-picture that we could possibly produce with the concepts and standards of reasoning that our culture makes available to us. We cannot in fact conceive the fourfold at all, because we cannot get control of its mirror-play. (So Heidegger's account in "The Thing" is not to be thought of as his "world-view," as if there were something for seeing to hold in place.) The gathering of the four into a fourfold ventures the world to which we belong whether we will or no. We cannot distance ourselves from the world in order to give an objective description of it. In this respect, the "step back" of which Heidegger frequently speaks would not be a distancing by which we could attain an analytical standpoint; on the contrary, the step back is a giving up of "the human will to explain." It is therefore the abandonment of philosophy. Heidegger's satirical point, however, is to ask what it is to dwell within a culture dominated by the will to explain. It is the mark of this dominance that for us giving up "the human will to explain" means giving up human reason itself. It is the same as commending ourselves to unreason and the babbling of lunatics. Think of poor Hölderlin's fate, or Nietzsche's.

Giving up "the human will to explain" means, for example, dropping the compelling question of how exactly the mirror-play of the fourfold works or what it looks like. Yet who isn't intrigued by this figure (if it is a figure)? Who doesn't want to know how it works? Who doesn't want to experience it? Why figure the togetherness of earth and sky, gods and mortals, as a *Spiegel-Spiel*? With all this wonderful word-play, this gambling game, who can keep from thinking of the magical act in which it is all done with mirrors (or with mere words)? It is too easy to say, of course, that Heidegger is a mere illusionist, but it is also the case that, like the magician, he makes it very difficult for us to map the categories of appearance and reality onto the results of his performance. Thus we are left not knowing exactly how to take the fourfold. We cannot quite take it seriously, cannot take it philosophically, but then again we cannot just summarily wave it aside as Heidegger's own private world-picture or mad mythology, the obscure vision of a fevered brain, as if Heidegger had caught Hölderlin's madness from his poetry. (Think of the simile of the magnet in Plato's *Ion*: poetry is mindlessness, that is, either stupidity or madness.) Earth and sky, gods and mortals, world and thing—Heidegger warns us that these are not "terms" in a conceptual scheme. Their task is not to represent a state of affairs either real or imaginary. Hence the unsuitability of referring to the fourfold as Heidegger's "cosmos." We will not get anywhere trying to form a picture of what Heidegger has in mind, because the fourfold is not a picture of anything and is not itself picturable. No picture of it could be true to its simpleness—*die Einfalt*, where *Einfalt* means singularity, simplicity, naiveté, and also the silliness in the antique sense of rustic (cf. ME *sely*).

There is no doubt, of course, that Heidegger wishes to put this rustic note into play as a way of diverting the simplicity of the *Geviert* from the sophisticated technology of the *Ge-stell*. One cannot help thinking here of Schiller, and perhaps there is good reason to identify Heidegger as one of the Last Romantics (for the fourfold belongs after all to his dialogue with Hölderlin). But we should understand that for Heidegger naiveté is not a property of consciousness; it is not primitive sensibility or Viconian "poetic logic." It is not opposed to the self-consciousness and abstraction of modernity. It concerns rather the unanalyzable, untheorizable, untranslatable character of the fourfold, whose mirror-play ventures the simple onefold that Heidegger calls the world. This venturing is not production; it is rather *Gelassenheit*, letting-go or letting-be.

So precisely at the point where an account of how this venturing works is called for, Heidegger gives us instead something altogether puzzling and strange—namely, the rustic "round dance" in which the four come together as in the celebration of their venturing or betrothal:

> The fouring presences as the appropriating mirror-play of the betrothed, each to the other in simple oneness [*Die Vierung west als das ereignende Spiegel-Spiel der einfältig einander Zugetrauten*]. The fouring presences as the worlding of world. The mirror-play of world is the round dance of appropriating [*Das Spiegel-Spiel von Welt ist der Reigen des Ereignens*: don't miss the pun here]. Therefore, the round dance does not encompass the four like a hoop. The round dance is the ring that joins while it plays as mirroring [*Der Reigen ist der Ring, der ringt, indem er als das Spiegeln spielt*]. Appropriating, it lightens the four into the radiance of their simple

oneness. Radiantly, the ring joins [*vereignet*] the four, everywhere open to the riddle of their presence [*überallhin offen in das Rätsel ihres Wesens*]. The gathered presence of the mirror-play of the world, joining [*ringenden*] in this way, is the ringing [*das Gering*]. In the ringing of the mirror-playing ring, the four nestle into their unifying presence [*schmiegen sich die Vier in ihr einiges und dennoch je eigenes Wesen*: note the play of einiges-eigenes]. So nestling, they join together [*fügen sie fügsam*], worlding the world. [VA 173/180]

This is dizzying. In place of pictures we get puns, which is what happens in the letting-go or gambling game of language. Thus, to take only one example, the key word, *Ereignis*, "ventures" the round dance, *Reigen,* but one cannot explain why: the connection between *Ereignis* and *Reigen* isn't a conceptual one; rather, it's just what a gamble is —a chance connection, as if *Reigen* were simply tossed off of *Ereignis* like a throw of the dice. Or, to change the metaphor, say that the two are joined in the manner of the hint, as when one fragrance, taste, or sound gives off or radiates the hint of another, no one knows why. Indeed, the whole passage—the whole essay—is impossible to explicate coherently because it is, structurally, a wayward mixture of metaphors. Heidegger's language doesn't cohere into a self-interpreting system. It is language that confounds the reader's training as the one who grasps, sees, or construes the relationship of part and whole—that is, the one who sees the point. But here we get punning "without why": as writing, the text is a play of contingencies—mirror-play, round dance, ringing, and radiance: "Radiantly, the ring joins the four, everywhere open to the riddle of their presence." Just so, Heidegger's is a riddling text, not in the literary sense of the riddle as a logical construction that can be analyzed into a solution, but as an enigmatic or earthly text that, like a Heraclitean fragment (or, for all of that, like a fragment from Hölderlin) blocks every effort we make to get behind or to the bottom of it. The text keeps us out in front of itself where Heidegger presumably wants us—for reasons not to be fathomed. Unless it were simply to emancipate us (or, more likely, the world) from "the human will to explain."

Dizzy as we are, we should nevertheless be able to see that what Heidegger is concerned with is something like the emergence of the thing into the open, which is an event, he says, that "stays—gathers and unites—the fourfold [*Das Ding verweilt das Geviert*]" (VA 172/181). Hofstadter's translation tries to explicate *verweilen,* to remain or stay, as a transitive verb, as if the thing were somehow productive of the fourfold; but the thing is not active in any causal or foundational way. It has no logical priority to the fourfold or world. Rather, the thing emerges into the round dance of the fourfold, where the dance itself would not occur without the thinging of the thing—which is an event (*Ereignis*) in which everything comes into its own, free of the categories of subsumptive thinking. The fourfold, after all, is not a system. It is not a totality in which earth and sky, gods and mortals are assigned their relative positions. They are not coerced into the round dance but join together as dancers will in a mutual belonging in which differences are not subsumed in a larger identity.[8] They are more players than parts.

"The thing," Heidegger says, "things world" (VA 172/181). In a moment we will ask about the relationship of thing and world—a question that will take us back at last to the lecture on "Language." The point here is that the fourfold is (or is called) the world in which things occur as things rather than as objects in a conceptual framework. This distinction between thing and object is important because it concerns the way we *are* with things rather than the way we *have* with them. Thus Heidegger speaks of "preserving [*Bewahrundung*]" the thing the way he spoke of preserving the work of art. *Die Bewahrunden* derives from *wahren*, to guard, and from *wahr*, true or real. There is an intimacy (which only a pun could register) between preserving and truth (*die Wahrheit*): to preserve the work means "to stay within the truth that is happening in the work. Only the restraint of this staying lets what is created be the work that it is" (Hw 54/66).

Similarly, "As we preserve the thing qua thing," Heidegger says, "we inhabit nearness" (VA 173/181)—meaning that we ourselves come into our own and take up our dwelling with things instead of taking hold of them and fixing them categorically before us. This preserving of the thing, letting it be, requires that we step back from it and allow it to be a thing and not what we construe it as or otherwise propose for it. The conceptual vagueness of Heidegger's thing is what comes of not approaching the thing as a product of representational consciousness; the thing is not an object in need of clarification so that we may see it better. Nothing requires to be made transparent. Our seeing does not need to be improved. "When and in what way do things appear as things?" Heidegger asks. "They do not appear," he says, "by means of human making. But neither do they appear without the vigilance of mortals. The first step toward such vigilance is the step back from the thinking that merely represents—that is, explains—to the thinking that responds and recalls [*in das andenkende Denken*]" (VA

174/181). Here thinking occurs in the mode of *Gelassenheit*. Heidegger goes on to say that the step back does not imply or produce a change in attitude, point of view, approach, or program of thinking. The step back is not a Heideggerian "project." It isn't anything that puts us in a better position with respect to our view of things; it doesn't elevate us to higher ground or to a higher level of awareness. The thing never "appears" as such. The step back has rather to do with our own world-liness; it has to do with how we are rather than with how we perform as knowing subjects. What is it to be in the mode of *Gelassenheit,* or *andenkende Denken?* This mode is not a state of mind. Almost certainly it is to be in the mode of *alētheia,* unforgetfulness as unconcealment rather than as the recuperation of memory or recognition; but it is also to be answerable to the calling which summons things from the remote into the nearness of the fourfold. Stepping back, letting things be, preserving, giving up the human will to explain, is thus related to homecoming—the return of mortals, and not of mortals only but of earth and sky and the return of the gods as well. This is the event (*Ereignis,* with its puns or hints of the round dance or coming into one's own) hinted at in Trakl's poem.

Dif-ference

Remember that the lecture on "Language" is concerned with what it is for language to speak. The speaking of language is at first a disap-pointment, because it doesn't produce anything; contrary to our pic-ture of how language is supposed to work, it doesn't leave any traces, and it doesn't cause anything to happen. There's nothing to trace back to it. It is itself a happening where naming occurs in the mode of calling rather than as designation or assignment in a system of terms. What matters in this event is not the identity of what is called but—whereto (*wozu*)? What is the "place of arrival" of what is called? The point of my digression from "Language" to "The Thing" was to make it possible to ask this question. Things are called, Heidegger says, not into unalloyed presence but into "a presence sheltered in absence" (US 22/199). And it is here that Heidegger links up the speaking of language with the mysterious or preposterous fourfold:

> The place of arrival which is also called in the calling is a pres-ence sheltered in absence [*ein ins Abwesen geborgenes Anwesen*]. The naming call bids things to come into such an arrival. Bidding is

inviting. It invites things in, so that they may bear upon men as things. The snowfall brings men under the sky that is darkening into night. The tolling of the evening bell brings them, as mortals, before the divine. House and table join mortals to the earth. Things that were named, thus called, gather to themselves earth and sky, mortals and divinities. The four are united primally in being toward one another, a fourfold. The things let the fourfold of the four stay with them. This gathering, assembling, letting-stay is the thinging of things [*das Dingen der Dinge*]. The unitary fourfold of sky and earth, mortals and divinities, which is stayed in the thinging of things, we call—the world. [US 22/199]

This passage roughly summarizes the essay on "The Thing." Remember that we cannot say, of a thing, that it *is;* rather, in Heidegger's strange lingo, the thing *things* as language speaks (*Die Sprache spricht*). This is not the same as saying that it exists; existence is a metaphysical category that Heidegger tries to finesse by speaking of the thing not as a being but as an event, that is, as what *things*: he deprives the thing of its substance as a subsistent entity; the noun thing disappears into the verb thinging. And if we ask, What is this thinging if it is not the existence of the thing?, Heidegger would madly reply with the word "staying [*Verweilung*]." The thing is called and it answers in the sense that it draws near the place of arrival, but instead of withdrawing again, as it might well do, it stays, but its staying is not just a hanging-around; it is also a gathering or assembling of the four, or the worlding of the world, where the world is not a system of identities but a play of differences, a round dance of the four in which each comes into its own (*eigen*) as something singular and strange.[9]

To the reader who does not linger with Heidegger's text but simply glances at it, or runs through it just to see what's in it, Heidegger seems merely to be throwing words around, but in fact his discourse is meticulous and painstaking in the care with which it unfolds. Letting-go of language does not mean letting-fly with words, although it may mean letting them fly of their own accord. Thus "The word 'world,'" Heidegger says, "is now no longer used in the metaphysical sense. It designates neither the universe of nature and history in its secular representation nor the theologically conceived creation (mundus), nor does it mean simply the whole of the entities present (kósmos)" (US 23–34/201). Moreover, the word "world" is no longer used quite in the same way as it was in "The Origin of the Work of Art," where it belonged to the rift of earth and world. In "Language" the key relation is not between earth and world but between world and thing —but relation is (again) not the right word. Indeed, the notion of "right word," of the proper assignment of terms, seems to have lost its force. But this does not mean that infinite care is not required in choosing one's words—as the following shows. How, after all, to speak of the "relation" of world and thing?

For world and things do not subsist alongside one another. They penetrate each other. Thus the two traverse a middle. In it, they are at one. Thus at one they are intimate. The middle of the two is intimacy—in Latin, *inter*. The corresponding German word is *unter*, the English *inter-*. The intimacy of world and thing is not fusion. Intimacy obtains only where the intimate—world and thing—divides itself cleanly and remains separated. In the midst of the two, in the between of world and thing, in their *inter*, division prevails: a *dif-ference* [*In der Mitte der Zwei, im Zwischen von Welt und Ding, in ihrem inter, in diesem Unter- waltet der Schied*]. [US 24/202]

And so we get another keyword: dif-ference. How are we to take this word?

Heidegger says, relentlessly warning us about his words, that the "word 'dif-ference' [*Unter-Schied*] is now removed from its usual and customary usage [*gewöhnlichen und gewohnten Gebrauch*]" (US 25/202). It is a familiar term but is now otherwise in a sense not explicated or determined. This is how it is with Heidegger and his words. But what is it for a word to become estranged from itself—without turning figurally into another word? Dif-ference, it appears, is an example of such estrangement. (I think of it as a parody of the term "difference," that is, not a new term but an old term that is beside itself, no longer itself or self-identical, thus more word than term.)

The problem with dif-ference—especially for English-speaking readers in literary study—is that "usual and customary usage" has changed since 1950 when Heidegger presented his lecture. Heidegger could not have foreseen Derrida and his word, *différance* (with an *a*).[10] In the years since Derrida introduced this word, *différance* has acquired what Walter Benjamin would have called an "aura." In literary study, perhaps more so than in the case of Derrida's own philosophical career, *différance* is the watchword of deconstruction, and for us there is no longer any way to register Heidegger's word independently of deconstruction and its history, which has fixed *Unterschied* with a powerful interpretation, one that reinserts it into the canon of "usual and customary usage"—and so places us under the obligation of reading Heidegger against himself (that is, as someone who is simply disguising his recuperation of the Same). For Derrida, *Unterschied* can be made to refer more or less single-mindedly to the "ontological difference between Being and beings" that Heidegger tries to recover or perhaps to think for the first time, since it is this difference that has been forgotten or repressed during the long reign of metaphysics. As Derrida explains, however, "the determinations which name difference always come from the metaphysical order. This holds not only for the determination of difference as the difference between presence and the present (*Anwesen/Anwesend*), but also for the determination of difference between Being and beings. If Being, according to the Greek forgetting which would have been the very form of its advent, has never meant anything except beings, then perhaps difference is older than Being itself. There may be a difference still more unthought than the difference between Being and beings"—older, in other words, than Heidegger's *Unterschied*.[11] This unthought, unthinkable difference is, we know, *différance*, which, "in a certain and very strange way, (is) 'older' than the ontological difference or than the truth of Being. When it has this age it can be called the play of the trace. The play of a trace which no longer belongs to the horizon of Being: the play of the trace, or the *différance*, which has no meaning and is not. Which does not belong. There is no maintaining and no depth to, this bottomless chessboard on which Being is put into play" (M 22).[12] (What does a "bottomless chessboard" look like?)

However, it isn't obvious that ontological difference or the question of Being is what concerns the later Heidegger in his lectures on language. Is Being a matter any longer for Heidegger's thinking? My thought is that the later Heidegger is reading himself against himself (later against earlier) when he says that, like the word "world," "the word 'dif-ference' [*Unter-Schied*] is now removed from its usual and customary usage," meaning that it is no longer a term of art in determining such things as the relation of Being and beings. "What it now names," Heidegger says, "is not a generic concept for various kinds of differences. It exists only as this single difference. It is unique. Of itself, it holds apart the middle in and through which the world and things are at one with one another" (US 25/202). Which would be to say that the *Unter-Schied* of the lecture on "Language" is no longer the metaphysical concept flushed out by Derrida, that is, no longer "the ontological difference of Being and beings," but only the "dif-ference" of world and thing, where world and thing are understood as events

rather than as entities. World and thing seem to me to be quite otherwise than Being and beings. World and thing cannot be translated
into philosophy. Anyhow dif-ference (with a hyphen) is no longer conceptual, that is, it is not differentiation within a conceptual or semiotic
ensemble; it is not logical or structural difference, that is, not any sort
of relationship that can be constructed or perceived among elements
in a total system. It is, at least, not a diacritical concept. It is removed
from totality as from usual and customary usage. "It is unique," unsubsumable, *otherwise than difference*, with a hyphen doing the weird
work of Derrida's *a*.

And not the hyphen only. Heidegger's way of removing dif-ference
from usual and customary usage is in fact more complicated and parodistic still. Instead of narrowing or fixing the meaning of dif-ference,
with its hyphen, as a term that will always work the same way every
time it is used, or which will carry an identity over from context to
context, Heidegger allows the word to unfold in his text through a
series of wild substitutions—wild, because none of them fits in with the
others to form anything like a coherent pattern, say a metaphorical
structure or theoretical narrative.

The substitutions, if that is the right word, are as follows:

1. *Diaphora*. The dif-ference, Heidegger says, is "the *diaphora*, the
carrying out that carries through. The dif-ference carries out world
in its worlding, carries out things in their thinging. Thus carrying
them out, it carries them toward one another. The dif-ference does
not mediate after the fact by connecting world and things through a
middle added on to them. Being the middle, it first determines world
and things in their presence, i. e., in their being toward one another,
whose unity it carries out" (US 25/202).

2. *Ereignis*. "The word [dif-ference] no longer means a distinction established between objects only by our representations. Nor is it merely
a relation obtaining between world and thing, so that a representation
coming upon it can establish it. The dif-ference is not abstracted from
world and thing as their relationship after the fact. The dif-ference
for world and thing *disclosingly appropriates* things into bearing a world;
it *disclosingly appropriates* world into the granting of things [*Der Unter-
Schied für Welt und Ding ereignet Ding in das Gebärden von Welt*, ereignet
Welt in das Gönnen von Dingen]" (US 25/202–03): it isn't clear why Hofstadter chooses to embellish *ereignen* by translating it as "disclosingly
appropriates"; why not just "appropriates"—if "appropriates" is the
correct translation?

3. *Dimension*. "The dif-ference is neither distinction nor relation.

The dif-ference is, at most, dimension for world and thing. But in this case 'dimension' also no longer means a precinct already present independently in which this or that comes to settle. The dif-ference is *the* dimension, insofar as it measures out, apportions, world and thing, each to its own [*Das Unter-Schied ist* die *Dimension, insofern er Welt und Ding in ihr Eigenes er-misst*]" (US 25/203). As if dimension were something other than a topological or topographical or geometrical concept. But if none of these, then what?

4. *Pain; or, der Riss.* Picking up on Trakl's line, "Schmerz versteinerte die Schwelle," Heidegger toys with the connection between pain and threshold, and asks:

> But what is pain? Pain rends. It is the rift [*Der Schmerz reisst. Er ist der Riss*]. But it does not tear apart into dispersive fragments. Pain indeed tears asunder, it separates, yet so that at the same time it draws everything to itself, gathers itself to itself. Its rending, as a separating that gathers, is at the same time that drawing which, like the pen-drawing of a plan or sketch, draws and joins together what is held apart in separation [*Sein Reissen ist als das versammelnde Scheiden zugleich jenes Ziehen, das wie der Vorriss und Aufriss das im Schied Auseinandergehaltene zeichnet und fügt*]. Pain is the joining agent in the rending that divides and gathers. Pain is the joining of the rift. The joining is the threshold. It settles the between, the middle of the two that are separated in it. Pain joins the rift of the dif-ference. Pain is the dif-ference itself [*Die Schmerz fügt den Riss des Unter-Schiedes. Der Schmerz ist der Unter-Schied selber*]. [US 27/204] [13]

Diaphora, Ereignis, Dimension, Schmerz: What is to be made of these characterizations of dif-ference? Our natural inclination is to shut our eyes tight and to try and picture some unifying concept that will resolve this mixture of metaphors, if that is what they are, into a whole, but it will not do, because Heidegger does not mind mixing his metaphors. For the idea is not to produce anything resembling an allegory of ideas. The effect of Heidegger's figural license is to block any attempt to reduce dif-ference to a unitary concept. The effort to say what dif-ference is, exactly, is misguided, or at all events doomed to fail. If we want to say what it is, we must say all of these things, possibly in no particular order: *diaphora, Ereignis,* and so forth.

Indeed, here might be the place to remark that Heidegger's texts have a curiously unrevised look about them, as if they were, not improvisations exactly, but something like a thinking-out-loud in which there is no looking back—no going back over previous ground in order to remove what doesn't belong, or which disrupts an order or series, or which can't be mapped onto a deep structure. The lecture on "Language" is not an essay but in fact remains a lecture that has not been reworked into the tightly-argued system that would otherwise count as philosophical discourse. This does not necessarily imply a tolerance for mistakes, although we know that there is no movement without errancy, and so perhaps there is a sense in which Heidegger takes up one figure after another without bothering to clean up after himself, leaving behind within the text itself instead of in smudged manuscripts in the desk drawer the *Nachlass* of uncorrected thoughts. It is this sort of errancy that methodical thinking tries to conceal by cleaning up after itself, subordinating its parts to a whole, but in Heidegger's case the text is not a system. The text is unconstructed, endlessly revised but never finished. So instead of thinking of *diaphora,* et cetera, as so many terms in a series, so many growing approximations of the idea, we should think in terms of adjacency (that is, according to the model of parody), with diaphora, appropriation, dimension, and rift or pain standing independently side-by-side, each on its own, throwing off hints in several directions at once. Of course, this makes us want to think of differing perspectives, as if each metaphor (if it is that) were not a hint but a point of view for seeing the thing itself under changing aspects; but it appears that Heidegger wishes the dif-ference to remain variously embedded in his text, now here, now there, always dif-ferent and so never the same (but how not the same if always dif-ferent with a hyphen?), so that it is not something we can come away with, extracted from its textuality, as a product or result of reading. The dif-ference is inextricable; it is not a portable concept. "It is unique" (its own) in each event. It makes sense nowhere (if at all) except in the ways it occurs in Heidegger's text. It is a good example of Heidegger's language, the more so because it is far from clear that *Unter-Schied* can be rendered simply as dif-ference. It's the sort of word Plato warned us about.

The wonder is that the word is not just nonsense, because it isn't, but we need to let go into the strangeness of it, entering into the abandon or gambling game, as if the sense were in the strangeness. So: World and thing: the one is not the container of the other, nor do things added together compose a world. So there is no speaking of a world of things. World is not *Umwelt.* Things themselves are worldless in the manner of the stone, separated from world by a threshold not to be crossed—hence the rift, or seam, that binds the two intimately together yet at the same time holds them apart, yet not in the logical mode of relation and distinction, but in the painful mode of earth and world, where there is antagonism, not to say hostility. World and thing belong together without coming together in any form; each comes into its own, carried out or through (thinging and worlding) in the dif-ference. The dif-ference carries through on this coming-into-one's-own of world and thing, their homecoming in the place of *Ereignis-Eigenes*, but it is not as though diaphora were a process of mediation within a unity. Diaphora, curiously, is a rhetorical figure, related to *metaphora*, or carrying-over in the sense of transference; but transference implies regions ready-made and waiting for something to travel across a boundary (as between literal and figurative), whereas diaphora has more to do with making good on a promise or coming through in a pinch, or just at that intersection (or is it the rift?) of the before and the after, without which nothing would take place, or without which time would be empty or nothing at all, and there wouldn't be anywhere for anything to occur: no *Ereignis*. Between the before and the after occurs the now, but, as Heidegger has shown in his commentary on Aristotle's notion of time, the now is not a present, that is, not an instance of presence: it is the dif-ference between before and after in virtue of which things thing, coming near without becoming familiar.[14] One cannot say that things abide in the now as in an interval of being between the not yet and the no longer; rather, the thinging thing is a lingering in which the thing stands on its own, not in the world but with it in the between held open by the now. There is no longer any question of anything in being.

Stillness

The truth, however, is that talk about the now as rift or the dif-ference between before and after is out of place here because Heidegger has put questions of time (and perhaps also therefore questions of Being and beings) behind him, or rather aside (possibly in the region opened up by parody). The later Heidegger is just no longer the author of *Being and Time*. At all events, nearness and the remote, the fourfold and world, thing and carrying-through, taking place, dimension and rift—this whole metaphorical mixture, this heterogeneous play, is spatial as well as temporal in ways that seem to parody these categories.[15] At first it looks like Heidegger is attempting something like a re-description of space. Certainly one is tempted to read the lectures on

"The Thing" and "Building Dwelling Thinking" in this light, but we know that things are growing strange when the thing is no longer to be conceived as an object in time and space. Inevitably, of course, we will continue to think of space as something laid out before us as a prospect, field, area, or landscape in which things have their place. We think of space as something to be comprehended. But Heidegger with his talk of the fourfold gives us something different from a spectator-theory of space in which a knowing subject is able to situate things. The question is whether he gives us a theory of space at all. The term "space" (*der Raum*) turns up in "Building Dwelling Thinking" (with spaces between words of the title), but only as an idea that gets put aside. Heidegger's point is that our relationship to space is no longer that of the spectator's. "Man's relation to locations," he says, "and through locations to spaces, inheres in his dwelling, strictly thought and spoken" (VA 152/157). What "strictly thought and spoken" can mean here is not easy to say. Would it sound too silly to say that Heidegger's notion of space is no longer, strictly speaking, "spatial"? The upshot anyhow is that Heideggerian space is no longer made of surface, volume, distance, depth, or size. There is a here and there, near and remote, but not an inner and outer nor an up and down (unless this is the same as high and deep, which it isn't, exactly). Space here has nothing to do with the logical space (topology) of the philosophers, which is to say, for example, the space of such indispensable concepts as extension and its corollary, intension. System, scheme, and frame go by the board, taking reference and inference and every sort of consecutiveness with them. *Der Raum* gives way to *der Ort* and to the "phenomena" (that can't be the right word) of gathering, staying, belonging, and rest. Space becomes an event, temporalized as a worlding and a thinging; literally it is a taking *place* (Ereignis), as at the table in Trakl's poem where bread and wine await the wanderer's return. To enter into the space of the fourfold is to enter into the repose of this event.

But repose is not to be thought of as something for the wanderer; it is not a subjective state (nor is it clear that the wanderer ever enters into repose or ceases to wander, although he or she may pause for a while). Repose seems rather more for the bread and wine, that is, for things: "The dif-ference," Heidegger says, "lets the thinging of the thing rest [*beruhen*] in the worlding of the world. The dif-ference expropriates [*enteignet*] the thing into the repose [*die Ruhe*] of the four-fold. Such expropriation does not diminish the thing. Only so is the thing exalted into its own, so that it stays world [*Est enthebt das Ding erst in sein Eigenes: dass es Welt verweilt*]" (US 29/206). Space, in other words, is taken up in the event; to enter into the space of the four-fold means coming into one's own. But shake loose from the idea that homecoming is an anthropological event.

It may seem that we are a long way here from the question of what it is for language to speak, but in fact we are in the midst of it. "The dif-ference expropriates the thing into the repose of the fourfold," Heidegger says. "To keep in repose is to still [*in die Ruhe bergen ist das Stillen*]. The dif-ference stills the thing, as thing, into the world" (US 29/206). The question of what the stillness is takes us into, or toward, the essence or truth—or, more accurately, the event (*Ereignis*) —of language.

Stillness is not, it turns out, simply the absence or negation of sound. It is not mere soundlessness, just as rest or repose is not simply motion-less and the near is not simply the eradication of distance. The question, "What is stillness?" (US 29/206) is not empirical. Call it, if you want, phenomenological. Stillness and rest are a plenitude, not in the metaphysical sense of a totality in which everything is contained (in place), but in the sense of a palpability for which there is no determi-nate object. The stillness is something you can hear if you listen for it. Stillness is, for example, a forest phenomenon, as Heidegger would know, gnarly creature of the forest that he is—indeed, one could say that the whole of the later Heidegger presupposes something like a phenomenology of the forest. If you call into the forest you will hear the stillness.

As we have seen, however, calling in this event is not the perfor-mative of any subject; it is not the subjective act of one who calls. It is the event of the dif-ference, a happening of the between, a rift of silence and sound in which neither is broken, each comes into its own. "In stilling things and world into their own," Heidegger says, "the dif-ference calls world and thing into the middle of their intimacy. The dif-ference is the bidder [*das Heissende*]. The dif-ference gathers the two out of itself as it calls them into the rift that is the dif-ference itself. This gathering calling is the pealing [*das Lauten*]. In it there occurs something different from a mere excitation and spreading of sound" (US 29/206). This something different is the speaking of lan-guage. It is the calling of the dif-ference of world and thing into the nearness of the fourfold. There is no collapsing of world and thing into one another in this event, or mere indeterminacy between them; rather, each comes into its own in the rift between them. The rift is the dif-ference, which is neither relation nor distinction but—calling.

The dif-ference calls. The rules of grammar would seem to cast the dif-ference into the role of a speaking subject, as if to allegorize the dif-ference in some fantastic mythology. But Heidegger wants to say that the dif-ference does not call as the subject of a predicate. The calling of the dif-ference is not any sort of agency. It is not a foundational act. Think of it in terms of the tolling of vespers in Trakl's poem, where calling is an event, not an act. Nor is this calling simply the sound of anything, just as the tolling of vespers is not the noise the bells make. Heidegger would say that the tolling of the bells *produces* sound, but what *occurs* is the stillness—a stillness so palpable one can hear it if one listens, but also a stillness that *stills* in the same strange way that things *thing* and world *worlds*. (Stilling has nothing to do with staying in place.)

Moreover, the stillness *stills* in the same strange way that language *speaks* (*Die Sprache spricht*). In fact, the stilling *is* the speaking of language. The famous line is: "*Language speaks as the peal of stillness* [*Die Sprache spricht als das Geläut der Stille*]" (US 30/207).

"Language speaks as the peal of the stillness": notice that this line tells us nothing about what language is. One has to say that language is not anything that is, does not exist, nor is it productive of things or worlds that are; rather, existence gives way to occurrence, the Being of beings to *Ereignis*. Language *occurs*, and its occurrence is the event of the fourfold, the calling of world and thing each into its own, that is, into the event (*Ereignis*) of the dif-ference. "The carrying out of world and thing in the manner of stilling," Heidegger says, "is the appropriative taking place [*Ereignis*] of the dif-ference. Language, the peal of stillness, is, inasmuch as the dif-ference takes place [*indem sich der Unterschied ereignet*]. Language goes on [*west*] as the taking place or occurrence of the dif-ference [*ereignende Unter-Schied*] for world and things" (US 30/207).

Certainly this is very strange, and deliberately, cunningly so. Heidegger's lingo, his strange way of speaking, is a rhetoric of bewilderment that puts us in the position of not knowing what to say about language. I mean that his strange idiom maneuvers us out of the theoretical attitude with respect to language. We are further than ever from getting a fix on it. We cannot ask what it is, for the whole grammar of proposition-making—*s* is *p*—has been displaced by a discourse without the copula: things thing, world worlds, stillness stills, and all of this is what occurs when language speaks. But what is it, exactly, that happens? We are very far from being in the know. We shall see that what happens does not occur for the benefit of our experience. We are being turned into skeptics with respect to language. (Does language exist?)

Just how far out of it we are is emphasized dramatically by Heidegger in a single line: "The peal of stillness," he says, "is not anything human" (US 30/207). We ought to allow this line to sink in. What Heidegger is saying is that language, which speaks as the peal of stillness, is not anything human. So it is no wonder that we are in the dark. I mean chances are we are in the dark not just because of Heidegger's mystifications, but because language does not have anything essential to do with us. It is something wholly other, alien and inaccessible to our customary ways, possibly even our strange ways, of speaking. Still, it is what occurs in speaking, even in our own. Language is not anything human, but we are for all of that *sprachlich* or linguistical, which is perhaps a way of accounting for our own strangeness with respect to each other. In *Totality and Infinity*, for example, Levinas speaks of discourse as "the experience of something absolutely foreign, a pure 'knowledge,' or 'experience,' a *traumatism of astonishment*." Levinas adds, however, that "it is only man who could be absolutely foreign to me, refractory to every typology, to every genus, to every characterology, to every classification—and consequently the term of a 'knowledge' penetrating beyond the object" (TI 73). For Levinas, strangeness remains within the region of the ethical, defines this region. Not so for Heidegger. Heidegger would want to say, by contrast, that the strangeness of man is possible only in virtue of the prior strangeness, the absolute otherness, of language itself. Discourse is indeed the experience of something absolutely foreign, a traumatism of astonishment—this is the subject of my next chapter—and as *sprachlich* we belong to this event in ways yet to be understood, but what remains absolutely foreign, refractory to every typology (or topology for that matter), to every genus, to every characterology or classification, is language.

The question is, if language is not anything human, what have we to do with it? The answer to this question lies in *Ereignis*, the word for event that is translated, however, with all the ambiguity of a pun, as appropriation. Heidegger speaks of our linguisticality as a condition in which we are taken up in the other—"appropriated," he says, "to the nature of language." The text here is difficult: "What has thus taken place, human being, has been brought into its own by language, so that it remains given over or appropriated to the nature of language, the peal of stillness. Such an appropriating takes place in that the very nature of language, the peal of stillness, needs and uses the speaking of mortals in order to sound as the peal of stillness for the hearing of mortals. Only as men belong within the peal of stillness are mortals able to speak in their own way in sounds [*Das so Ereignete, das Menschenwesen, ist durch die Sprache in sein Eigenes gebracht, dass es dem Wesen der Sprache, dem Geläut der Stille, übereignet bleibt. Solches Ereignen ereignet sich, insofern das* Wesen *der Sprache, das Geläut der Stille, das Sprechen der Sterblichen* braucht, *um als Geläut der Stille für das Hören der Sterblichen zu verlauten. Nur insofern die Menschen in das Geläut der Stille gehören, vermögen die Sterblichen auf* ihre Weise *das verlautende Sprechen]*" (US 30/208).

The rest of this book will be an attempt to work out what is said in these three sentences. It is just possible that all that Heidegger has to say about language is contained in them. What is it, after all, for us to belong [*gehören*] to language? What is belonging when *gehören* is a pun on listening? What is it for us to be taken up or appropriated to language in the event called *Ereignis*? What does the expression, "the nature of language [*das Wesen der Sprache*]" mean when it is characterized as "the peal of stillness"? What is it to be brought into our own? And what is it to be called mortals?

Above all, what is it (for us) to speak? Heidegger answers this question with the word for (the event of) poetry: *Dichten*. "Mortal speech," he says, "is a calling that names, a bidding which, out of the simple onefold of the dif-ference, bids things and world to come [*Das sterbliche Sprechen ist nennendes Rufen, Kommen-Heissen von Ding und Welt aus der Einfalt des Unter-Schiedes*]." So we have a say in the event that calls world and thing into the nearness of the fourfold—a *mortal* saying that occurs in the event of poetry. "What is purely bidden in mortal speech is what is spoken in the poem [*Das rein Geheissene des sterblichen Sprechens ist das Gesprochene des Gedichtes*]" (US 30–31/208). But what is poetry (*Dichten*: poetic speaking, if it is a speaking)? Or, rather, what is it for such "speaking" to occur? All that Heidegger says at this point is that "Poetry proper [*eigentliche Dichtung*] is never merely a higher mode (*Melos*) of everyday speech [*der Alltagssprache*]. It is rather the reverse: everyday language is a forgotten and therefore used-up poem, from which there hardly resounds a call any longer" (US 31/208). This does not mean that there is any *formal* difference between poetic and everyday speaking that one could identify analytically. The question of poetry has rather to do with our relation with language as speaking, that is, language as the peal of stillness; it is *not a question of knowing how to speak poetically* in contrast to how we speak in everyday occurrences; that is, it is not a question for poetics or a question that poetics knows how to formulate.

On the contrary, Heidegger concludes his lecture on "Language" by emphasizing once more that our relation with language does not put us in the position of speaking subjects. Our relation with language, he says, is one of listening rather than speaking—except that in this event the relation of speaking and listening is no longer a difference that can be captured in a formal distinction. "Mortals speak," Heidegger says, "insofar as they listen. Listening [*Hören*] draws from the command of the dif-ference what it brings out as sounding word [*lautende Wort*]. This speaking that listens and accepts is answering [*Das hörend-entnehmende Sprechen ist Ent-Sprechen*]" (US 30/209). Which is to say that our relation with language is, in some sense, not yet understood, dialogical; that is, we are caught up in a relation that is something like a dialogical realm where speaking and listening are impossible to isolate from one another analytically in a way that could identify them as separate acts or experiences of a subject. We are not caught up in this dialogue as subjects endowed with linguistic competence; rather, we are called upon and put under a claim that we must acknowledge. This, or something like this, is what answering means: "*Das Entsprechen ist als hörendes Entnehmen zugleich anerkennendes Entgegnen*" (US 32/209). Perhaps we will be able to think of poetry (*Dichten*) as our belonging and listening to language, our answering and accepting (in the sense of being open to the otherness or mystery of) language. However, to understand what this means will take some time. We will need to work our way through the rest of Heidegger's writings on language. And even then there is no assurance that we will find ourselves at home in what he has to say.

Chapter Four
The Poetic Experience
with Language

... we are moving within language,
which means
moving on shifting ground.
—What Is Called Thinking?

Experience

One therapeutic effect of Heidegger's first essay on language is that
it disconnects us—estranges or alienates us—from the very idea of
language, especially as this comes down to us in idealist and analytic
philosophies of language, linguistics, semiotics, various criticisms, and
so on; and this also means alienation from what we might call the
social theory of language, where the idea is not to retrieve the deep
grammatical, semantic, or propositional structure of human expression, but just to study how people talk, what they say when, their
language games, their discursive practices and institutions, their forms
of life. Language, Heidegger says, as if to sweep all this aside, "is not
anything human"; it is absolutely other. As if there were no such thing
as language.

However, having gone this far and having determined, if that is the
right word, the otherness of language, Heidegger turns to the task
of reconnecting language and those of us—mortals, he calls us—who
speak it, although it can no longer be said exactly that we "speak"
language (on the contrary, language does all it can to keep us from
speaking it). This reconnection is in part the job of "The Nature of
Language," which comprises three lectures delivered at Freiburg during the winter of 1957–58. These lectures do not appear to add anything new to what Heidegger has to say about language. They don't
represent an improvement or advancement upon what is said in the
lecture on "Language"; they don't carry us a little farther down a road,
as if the way to language were in fact something that enabled us to approach it, draw near enough for a look or glimpse. In other words, the

lectures in "The Nature of Language" don't add up to a rethinking or progression beyond an already established position; rather, they are what Heidegger would call a "lingering" in a region opened up within language—a *Gegend* within which language will avail itself to us, or of us, whatever that might turn out to mean. For our part there is now, at least, the advantage of having sweated through the lecture on "Language," and of being, therefore, within open if still uncertain surroundings.

Indeed, Heidegger even begins by introducing a familiar and always reassuring concept: experience. "The three lectures that follow," he says, "bear the title, 'The Nature of Language.' They are intended to bring us face to face with the possibility of undergoing an experience with language [*mit der Sprache eine Erfahrung zu machen*]" (US 159/57). This is surely what we've been hoping for—some possibility of arriving independently at what Heidegger is talking about: not having to struggle against his weird, unheard-of lingo but able to see things for ourselves. Except that Heidegger doesn't think of experience in this way, that is, in the familiar way of empirical verification or the independent testing of concepts. *Erfahrung* means something like living-through rather than knowledge-of. It is obviously more of a Hegelian and Diltheyan than a Lockean concept—*Erlebnis* rather than *Empfindung*. But of course it is not just Diltheyan or Hegelian, either. "To undergo an experience with something," Heidegger says, "—be it a thing, a person, or a god—means that this something befalls us, strikes us, comes over us, overwhelms and transforms us. When we talk of 'undergoing' an experience, we mean specifically that the experience is not of our own making; to undergo here means that we endure it, suffer it, receive it as it strikes us and submit to it. It is something itself that comes about, comes to pass, happens" (US 159/57). Experience in this sense will seem less like an inductive process than like an epistemological crisis; it isn't an event that is likely to confirm anything, rather it is likely to leave us dumbstruck and dispossessed as in a tragic calm. It is experience as reversal and estrangement: experience which has nothing to do with knowledge, unless it is just the negative insight that everything is otherwise. As Gadamer says in his reflection on hermeneutical experience in *Truth and Method*, experience is not knowledge but *being experienced:* it means, not being in the know, but being open to what happens. But this is a radical openness or exposure from which there is no refuge (TM 319).[1]

Hence the strange locution: experience *with*, not experience *of*. Language is not to be made an object of experience. Quite the contrary.

What is it to be experienced with language? It is not, it turns out, the same as wit, eloquence, rhetoric, or readiness with words. Indeed, Heidegger makes a special point of remarking that experience *with* language never occurs in the speaking of it: "at whatever time and in whatever way we speak a language, language itself never has the floor. Any number of things are given voice in speaking, above all what we are speaking about: a set of facts, an occurrence, a question, a matter of concern. Only because in everyday speaking language does *not* bring itself to language but holds itself back [*an sich hält*], are we able simply to go ahead and speak a language, and so to deal with something and to negotiate something by speaking" (US 161/59). Rather, the experience *with* language is likely to occur when language withholds itself in a radical way, that is, when we are at a loss for words and are forced to leave something unsaid; it occurs when language *fails* us, or when our linguistic competence breaks down. It is when we have lost control of language—when we are no longer in command of it but have been left speechless by its departure or by the words it withholds from us—*then*, Heidegger says, language will avail itself to us (US 161/59). As if there were a connection between the experience *with* language and the historic "weakness of the logos." Not that this means that we will therefore or henceforward know what language is; on the contrary, we may well be less in a position than ever before to produce a theory of language. An experience with language does not produce any knowledge of any sort; it is not an event of cognition.[2]

Actually, this ought not to seem so strange to us. After all, a basic topos of modern writing—from the Romantics to Mallarmé to Beckett —is the link between poetic experience and the failure of words, that is, the breakdown of expression and the palpability of silence or the whiteness of the blank page.[3] So it is not surprising that, in order to give us some sense of what it is to undergo an experience with language, Heidegger introduces a poem by Stefan George, which is very much in this modern tradition:

DAS WORT

Wunder von ferne oder traum
Bracht ich an meines landes saum

Und harrte bis die graue norn
Den namen fand in ihrem born—

Drauf konnt ichs greifen dicht und stark
Nun blüht und glänzt es durch die mark . . .

Einst langt ich an nach guter fahrt
Mit einem keinod reich und zart

Sie suchte lang und gab mir kund:
"So schläft hier nichts auf tiefem grund"

Worauf es meiner hand entrann
Und nie mein land den schatz gewann . . .

So lernt ich traurig den verzicht:
Kein ding sei wo das wort gebricht.

*

THE WORD

Wonder or dream from distant land
I carried to my country's strand

And waited till the twilit norn
Had found the name within her bourn—

Then I could grasp it close and strong
It blooms and shines now the front along . . .

Once I returned from happy sail,
I had a prize so rich and frail,

She sought for long and tidings told:
"No like of this these depths unfold."

And straight it vanished from my hand,
The treasure never graced my land . . .

So I renounced and sadly see:
Where word breaks off no thing may be.

[US 162–63/60]

"The manner in which we shall converse with this poem," Heidegger says, "does not claim to be scientific" (US 162/60). This is fair enough. We have already got wind of Heidegger's hermeneutics, where the reader steps back from the text, ceasing to be a reader in any formal or analytical sense but rather taking off from what the text says, or does not say, as one might pick up on a pun or play of words or take a hint as to one's next move. The poem is not by itself the object of much exegetical interest. Interest instead is always in a subject matter (*Sache*), which has a life and a claim of its own apart from the text.

There is no poetry for its own sake in Heidegger's reflections. For Heidegger, it is always in response to the matter of thinking that we come before, or away, from any text.

Heidegger's hermeneutics has to do with the relation of poetry and thinking, where thinking does not take poetry as its object of study, nor does poetry serve as a way of illustrating or clarifying what is thought. For example, in the case of Stefan George's poem, Heidegger has positively to restrain himself from condensing the poem's meaning or point into its final line: "Where word breaks off no thing may be." This line means almost *too much* to Heidegger, because in fact it summarizes what he believes (or once took) to be the case. He says, correctly, that one can take this line as making the following statement: "something *is* only where the appropriate and therefore competent word names a thing as being, and so establishes the given being as being" (US 165/63). Heidegger had worked out this poetics of establishment in his essay on "Hölderlin and the Essence of Poetry." The poet by his naming establishes the being of beings (*das Sein dem Seienden*); that is, his word nominates the being as what it is (ED 41/281). And in "The Nature of Language" Heidegger is quick to register his continuing agreement with this earlier idea. He says, glossing the last line of George's poem, "The being of anything that is resides in the word. Therefore this statement holds true: Language is the house of being" (US 166/63).

In "The Nature of Language," however, Heidegger wants to put aside the method of reading that simply seeks to underwrite a doctrine by means of poetry. By means of such a method, he says, "we would seem to have adduced from poetry the most handsome confirmation for a principle of thinking which we had stated at some time in the past —and in truth would have thrown everything into utter confusion. We would have reduced poetry to the servant's role as documentary proof for our thinking, and taken thinking too lightly; in fact we would already have forgotten the whole point: to undergo an experience with language" (US 166/63). The point, in other words, is not simply to contextualize the poem's meaning. The difficulty, however, lies just in this, that the poem's meaning is powerfully seductive. One cannot —Heidegger cannot—forbear summarizing its essential idea: "The decisive experience," he says, "is that which the poet has undergone with the word—and with the word inasmuch as it alone can bestow a relation to a thing. Stated more explicitly, the poet has experienced that only the word makes a thing appear as the thing it is, and thus lets it be present. The word avows itself to the poet as that which holds and sustains a thing in its being. . . . But the word is also that possession with which the poet is trusted and entrusted in an extraordinary way. The poet experiences his poetic calling as a call to the word as the source, the bourn of Being" (US 168–69/65–66).

But the important message of the poem is that this experience does *not* occur in the fullness of the poet's expression; on the contrary, the poet experiences the power of the word precisely at the moment when his own relationship with the word undergoes a decisive break. Here it is quite plain that Heidegger diverges from "Hölderlin and the Essence of Poetry." At first, the poet's relation to the word had been as to a cornucopia: there was nothing he could not say. All was given to him in the way of discourse; there was a plenum of expression. Language placed itself entirely in his possession. And this, according to Heidegger, is what the first five stanzas of the poem are about. However, the power of the word had no reality for the poet until, Heidegger says, that moment "when the conventional and self-assured poetic production suddenly breaks down" (US 172/68):

> And straight it vanished from my hand,
> The treasure never graced my land.

Here the poem converges upon its conclusion: the poem is finally not about the power of the word but about our proper relationship with it. This relationship is not that of expression or use; it is one in which renunciation replaces enunciation or pronouncement. The poet gives up his possession of the poetic copia:

> So I renounced and sadly see:
> Where word breaks off no thing may be.

"What does renunciation mean?" Heidegger asks (US 168/65). It means, literally, abdication in the double sense of refraining from speech, keeping silent, and giving up power. The two go together. "*Der Verzicht ist ein Entsagen*" (US 168/65).[4]

The poem, in other words, is about the breaking-off of *poiēsis*. It can be read as a secret allegory of *Gelassenheit* or letting-go. The experience with language occurs in the moment that language withdraws itself; it is not an experience *of* language, because language is no longer the copia or copious inventory, no longer the cornucopia of words and things in which everything emerges as a plenum. Instead of the plenum there is a Mallarméan abyss. Language now avails itself to us, not *for* speaking, not for poetic speaking or production, but *as* language (if language is the right word); it avails itself, that is, in poetic abdication or renunciation, the nonspeaking, the not-having-anything-to-express. One cannot help thinking here of Samuel Beckett's writer who withdraws from the "plane of the feasible," the plane of production, preferring instead the "expression that there is nothing to express, nothing with which to express, nothing from which to express, no power to express, no desire to express, together with the obligation to express."[5] Or, better, here would be the context in which to study Maurice Blanchot's great essay, "Literature and the Right to Death" (1949), which plays Heidegger's notion of *Entsagen* off against the Hegelian idea of annihilating predication, the word that kills—the word that takes possession and destroys:

> I say, "This woman," and she is immediately available to me, I push her away, I bring her close, she is everything I want her to be, she becomes the place in which the most surprising transformations occur and actions unfold: speech is life's ease and security. . . .
>
> For me to be able to say, "This woman," I must somehow take her flesh and blood reality away from her, cause her to be absent, annihilate her. The word gives me the being, but it gives it to me deprived of being. The word is the absence of that being, its nothingness. . . .
>
> Of course, my language does not kill anyone. And yet: when I say, "This woman," real death has been announced and is already present in my language; my language means that this person, who is here right now, can be detached from herself, removed from her existence and her presence and suddenly plunged into a nothingness in which there is no existence or presence; my language essentially signifies the possibility of this destruction; it is a constant, bold allusion to such an event. My language does not kill anyone. But if this woman were not really capable of dying, if she were not threatened by death at every moment of her life, bound and joined to death by an essential bond, I would not be able to carry out that ideal negation, that deferred assassination, which is what my language is.[6]

For Blanchot, there is an inescapable linkage between meaning and death: "Death allows me to grasp what I want to attain," he says; "it exists in words as the only way they can have meaning." Literature, however, is a withdrawal of language from annihilating discourse: in literature, "language . . . tries to become senseless" (GO 46). It lets things be; it does not seek to overcome them by an act of conceptual determination but steps back, away from the proposition, to that moment before speech when things are self-possessed as things, not yet objects present at hand but self-standing and free. Poetry is renunciation (*Verzichten*) of meaning as that which grasps and fixes, that which produces determinate objects. Poetry lends itself, avails itself, to the abyss. "The ideal of literature," Blanchot says, "could be this: say nothing, speak and say nothing [*L'idéal de la littérature a pu être celui-ci: ne rien dire, parler pour ne rien dire*]" (GO 43).

The kinship between the later Heidegger and Blanchot is uncanny and profound, and I can't explain it; but the point here would be that Stefan George's poem needs to be read in relation to someone in the Mallarméan tradition like Blanchot rather than as someone in the romantic tradition of Hölderlin. For Heidegger, at all events, "Das Wort," taken in this wise, is doctrinally a crucial poem. It speaks for Heidegger. It is, one might say, what he is thinking.

"And yet," Heidegger says, "in making these statements, however broad their implications"—however true they are, affirmable (for sound philological reasons) as *statements*—"we have done no more than sum up the experience the poet has undergone with the word, instead of entering into the experience itself" (US 170/67). In other words, all we have done is to give a basic schoolroom reading of the poem. Nothing wrong with that, but the *truth* of the poem is not contained in its content; it cannot be put into the form of a statement or doctrine. It does not lie in any correspondence to some prior experience on which the poem is based or which it tries to represent; it cannot be extracted by diligent or creative reading. Rather, it lies in front of the poem, in the bearing of the poem upon the situation in which we find ourselves, that is, the situation in which we find ourselves *with language*. In this respect, it must remain an open question whether we can claim to have understood the poem at all if we simply go on imagining ourselves in the readerly posture of grasping something contained or concealed or produced by the text, that is, as subjects occupied in the project of "unpacking" language. Certainly from the standpoint of hermeneutics understanding will consist in the way in which, in virtue of the poem, we now comport ourselves with language, much the way our understanding of a law will show itself in how, in virtue of the law, we act in the world, that is, how we respond to situations in which we find ourselves in consequence of the law. Understanding the law is not a case of mental agreement with anything; it is a practical and not merely conceptual condition of being. Just so: What follows? Where are we? or How do we stand? Whereto? These are the basic questions of Heideggerian hermeneutics.

Heidegger says: "it must remain open whether we are capable of entering properly into this poetic experience. There is the danger that we will overstrain a poem like this by thinking too much into it" (US 172/69). The point (again) is that the experience with language is not anything to be recovered from the poem. This experience lies not behind the poem but in front of it, or indeed in front of us in our concern with language. Thus we should not try to enter into the poem in order to reexperience the experience that presumably underlies it. This would be the way of romantic hermeneutics, whose key term is the Diltheyan *Nacherleben*. Heideggerian hermeneutics takes the opposite tack, taking off from the poem, not trying to get behind the poem's back but setting off on a path opened up by the poem.

Another way to put this would be to say that the experience with language is not an event of subjectivity that can be objectified by means of expression. It is not something that goes on inside of you as a result of impact with the outside world. If you ask where it occurs, Heidegger wants to say: "in the neighborhood of poetry and thinking." All by itself this is not very helpful, but the question is where it leads. Heidegger says that "the true experience with language can only be a thinking experience" (US 173/69). But if so, why all this talk about poetry? The answer, according to Heidegger, is that thinking is something that occurs only in the company of (or with) poetry.

But what is (called) thinking?

Thinking

Heidegger's first lecture in "The Nature of Language" is a text that doesn't take us very far. In fact, it concludes by starting over, as if the whole lecture were simply a slow realization that a mistake had been made at the outset; so Heidegger ends by returning to his first two sentences and rewriting them. "This series of lectures," he says, "bears the title, 'The Nature of Language.' It is intended to bring us face to face with the possibility of undergoing a *thinking* experience with language" (US 174/70). And what is thinking? As it turns out, it is not ratiocination—not a deductive process (US 175/71). It is not a quest for ultimate foundations (US 175/71). It is not even a questioning (US 175/72), which is a surprising thing for Heidegger to say, because he had once very prominently taken recourse to the question as an alternative to the style of rationality appropriate to the *Gestell*. Questioning is different from calculative and representational thinking. Questioning is not en-framing but de-framing, the unsettling of meanings or boundaries, the opening up of what is closed. Questioning is vigilance in behalf of freedom. It unmoors things, lets them go. It is opposed to manipulation and control. It exposes (exposes thinking to) the ambiguity of what is supposedly or assertedly fixed and certain. As Gadamer has shown, the question is the mode of rationality of the conversation; it is that force in the conversation which "protects words from dogmatic abuse" (TM 332). It historicizes the finality of monological reasoning, undoes the seams of such discourse, and so allows the conversation to take place. As such, it has nothing to do with such monologues as Cartesian doubt, the hermeneutics of suspicion, or the negative questioning of sophistic rhetoric that tries to put thinking at an impasse—tries to catch it in the double bind that will put a stop to it altogether. Rather, questioning itself is a mode of understanding in which there is always a difference—always another sense, always multiple and endlessly exfoliating senses—in which something is to be taken. Or say that it is a mode of understanding that goes on at the limits of sense where intelligibility is in the balance and about to get away from us. Questioning is openness to difference, otherness, or the strange. It is what is implied in Gadamer's famous line, "It is enough to say that we understand differently if we understand at all" (TM 264).

Moreover, it is clear that the whole purpose of the first lecture in "The Nature of Language" has been to put everything in question, not just all prior speaking of language, but even such formulas as the title of the lecture series itself, with its famous philosophical terms. "Let us give the title a question mark," Heidegger says, "such that the whole of it is governed by that mark and hence has a different sound. It then runs: The Nature?—of Language? Not only language is in question now, but so is the meaning of nature [*Wesen:* that is, being or essence]—and what is more, the question now is whether and in what way nature and language belong together [*mehr noch: in Frage steht, ob und wie Wesen und Sprache zueinander gehört*]" (US 174/70).

Indeed, even the words "language" and "nature" are opened up: "the possibility may emerge," Heidegger says, "that we shall at the proper time substitute another word for 'language' as well as for 'nature'" (US 1765/72). This will indeed be a crucial moment. Indeed, it is characteristic of Heidegger's thinking to allow familiar terms to

slip away into other senses. For the present, however Heidegger simply substitutes another poem for Stefan George's "Das Wort," not so
much to change senses as to release them. After all, he had been working George's poem pretty hard. He says: "In order that we may hear
the voice of Stefan George's poetic experience with the word once
more [but] in another key [*in einem anderen Ton*], I shall in closing read
Gottfried Benn's two-stanza poem. The tone [*der Ton*] of this poem
is tauter [*gestraffter*] and at the same time more vehement, because
it is abandoned and at the same time resolved in the extreme [*weil
preisgegeben und zugleich ins Äusserste entschieden*]. The poem's title is
a characteristic and presumably intentional variation [*überschrieben*]"
(US 177/72):

EIN WORT

Ein Wort, ein Satz—: Aus Chiffern steigen
erkanntes Leben, jäher Sinn,
die Sonne steht, die Sphären schweigen
und alles ballt sich zu ihm hin.

Ein Wort—ein Glanz, ein Flug, ein Feuer,
ein Flammenwurf, ein Sternenstrich—,
und wieder Dunkel, ungeheuer,
im leeren Raum um Welt und Ich.

*

A WORD

A word, a phrase—: from cyphers rise
Life recognized, a sudden sense,
The sun stands still, mute are the skies,
And all compacts it, stark and dense.

A word—a gleam, a flight, a spark,
A thrust of flames, a stellar trace—
And then again—immense—the dark
Round world and I in empty space.

[US 177/73]

Benn's poem is indeed an apt companion of Stefan George's "Das
Wort." The poem is, once more, about the power of the word, and,
once more, the experience with the word occurs in the break that
results from the word's withdrawal:

And then again—immense—the dark
Round world and I in empty space.

Benn's poem, to be sure, is more apocalyptic than George's. It is a poem about the disappearance of foundations, the *Abgrund*. But no matter: Heidegger does not quote the poem in order to perform an exegesis of it. Rather the poem occurs here as part of Heidegger's dramatic self-questioning in which he throws his whole first lecture into the air: "the true stance of thinking," he says, "cannot be to put questions" (US 176/72). It is not, after all, the nature of language that is in question; what is in question *are those very words*—the *nature* of *language*—and with them our whole customary way of trying to open up the possibility of such a thing as "experience with language." What Heidegger is saying is that this experience will remain closed to us if we simply go on putting ourselves in the subjective posture of interrogating an object, a text or "piece" of language.

So the second lecture in the series is a beginning-all-over-again. Heidegger begins, interestingly, with a characterization of his audience: "because most of you here," he says, "are primarily engaged in scientific thinking, a prefatory remark is in order" (US 178/74). The remark is to the effect that nothing of what follows is going to make any sense to you. This is, he says, because the sciences know only one thing: method. "Method, especially in today's modern scientific thought, is not a mere instrument serving the sciences; rather, it has pressed the sciences into its own service" (US 178/74). Heidegger quotes Nietzsche on scientific formalism: "It is not the victory of *science* that distinguishes our nineteenth century, but the victory of scientific *method* over science" (US 178/74: *The Will to Power*, no. 466). The end of science is no longer knowledge but methodological efficiency, where knowledge turns into know-how and getting the most out of your where-with-all. Science functions, operates, and proceeds; its watchwords are innovation and breakthrough, and so it goes without saying that it advances, always emancipating itself from obsolescence and varieties of false consciousness. Science gets it together; science is under control. But it does not think.

In place of method, Heidegger proposes—and here we must imagine his audience stiffening in its seats—*die Gegend:* region or country. "In thinking," Heidegger says, "there is neither method nor theme, but rather region [*Gegend*], so called because it gives its realm and free reign to what thinking is given to think [*die so heisst, weil sie das gegnet, freigibt, was es für das Denken zu denken gibt*]. Thinking abides in that country [*hält sich in der Gegend auf*], walking the ways of that country. Here the way is part of the country and belongs to it" (US 179/74–75). To which Heidegger adds, quite unnecessarily: "From the point of view of the sciences, it is not just difficult but impossible to see this situation" (US 179/75).[7]

Heidegger's *Weg* is a return of method to its etymological sense, which is hardly a sense at all (call it a slippage of sense). Indeed, from an analytical point of view, Heidegger's whole enterprise is a program of colossal regression. Bad enough that the region or country in which thinking abides turns out to be poetry—bad enough, this, but even worse is Heidegger's characterization of thinking as passive and uncritical acceptance: "to think," he says, "is before all else to listen, to let ourselves be told something [*Sichsagenlassen:* literally, to let saying happen to us] and not to ask questions" (US 180/76). Is Heidegger trying to insult his audience? What he proposes looks for all the world like a headlong retreat from critical reason: "to listen, to let ourselves be told something and not to ask questions"—this is Gnosticism, not Enlightenment. Thinking for Heidegger appears to presuppose the eradication of suspicion. From the standpoint of Enlightenment this can only lead to the restoration of myth and superstition. No wonder, then, Heidegger's talk of earth and sky, gods and mortals! No wonder the mystification, no wonder the delight in fragments of discourse from another world and in words whose meanings we no longer know. No wonder the indifference to the slippage of sense.

Moreover, this substitution of listening for questioning as a characterization of thinking has this peculiar effect on Heidegger's lecture: it seems to stop it in its tracks. That is, Heidegger himself gives up questioning for listening. I mean his lecture does not formally shape itself as a questioning or inquiry that pursues its subject as it would a prey or quarry (an object of thought). There is no movement, no plot, no progress toward a goal, not even the suggestion of effort; rather, the lecture shapes itself as a listening, say a lingering or pause (as between lectures one and three), in which nothing much happens, that is, nothing gets said—until near the end, when suddenly something strikes Heidegger (not quite out of the blue) and awakens him, as he says, from "a slumber of hastily formed opinions" (US 193/87). Until this moment the lecture is nothing if not muted. It is very far from taking the form of a coherent essay. Nothing is put into play—certainly not anything like an argument waits to be advanced, there is nothing so active or strenuous as an intellectual movement against an adversary or a problem. Nothing we would recognize as thinking is taking place.

Of course, our norms of rationality accustom us to the idea that thinking is something dynamic and aggressive—being tough-minded, making impregnable, solid, or rigorous arguments, tackling hard cases, probing complex issues, being philosophically penetrating, solving insurmountable problems, undertaking strenuous tasks, taking bold positions, having strong views, overthrowing established opinions and entrenched schools, dismantling systems: the life of the mind is nothing if not a struggle against the forces of ignorance, superstition, error, illusion, dogmatism, or outmoded views. This is why we think of thinking as something masculine, whereas poetry (in the same metaphorical stroke) is something feminine or gay—passive, receptive, attentive, philosophically naive, listening for the word of inspiration, sensitive to the gentle impulse or, alternatively, being rapt with a passion or carried away by the spontaneous overflow of powerful feelings. However, what Heidegger throws into the air is just this metaphorical latticework to which our norms of rationality cling.

It is not to be thought, in other words, that Heidegger stops thinking just because he is no longer in the mode of problem solving. Language for Heidegger isn't a problem; rather, as Marcel would say, it is a mystery.[8] A mystery isn't anything anyone can solve. One doesn't probe a mystery; one cannot approach such a thing analytically, or at all. One can never get outside a mystery in order to comprehend it from a certain point of view; instead, a mystery is what one always finds oneself in the midst of, like falling in love or being a father or suffering a tragedy. One lives through a mystery, and what matters is whether one is open or oblivious to what happens. Openness in this event is radical in the manner of exposure; it is a venture or risk. In the nature of the case, our relation to mystery, insofar as we enter into it, is always reflective rather than investigatory, ruminative rather than probative, improvisatory and ad hoc rather than methodical, systematic, or productive of clean propositional results. In our relation to mystery there is always blindness, perplexity, and the sense of being in an indefensible position—but also, as if by way of bewilderment and logical weakness, there is also the possibility of insight (since in such a state nothing is foreclosed). But of course talking this way may only be further mystification to cover up the hard or dirty truth about Heidegger, which is that he has regressed from Enlightenment to Darkness, from Criticism to Witchcraft, from white to black theology, from Philosophy to Poetry. As in a sense he has.

Zusage—Zuspruch—Sage

So lecture two is a sort of standing and waiting, as if on the brink of enthusiasm; but it is not therefore empty—there are things one ought to pick up on. For example, to think is to listen—but listen to what? It appears that there are two answers to this question, neither one, to be sure, terribly illuminating in itself, but perhaps they will help us to get into the spirit or play of Heidegger's venture. The first answer entails (as does everything in the later Heidegger) a pun: "Every question posed to the matter of thinking," he says, "every inquiry for its nature, is already borne up by the grant [*Zusage*] of what is to come into question. Therefore the proper bearing of the thinking which is needed now is to listen to the grant, not to ask questions [*Darum ist das Hören der Zusage die eigentliche Gebärde des jetzt nötigen Denkens, nicht das Fragen*]" (US 180/75).

What is this *Zusage*?

Peter Hertz translates it as "grant," but in a note he judiciously adds that Heidegger's word "exceeds the meaning of the translation" (76). In fact, the word is untranslatable in the present context. Its excessiveness entails, for example, the pun on the word *Sage*, Saying. Recall Heidegger's warning or promise that he might shortly substitute another word for "language." Here is that substitution, that slip-sliding into another sense, beginning to take place: "the listening we have now in mind," Heidegger says, "tends toward the grant, as Saying to which the nature of language is akin [*das hier gemeinte Hören ist der Zusage als der Sage zugeneigt, mit der das Wesen der Sprache verwandt ist*]" (US 180/76). *Sage*, Saying, becomes the keyword of lecture three, displacing (or escaping) *die Sprache* almost completely, but here in lecture two it is not yet *Sage* but only the promise of such a thing: *Zusage* means "promise" as much as "grant," although the phenomenon of promising implies a taking-for-granted, as in the giving of one's word, which is taken as granted, accepted in good faith, say taken as given. There is in fact a play on philosophical givenness beginning here, and in a moment this play will take place in earnest.

Zusage is, in a sense, a *Sage* that remains unsaid, or just out of hearing, a promise of something yet to come: "If we are to think through the nature of language," Heidegger says, "language must first promise itself to us [*muss sich die Sprache zuvor uns zusagen*]" (US 180/76). Heidegger then adds the following, now substituting the word *Zuspruch* for *Zusage*:

Language must, in its own way, avow to us itself—its nature. Language persists as this avowal [*Die Sprache muss auf ihre Weise sich selber—ihr Wesen uns zusprechen. Die Sprache west als dieser Zuspruch*]. We hear it constantly, of course, but do not give it thought. If we did not hear it everywhere, we could not use one single word of language. Language is active as this promise [*Die Sprache west als dieser Zuspruch*]. The essential nature of language [*das Wesen der Sprache*] makes itself known to us as what is spoken, the language of its nature [*die Sprache ihres Wesens*]. But we cannot quite hear this primal knowledge, let alone "read" it [*Aber wir können diese Ur-Kunde weder recht hören noch gar "lesen"*]. It runs: The being of language—the language of being [*Sie lautet: Das Wesen der Sprache: Die Sprache des Wesen*]. [US 180–81/76]

This is not an easy passage to understand, not even for a Heidegger text. It is a text that disconnects itself from its language, which it allows to float away. Hertz translates *Zuspruch* as "promise" and "avowal," thus easing somewhat the slippage that occurs in the substitution of *Zuspruch* for *Zusage*. But perhaps the best recourse is simply to take both *Zusage* and *Zuspruch* as literally (or as etymologically) as possible, that is, in the sense of a *saying-to* (someone), which at least catches the dialogical character of such events as giving someone one's word, handing down a verdict, handing on a proverb or a saying, language disseminating itself—where in each case language avails itself to us as an event of giving. What is given in such an event? In part this remains to be seen—what is given is the gift of *es gibt* (an excessive gift). *Es gibt*, of course, is a piece of uncanny discourse and a concept of dissemination. For now, however, it is enough to say (as Heidegger does) that if language did not give of itself (give its giving, its speaking), we would never be in a position to speak a language, there would be nothing for us to say. This giving of itself is a saying (*Zuspruch*) we should listen for, even though we are not yet able to hear anything. "We cannot quite hear this primal knowledge"—but Hertz's translation here normalizes Heidegger's text a little too philosophically: the word for Hertz's "primal knowledge" is *Ur-Kunde*, where *Kunde* means something like news in the sense of tidings (v. headlines). Whatever it is, *Ur-Kunde* is a word made strange, a word in excess of itself, very much like *Zusage* and *Zuspruch:* a word in which another word resounds in the manner of punning and parody, a word that we cannot quite take hold of by the usual means of exegetical reading that would properly fix its meaning. "We cannot quite hear this Ur-Kunde," Heidegger says, "let alone 'read' it." It *runs* (*lautet:* another pun, and one of Heidegger's favorites; cf. *Erläuterung*), and there is nothing for it but to let it go. What it gives us is the transformation of Heidegger's philosophically resounding title into so many figures of speech (chiasmus; parataxis): *Das Wesen der Sprache: Die Sprache des Wesens.*

"The transformation of the title," Heidegger says, "is of such a kind that it makes the title disappear" (US 181/71).

And with it go the last signs that what we are getting from Heidegger is a philosophical essay about the nature, essence, or being (or whatever) of language, much less an essay about the language of Being, whatever that might be. This ought to eliminate once for all the confusion or misunderstanding about "the language of Being"—as if there existed a language that Being (*Sein*) would use if it could speak. I think Hertz would agree that *Das Wesen der Sprache: Die Sprache des Wesens* is not really translatable as "The Being of Language: The Language of Being." Nowhere in Heidegger is there any notion of Being (*Sein*) expressing or disclosing itself in language, as if the revelation of Being were the function of language. This is Paul de Man's mistake in "Heidegger's Exegeses of Hölderlin," where the problem that is said to occupy Hölderlin and Heidegger is not only how one can speak *of* Being (*Sein*), "but say Being itself," without mediation.[9] For de Man, the very idea of language contradicts the possibility of unmediated revelations of Being ("stating Being," he calls it), because language is nothing if not mediation. But for Heidegger Being was never the content of revelation in this epistemological sense, that is, as an event involving consciousness and its mediations. And now it is certainly clear that language is no longer a Kantian system of mediations that one could describe analytically, say in a philosophy of symbolic forms.

"What follows," Heidegger says, as if beginning again, and not for the last time, "is not a dissertation on language under a different heading. What follows is an attempt to take our first step into the country which holds possibilities of a thinking experience with language in readiness for us. In that country, thinking encounters its neighborhood with poetry" (US 181/77). I want to come back to this sentence in a moment, since it calls (as Heidegger admits) for an explanation. Yet explaining must give way to listening—but listening to what? I said that there were two answers to this question. The first involves us in the puzzling series of dialogical substitutions or puns: *Zusage—Zuspruch—Sage.* The second answer requires only a single word: poetry (that is, the event of poetry, *Dichten*, which entails a pun on density or thickness). Not the idea of poetry; not poetics or the art of *Poesie*, but something otherwise than *poiēsis* or the production of *Dichtung*. In lieu of an explanation, Heidegger gives us something to listen to, namely fragments from Stefan George, Hölderlin, and Nietzsche—but particularly from Stefan George, the whole last section of whose collection *Das Neue Reich* (in which "Das Wort" appears) continues to ring in Heidegger's ear. In fact, the metaphor of a ringing in the ear turns up twice in this context—*"im Ohr"* (US 183/78), *"im Gehör"* (US 185/80)— and not by accident.

lōgos, dichten, phūsis

What is it for a poem (or anything) to ring in the ear? One does not actually hear anything in such an event, that is, one doesn't empirically register any sound; there is only the resounding of something, an echoing, a lingering, a haunting or conceivably even a nagging— whatever it is, it isn't there, but neither will it go away, it is excessive but inaccessible, which is also the case with Heideggerian "calling." Ringing in the ear is another mode of uncanny discourse. It is like stillness and riddling, punning and parody, and it appears that for Heidegger it is also the mode of being, or mode of sounding, of the poetic event (*Dichten*).

Here again one might appeal for clarification to Gerard Manley Hopkins, who thought roughly along Heideggerian lines when he suggested that the reader's task with respect to poetry is not to decipher the poem (which not infrequently is indecipherable in any case) but to keep it in one's memory, where one day it just might "explode." [10] Poetry, Hopkins said, should never be merely read, that is, one's relation to poetry should never be exclusively visual, analytic, or aesthetically distanced; he preferred to have his own verse read aloud, because it is in its echo and re-echo that the force of the poem, if not its sense, will make itself felt. Reading with the eye is safe; reading aloud leaves one exposed. Here the poem is not an object in front of us, under our gaze and our control, but an indeterminate voice, the voice of the other, disembodied and possessive. Poetry in this sense is what Plato warned us about, poetry as a mode of obsession in which one is no longer in one's right mind because one has been taken over by something else, something other, something not human—not an *alter ego* like the *daimon* of Socrates but something overwhelming and uncanny that takes over one's speaking, transforms and transports it, carries it away (and oneself in the bargain).

Heidegger recurs to something like this idea in an important section of *An Introduction to Metaphysics* (1935), where he pauses to consider that riddle of riddles, the origin of language. "The origin of language," he says, "is essentially mysterious. And this means that language can only have arisen from the overpowering, the strange and terrible [*aus dem Überwältigenden und Unheimlichen*], through man's departure into being. In this departure, language was being, embodied in the word: poetry. Language is the primordial poetry in which a people speaks being [*In diesem Aufbruch war die Sprache als Wortwerden des Seins: Dichtung. Die Sprache ist die Urdichtung, in der ein Volk des Sein dichtet*]" (EM 131/144). Heidegger's language here is very obscure. Manheim struggles to make sensible English out of it, but it is by no means clear that *die Sprache als Wortwerden des Seins* is to be rendered in the language of embodiment and expression, as if poetry were a form that signifies or reveals or makes sensible something hidden in a supersensible dimension—as if poetry were the mediation of language and being. Clearly it is not the case that in poetry something inexpressible (call it "Being") gets "turned into" language. Poetry as it is understood here is an event, more *Dichten* than *Dichtung*, more estrangement than revelation; it is an encounter with the other, where (in contrast to the later writings) the other is (still) Being, or perhaps already "older than Being." For in fact the event of poetry is very like the overwhelming and uncanny "experience with language" that Heidegger takes for his subject in "The Nature of Language."

It is crucial to Heidegger's account of language and poetry in *An Introduction to Metaphysics* that poetry is uncontainable within a theory of the logos. Heidegger re-mystifies or re-enchants poetry, but not in the mode of romantic primitivism (for example, as a Viconian "poetic logic" or animistic thinking, a primordial logos). In fact Heidegger is very careful to avoid the romantic language of the Spirit that turns poetry's possessiveness (its otherness) into a case of merely psychic indwelling, or the visitation of unseen powers, faculties, demons, spirits, familiars, or ideal entities from a transcendental realm. Poetry is mystified in the sense of becoming radically strange, not just not human but not even figurable in terms of non- or superhuman powers like romantic Imagination. In *An Introduction to Metaphysics*, Heidegger concentrates this otherness in the Greek word, *deinos*, which he picks up on from its appearance in the famous chorus from *Antigone* about the strangeness of man. Heidegger offers a long commentary on this word (EM 113–20/124–32), taking it not in the still-human sense of "fearful" or "terrible," which would have been the preference of normal philology and (for all we know) of Sophocles himself, but rather as *Überwältigung* and *Unheimlich,* overpowering and uncanny. In Heidegger's abnormal or radical philology, *deinos* becomes an event of incomprehensible violence that shakes man loose from everything safe and familiar, which disconnects him from his ground and transports him to a place where everything is otherwise. We should be able to recognize this notion of estrangement from its appearance in "The Origin of the Work of Art," which dates from this same period in Heidegger's thinking. Only here the note of violence and struggle is intensified—and is reflected even in Heidegger's own reading.[11]

The violent reading goes like this: poetry is language impinging or impacting on human existence, laying it open, exposing it to the uncanny, estranging it from its comfortable fixities, disclosing *Da-Sein* as *deinotaton,* strangest of all. *Dichten* is an event of radical estrangement in which *Da-Sein* is shattered against the uncanny. But it doesn't end there. What follows this shattering event is a struggle for control, a power struggle. Heidegger suggests that the Greeks tried to register their encounter with the uncanny in tragedy, as if tragedy were first philosophy or original metaphysics. Tragedy is a first attempt to give representation to the uncanny; it is also, therefore, a first taming of the uncanny, turning it to account, governing it. This appropriation of the uncanny is the work of the logos. The logos is the way *Da-Sein* brings the overpowering and the strange (that which is shattering) under control—an overpowering of the overpowering. But poetry shows that language is not logos, that is, not wholly identifiable or reducible to it, rather it is excessive and uncontainable, although there could be no Logos without it. Language as logos is gathering, ordering, controlling, making sense; it is foundational and just. By contrast, language as poetry is something else—*Überwältigung, Unheimlich, adike.* It is something other—no saying *what,* but we must imagine language resisting its own gathering, withholding itself, and refusing itself, always threatening to explode its own forms.

What Heidegger gives us in this section of *An Introduction to Metaphysics* (part 4, section 3: "Being and Thinking") is a critique of the Logos as that which overcomes language, tames it, bends language to the human will-to-power. "*It is by no means evident,*" Heidegger says, "*that language is logos*" (EM 131/144: my emphasis). Logos here means that which gathers, orders, makes sense of things; it is that which makes possible the unity of being in the construction of logical categories. It makes possible the building of the proposition, or the language of philosophy. Hence the logical function of the sign, which is to take over what language gives it and to hold it in place, stabilizing it, fixing it for the assertions and frameworks of the logos:

> The word, the name, restores the emerging being [*stellt das sich eröffnende Seiende*] from the immediate, overpowering surge [*überwältigenden Andrang*] to its being and maintains it in this openness, delimitation, and permanence. Naming does not come afterward, providing an already manifest being with a designation and a hallmark [*mit einer Bezeichnung und einem Merkzeichen*] known as a word; it is the other way around: originally an act of violence, the word sinks from this height to become a mere sign, and this sign proceeds to thrust itself before the being [*das Wort sinkt aus der Höhe seiner ursprünglichen Gewalt-tat als Eröffnung des Seins zum blossen Zeichen herab, so zwar, dass dieses selbst sich dann vor das Seiende schiebt*]. Pristine speech [*ursprünglichen Sagen:* originary Saying] opens up the being of the being [*das Sein des Seienden*] in the structure of its collectedness. And this opening is collected in a second sense: the word preserves what was originally collected and so administers the overpowering power [*wonach das Wort das ursprünglich Gesammelte bewahrt und so das Waltende, die* phūsis, *verwaltet:* notice the Greek word, *phūsis,* which Manheim leaves out of his translation]. Standing and active in Logos, which is ingathering [*Sammlung*], man is the gatherer. He undertakes to govern and succeeds in governing the power of the overpowering [*Er übernimmt und vollbringt die Verwaltung des Waltens des Überwältingenden*]. [EM 131–32/144]

This is a fascinating text, and it is crucial for any understanding of the later Heidegger. In place of a theory of the origin of language, Heidegger gives us an account of the origin of the logos and of the sign as that which designates, brings under control, grasps and fixes that which emerges in the opening of language as Saying (*im ursprünglichen Sagen*). In other words, he gives us an account of what, according to tradition, we take language to be; but language is something else, something other, something that withdraws, and in this text that other is characterized by the Greek word that Manheim drops from his translation (as if it were excessive, which it is): namely, *phūsis,* or that which, as Heraclitus said, loves to hide (*phūsis krūptesthai philei* [Fr. 123]). To put it as bluntly as one can: Language is not logocentric. As Heidegger says: "*All by itself the logos does not make language*" (EM 132/

145; my emphasis). Language is *phūsis* as well as *lōgos;* that is, language is not reason and order but overpowering and uncanny, uncontrollable and wholly other, irreducible to the Same—all this as well as (and even older than) that which we experience as grammatical, syntactical, diacritical, propositional, capable of putting all that is into a statement or into the conceptual frameworks summarized by the word metaphysics.[12] And the idea seems to be that poetry remains open to the *phūsis* of language, whereas philosophy (which is to say metaphysics) is the sealing off of *lōgos* from this other. So poetry is darkness against the philosophy of light; it is license against the rule of the logos; it is waywardness or ambiguity, endless dissemination as against the placing of things in their proper categories or the subsumption of things within a total system.[13]

It remained for the later Heidegger to work this out, but there is no doubt that the account of the "breaking apart" of *phūsis* and *lōgos* in *An Introduction to Metaphysics* is a crucial gloss: "the poetic experience with language" is an encounter with the *phūsis* of language, where *phūsis* is no longer translatable simply as the nature, essence, or being of language, rather it is the resistance of language to nomination: it is that which shows itself, for example, in the "weakness of the logos," that is, in the inability of language to keep things (including itself) under control. Rather than give it a name, we should call it simply the otherness of language. And the idea is, if I understand, that poetry is the preserve of this otherness. It is the renunciation of the violent logos as that which overpowers the overpowering (EM 132/144). Poetry is the language of *phūsis* and the *phūsis* of language. It is the letting-go or releasement of language into its own. Poetry is *Gelassenheit.*

The point for now is that in the second lecture in "The Nature of Language" (or, for that matter, in the whole of the later writings) Heidegger's subject is this otherness of language first glimpsed in *An Introduction to Metaphysics*, that is, language in its reserve, its excessiveness with respect to the logos (to logical or propositional form), its wildness or waywardness, its resistance to sense, its *phūsis.* From the beginning, he says, that is, "since the early days of Western thinking," much has been said about language, but nevertheless "the being [*sic*] of language nowhere brings itself to language as the language of being [*das Wesen der Sprache sich überall nicht als die Sprache des Wesens zur Sprache bringt*] (US 186/81). What would it be for language to bring itself as language to language? Heidegger addresses this question directly in "The Way to Language" (1959). But in the present context what matters is the self-refusal of language, its nature, or essence, or *phūsis:*

There is some evidence that the essential nature of language [*das Wesen der Sprache*] flatly refuses to express itself in words —in the language, that is, in which we make statements about language. If language everywhere withholds its nature in this sense, *then such withholding belongs to the very nature of language* [*dann gehört diese Verweigerung zum Wesen der Sprache;* my emphasis]. Thus language not only holds back when we speak it in the accustomed ways, but this its holding back [*dieses ihr Ansich-halten*] is determined by the fact that language holds back its own origin and so denies its being to our usual notions. *But then we may no longer say that the being of language is the language of being, unless the word "language" in the second phrase says something different, in fact something in which the withholding of the being of language—speaks* [*Für diesen Fall dürfen wir aber dann auch nicht mehr sagen, das Wesen der Sprache sei die Sprache des Wesens, es sei denn, das Wort "Sprache" besage in der zweiten Wendung etwas anderes und sogar solches, worin die Verweigerung des Sprachwesens—spricht;* my emphasis]. Accordingly, the being of language puts itself into language nonetheless, in its most appropriate manner [*auf seine eigenste Weise*]. We may avoid the issue no longer; rather, we must keep on conjecturing what the reason may be why the peculiar speech of language's being [*die eigentumliche "Sprache" des Sprachwesens*] passes unnoticed all too easily. Presumably part of the reason is that the two kinds of utterance *par excellence*, poetry and thinking, have not been sought out in their proper habitat, their neighborhood [*Vermutlich liegt dies mit daran, dass die beiden ausgezeichneten Weisen des Sagen, Dichten und Denken, nicht eigens und d. h. in ihrer Nachbarschaft aufgesucht wurden*]. [US 186/81]

So the question is not simply what it is for language to speak; rather, what is it for the withholding or refusal of language (*die Verweigerung des Sprachwesens*)—to speak? I take this passage to be Heidegger's call for thinking to step back from the logos and to seek its experience with language as *phūsis*, or that which loves to hide. This is the same as saying that, in a way that remains to be understood, thinking needs to link itself up with poetry. For it is in poetry that language as *phūsis* is preserved as that which cannot be subsumed or assimilated into our orders of signification and which we otherwise experience as excessive and irrational, the *délire* of discourse. If the logical task of thinking is to take over what language gives it and to hold it in place, cleaning and paring, stabilizing and fixing it for the mind in a conceptual determination, the task of thinking with respect to language must be something else, something different, because language does not give itself, as itself, to thinking in this logical way. It is not something that can be appropriated by the language of signs or the philosophical language of propositions and conceptual systems. It is not something about which one can frame a discourse. "What follows is not a dissertation on language."

This is surely why the poems by Hölderlin and George that ring in Heidegger's ear seem conceptually unproductive: despite their hold on us (anyhow on Heidegger), they don't tell us anything in the sense of giving us something we can come up or away with: an echo cannot be contained. Heidegger says that in them the poets register their *poetic* experience with language, but the force of this experience is not anything the poems themselves convey (unless it is just in their native darkness, which exegesis can overcome in a twinkling). On the contrary, "The experience of this poet with the word," Heidegger says of Stefan George's "Gesang" (the final section of *Das Neue Reich*), "passes away into darkness, and even remains veiled itself." To which Heidegger adds: "We must leave it so" (US 184/79). Let it go. But within the provenance of such poetry, Heidegger is sure, we can, if we listen, hear language "avowing" itself to us in its own appropriate way—not as *die Sprache* but as *Zuspruch*, not (yet) as *Sage* but as *Zusage*, or that in which language promises itself to us. We do not yet know what this promise holds for us, if promise is the word. Indeed, the upshot of Heidegger's funny words for language appears to be that they are words that play with the withholding of language, its endless deferral of itself, the way it beckons and withdraws, thus inscribing the structure of the promise, that most elusive of utterances.

Chapter Five
Words and Sounds
in Heidegger

To think is surely a peculiar affair. The word of
thinkers has no authority. The word of thinkers
knows no authors, in the sense of writers. The
word of thinking is not picturesque; it is
without charm. The word of thinking rests in
the sobering quality of what it says. Just the
same, thinking changes the world. It changes it
in the every darker depths of a riddle, depths
which as they grow darker offer promise of a
greater brightness.
—"Logos (Heraclitus, Fragment 50)"

The Neighborhood of Poetry and Thinking

I said at the end of the last chapter that "thinking needs to link itself up with poetry," but obviously this is a careless way of talking
—and misleading in the bargain, especially if we go on to imagine
that if language cannot avail itself to us logically, then it must do so
preconceptually, intuitively, practically, or by some primordial process
of knowing that logic might subsequently come along to verify; but
this isn't what Heidegger is talking about at all. It is not that there
are, for example, two categories of mental operation, one primitive
and one enlightened, one capable of inference and the other of insight. Questioning and listening, for example, are not to be thought
of as mental operations. (Indeed, our shock at Heidegger's statement
that thinking is listening rather than questioning is very likely rooted
in our mistaken assumption that questioning and listening are alternative methods of thinking between which we are free to choose or
which we may pick up and put down at will.) Poetry on this same
line is not a primitive logic that thinking could regress to as if to an
unmediated epistemological state in which an undistorted vision, or
some mystical access to the object, say language or world, would be

possible. So there is no obvious connection between poetry and negative theology. Rather, in place of a formal philosophical or prephilosophical state, Heidegger speaks of *Gegend,* region or country, which is another baffling word from the Heideggerian lexicon of nearness, belonging-together, wandering, and rift. Poetry and thinking are regional somethings (one doesn't know what to call them if they are not to be thought of as mental or linguistic operations). They are near one another, belonging to the same neighborhood.

"We will," Heidegger says, "immediately demand an explanation of what 'neighborhood' is supposed to mean here, and by what right we talk about such a thing" (US 186/81–82). By now, of course, we should be on to Heidegger and explanation, that is, we know how to cope with such demands, namely by letting-go and taking a step back; but in fact we should never lightly dismiss demands for explanation, especially not with a superior or knowing smile, and especially as this demand comes (as it surely does in this case) from one's audience, before whom one has the traditional obligation to be clear, or anyhow not devious, even when one's devious subject refuses to be converted into transparent discourse. Heidegger's response to this demand for explanation, however, is characteristic: "the phrase of the neighborhood of poetry and thinking means that the two dwell face to face with each other, that the one has settled facing the other, has drawn into the other's nearness" (US 186/82). He then adds this reflexive note: "This remark about what makes a neighborhood is by way of figurative talk [*in einer bildlichen Redeweise*]. Or are we already saying something to the point [*von der Sache:* on the subject, that is, literally and not in terms of something else]? What, really, does 'figurative talk' mean? [*Was heisst denn 'bildlichen Redeweise'?*]" (US 187/82).

Or, in other words, when I use the expression, "neighborhood of poetry and thinking," I'm speaking metaphorically. Or am I? What is it to do such a thing, speaking one way rather than another? *Was heisst 'bildlichen Redeweise'?*

Here Heidegger raises the question of the metaphoricality of his own language, not perhaps for the first time—recall that in the lecture "Language" from 1950 he introduced his tautology, "Language is language," in order to avoid speaking about language in terms of something else, something that is not language (reason, for example). As if he were determined to address language literally *as language,* rather the way language speaks as language when *Die Sprache spricht,* saying only itself, saying nothing (not conveying anything by means of words). Here, however, the question is simply whether "neighborhood" is a metaphor of the relationship of poetry and thinking. As is his usual way, Heidegger responds to this question by questioning the legitimacy of its terms: "What, really, does 'figurative talk' mean?" He adds: "We are quick to give the answer, never giving it a thought that we cannot claim to have a reliable formulation [*einer verlässlichen Form*] so long as it remains unclear what is talk and what is imagery [*was Rede ist und was Bild*], and in what way language speaks in images, if indeed language does so speak at all" (US 187/82). Think of how normal it would sound to say that, after all, in its deep structure language is propositional (language speaks in propositions), and that metaphor is just a sort of proposition with funny truth conditions. So all we have to do is to determine these conditions, that is, determine the sense in which it is true to say, "neighborhood of poetry and thinking." Or, alternatively, say with Nietzsche that the propositions of language are all sedimented metaphors, that we have no way of sorting out the literal from the figurative, that language is figurative (as the saying goes) "all the way down," and that nothing is true or false except under conditions laid down by language, including the statement that language is figurative all the way down. So the question of whether "neighborhood" is a metaphor of the relation of poetry and thinking is trivial. If language could talk, what would *it* say? Or, rather, if it could talk, *how* would it talk?

Heidegger's answer to this is the schoolmaster's despair. He says: "leave everything open" (US 187/82). It isn't necessary to decide about the metaphoricality of the neighborhood, or about the metaphoricality of any relation at all. We aren't, Heidegger says, in a position to decide the matter, because we are ourselves in the neighborhood, we belong to it, and so, Heidegger says, "the neighborhood is invisible."

> The same thing happens in our daily lives. We live in a neighborhood, and yet we would be baffled if we had to say in what that neighborhood consists. But this perplexity is merely a particular case, though perhaps an exceptionally good one, of the old encompassing perplexity in which all our thinking and saying finds itself always and everywhere. What is this perplexity we have in mind? This: we are not in a position—or if we are, then only rarely and just barely—to experience purely in its own terms [*rein aus ihr selbst her zu erfahren*] a relation that obtains between two beings. [US 188/83]

It's no trouble to take the neighborhood as a metaphor of the relation of poetry and thinking, but it is one that allows the relationship to remain indeterminate (there's no telling where one leaves off and another begins); so that neighborhood is only loosely metaphorical, in the sense that it doesn't quite stand for anything else, some (literal?) relation, say, that could be conceptually determined if only we could unpack the metaphor, find some language into which to translate it, or words to that effect; which is just to say that neighborhood is loosely literal, in the sense that it is not just another way of speaking, putting something in different terms, but a way of speaking that allows us *not* to determine the relation of poetry and thinking: a way of not saying or of withholding the relation from that which would fix it. Neighborhood, after all, is a figure (or place) of indeterminacy, that is, it preserves the absence of clear lines and firm boundaries. Which is as much as to say: Don't take sentences about "the neighborhood of poetry and thinking" literally, but don't take them figuratively, either. Perhaps neighborhood is a metaphor of this undecidability (or, better, refusal to decide or be decided). "Leave everything open."

"Leave everything open": this is a basic rule for reading the later Heidegger.

So Heidegger: "We cannot here decide flatly whether poetry is really a kind of thinking, or thinking really a kind of poetry. It remains dark to us what determines their real relation, and from what source what we so casually call the 'real' really comes" (US 189/83). Here is a sentence worth thinking about. We have nothing proper against which to measure the metaphoricality of Heidegger's discourse. This leaves open the question, which Nietzscheans pursue, of whether we can ever measure the metaphoricality of any discourse. Heidegger goes further by asking why we should want to measure such things in the first place. What is it that makes such an analysis, or decision, seem important or desirable? Heidegger's answer appears to be: logic. Logic is the motive of metaphor. The distinction between the literal and the figurative belongs to the region of representational-calculative thinking, the *Ge-Stell* or En-framing of technology. It is this framework that calls for metaphor; it is only within this framework that statements answer to the name of metaphor. This is what Heidegger means when he says, in a famous line, that "Only within metaphysics is there the metaphorical" (SG 89).[1] And perhaps this is why one can never tell the difference between a literal and a metaphorical statement just by looking at it, that is, just by analyzing its formal properties. As Donald Davidson says, "Metaphor runs on the same familiar linguistic tracks that the plainest sentences do."[2] This may be why most attempts to get at metaphor analytically turn into puzzles about whether the cat is on the mat. And it is why the theory of metaphor, like the theory of jokes, always threatens to dissipate its subject matter, as Paul Ricoeur has shown, perhaps inadvertently, in *The Rule of Metaphor*, which follows the prudential rule that if you want to write coherently about metaphor, you must be careful to give neither an example nor a theory of one; and so what Ricoeur gives us is a relatively example-free history of the theory of metaphor that concludes, interestingly, with the later Heidegger, whom Ricoeur values to the extent that he continues, however obscurely, to "think being," but whom he repudiates in the same stroke for his attempt "to sever discourse from its propositional character" (RM 313). Ricoeur, who wants to think of metaphor as semantic innovation at the level of the sentence, sees very clearly the danger to metaphor that the later Heidegger poses. For it follows from Heidegger that a good theory of metaphor would be one which concludes with the question, "Do metaphors exist?" The Heideggerian answer to this would be to put metaphor between quotation marks, as if to say: "Yes, but not quite. Leave everything open."

Here, however, is something worth remarking: as part of his woolgathering about neighborhood—is it a metaphor or isn't it?—Heidegger momentarily substitutes the word "element" [*Element*] for "neighborhood": "Poetry," he says, "moves in the element of Saying [*Sage*], and so does thinking. When we reflect on poetry, we find ourselves at once in that same element in which thinking moves" (US 188/83). This is clear enough, in its way—but then suddenly Heidegger has a second thought about the word "element": "Saying," he says, "is the same element for both poetry and thinking; but for both it was and still remains 'element' in a different way than water is the element for fish or air for the bird—in a way that compels us to stop talking about element, since Saying does more than merely 'bear up' poetry and thinking, more than afford them the region they traverse" (US 189/84).

This is a good example of Heidegger's way with words. He introduces the word "element" as a substitute for "neighborhood," but then throws it into question—estranges it: don't take the word as you usually do, which is to say: don't take it figuratively, but don't take it literally, either. Take it, say, as a misstatement, a piece of errancy ("stop talking about element")—but if it is a misstatement, why leave it in the text? Why not revise it out? The fact is that we are *not* told how to take it, only that there is no way to take it—it is to be used so differently that it no longer makes sense to use it (but this doesn't stop Heidegger from using it). It is the part of Heidegger's style to be always declaring that he is using words differently from their usual or customary (*gewöhnlich*) sense without specifying the difference. Possibly the word "element" is simply meant to take the exegetical heat off the word "neighborhood." For it is not just that poetry and thinking swim together in the same sea, although plainly they do; it is that they are "near" one another, dwelling together, as fish may not (fish belong to schools); whereas dwelling place (the neighborhood) is not simply a habitat (certainly not a school) but a place where things come into their own. But what this means we are still in no position to say.

No matter. As Heidegger says, pressing to exasperate his audience even further: "All this is easily said, that is, put into words, but difficult to experience, especially for us moderns" (US 189/84). We want to speak the familiar language of analytical distinctions, binary oppositions, signifier and system, subject and object, literal and figurative, poetry and philosophy. But poetry and thinking do not come together in this way, say as a division in the school. It is not quite right to speak of a "relation" between them at all. The meaning of the expression, "the neighborhood of poetry and thinking," is not anything we can figure out or conceptually determine. It belongs to a way of speaking designed to unsettle the normal procedures by which meanings get framed or fixed; it is designed to "leave things open." So Heidegger says, in effect, that the point is not to figure out the neighborhood, but to enter into it—or, what amounts to the same thing, to wake up to where we already are: "We must first turn," he says, doubtless playing with the metaphor for metaphor, "We must first turn, turn back to where we are in reality already staying" (US 190/85).

Do Words Exist?

This inquisition into the figurality or nonfigurality of the neighborhood of poetry and thinking—whether the neighborhood belongs to poetry, and is therefore metaphorical, or whether it belongs to thinking, and so is to be taken literally—this inquisition has been an error, not in the sense that things have been got wrong, but because such an inquisition is not the way into the neighborhood—not the way actually to enter this region or place (where, remember, "the possibility of a *thinking* experience with language" may avail itself to us). The neighborhood of poetry and thinking cannot be turned into a technical problem of exegesis proper to the domain of grammar, rhetoric, and logic; it is a place of its own where the arts of language lose their force, or where everything is otherwise.

Heidegger puts it this way: "we must not break off prematurely the dialogue we have begun with the poetic experience we have heard" (US 191/85). The lure of analysis and explanation, the temptation to do what we do so well—namely, worrying the difference between the literal and the metaphorical—has taken us away from the poem, Stefan George's "Das Wort," with its lines that refuse to go away:

> So lernt ich traurig den verzicht
> Kein ding sein wo das wort gebricht.

There is nothing for it but to turn back and attempt one more beginning, which is what Heidegger does now, in the midst of his second lecture in "The Nature of Language." He returns to these lines from "Das Wort," taking care, as he says, *not* to construe them as a "statement" (*Aussage*) or as a "theorem" (*Lehrsatz*), even though it is almost impossible not to do this—almost impossible not to take these lines as proposing a theory about the power of the word.

Heidegger in any case turns back from the mode of explanation to the mode of dialogue, which means, as we know, picking up on what is said, hearing the unsaid. This time Heidegger picks up on the word "word" in the poem's last line. What is this word called "word"? It is not, evidently, the name of anything that *is;* that is, the word *isn't* (is it?) quite in the same sense as things are said to *be* (as if in virtue of the word). Of course, this is silly, asking about the word, since there cannot be any mystery as to what a word is; it is common knowledge, that is, we are as a matter of common or everyday practice on such intimate terms with words that it just doesn't make any sense to ask about the word in this way (as if it were a thing). Neither is there any mystery about what the poet Stefan George is saying: he's talking about the priority of words over things. Words are foundational for things: no word, no thing—what could be more simple or more in keeping with tradition or with what we know?

But do we, after all, know? "We suppose that we have understood the poet on first hearing," Heidegger says, "but no sooner have we so to speak touched the line thoughtfully [*aber kaum haben wir den Vers nachdenkend gleichsam angerührt*], than what it says fades away into darkness" (US 192/86). What a strange touch this is! Normally, to have "the touch" means to be able to bring things off—think of the "magical touch" that makes things appear out of thin air or gets things going when all else has failed. The world looks over the shoulders of those with the "right touch." But this "nachdenkend Anrühren" is negative in its results, because the line under scrutiny, the line that thinking touches, "fades away into darkness," closes itself up, withdraws itself, turns into an enigma.

However, we should understand by now that this nonexegetical event is the essence of Heidegger's uncanny hermeneutics. In this hermeneutics, we are not plunged ourselves into darkness, but that which we seek to understand withdraws itself, holds itself back, eludes our grasp. Recall Heidegger and his privileging of the Heraclitean fragment—his elevation of the inscrutable trace of a lost utterance to the status of philosophical language. It is only in the company—in the neighborhood—of such an enigma that understanding can come into its own as something other than a weak or ungrounded species of representational-calculative thinking. As if it were only the dark saying, whose words we no longer know, that could give off light. The more we reflect upon a word or poem, the more we turn back to it, the longer we abide with it, the less it will seem to compose itself into a statement, the less it will seem a textual object for us, the stranger it will become. This hermeneutical phenomenon of estrangement—and I should think that every serious reader of poetry knows this estrangement intimately—appears to harbor the possibility of the experience with language that Heidegger wants to open up.[3]

What is it that we call a "word"? The moment we ask this question, the word withdraws itself. "The word," Heidegger says, "which itself is supposed not to be a thing, not anything that 'is,' escapes us" (US 192/86). Strictly speaking, there is no "word" for word: "The word for word," Heidegger says, "can never be found in that place where fate provides the language that names and so endows all beings, so that they may be, radiant and flourishing in their being" (US 192/86–87). Just now I asked: "Do metaphors exist?" An even more preposterous question, but also more serious, is: "Do words exist?" This is not a question that philology can sensibly ask: It *is* an open question:

> When thinking tries to pursue the poetic word, it turns out that the word, the saying, has no being [*das Wort, das Sagen, hat kein Sein*]. Yet our current notions resist such an imputation. Everybody, after all, sees and hears words in writing and in sound. They are; they can be like things, palpable to the senses. To offer a crude example, we only need to open a dictionary. It is full of printed things. Indeed, all kinds of things. *Plenty of terms, and not*

a single word. Because a dictionary can neither grasp nor keep the word by which terms become words and speak as words. Where does the word, where does Saying, belong [*Wohin gehört, wohin das Sagen*]? [US 192/87]

Lauter Wörter und kein einziges Wort: as if terms were louder than the peal of stillness.

We have already encountered Heidegger's distinction between *Wort* and *Wörter*, that is, between the word as word or Saying (*das Sagen*) and the word as term. What are we to make of this distinction?[4] It appears that terms have a sort of ready availability, in stark contrast to the word as Saying, which is apt to be just out of reach or out of hearing (one has to listen for it in order to catch it, as one does a hint, as it goes by). Terms belong to the space between two Heideggerian categories, the ready- and the present-at-hand, where what is present has been conceptually determined and possesses the logical status of an object, whereas what is ready-at-hand is just there, around us, part of our practical concern with the world. Everyday life, the region of untheorizable practice, goes on by means of what is always ready-at-hand, including the languages that we learn as part of our belonging or being-with one another and the world. Understanding as a social practice is in part just this Wittgensteinian sense of how to use the languages available to us in our forms of life and our institutions, including the technical languages of government, business, technology, and the schools, with their special languages of philosophy, science, law, literary study, and so on. Most of our formal attention to language figures language in terms of its discrete elements as a giant vocabulary, or set of vocabularies—canons of names, systems of signifiers, poetic dictions, even (as Borges might imagine) a circle of signs whose center is everywhere and whose circumference is inaccessible. I've been going on in an ill-natured way about grammar, rhetoric, logic, linguistics, semiotics, the formalisms of literary study, analytic philosophy of language, but of course one has to say that there's nothing wrong with these disciplines—nothing Heidegger says suggests that they ought to be practiced differently or, God forbid, got rid of. These disciplines are the sciences of the term and of all of its manifold possibilities of positive and negative combination. They are attempts to theorize the linguisticality of our world. They seek a transition from language as ready-at-hand to language as present-at-hand, that is, language in its logical status as a conceptual object about which we can make statements and frame theories.

By contrast, Heidegger's word, *Sage,* is inaccessible to these disciplines; in fact, as with much of the later Heidegger's lingo, the word *Sage* just sounds silly to the disciplined ear.[5] Call it a portentous piece of logocentric nonsense. But Heidegger wants to say that *Sage* belongs to a different realm, and it is this difference that we shake our heads at or brush aside as preposterous. For Heidegger, however, *Sage* belongs to *what is never at hand (das Sagen).* He asks: "Where does the word, where does Saying, belong?" We cannot say—not, at all events, in any of the formal languages of the school, and perhaps not ever in any language; in fact we cannot even put this question—the question itself is silly. But we can, Heidegger keeps saying, enter into this different realm, this region of the other—perhaps we are there already, silly as it sounds to say so.

What occupies Heidegger at the moment, however, is the sudden connection that he makes between the word "word" and the word "is": neither, it turns out, has any referent. Neither refers to anything, any being, there is nothing for either to determine, and so neither can be characterized (or used) as a *term.* "The 'is,'" Heidegger says, "cannot be found anywhere as a thing attached to a thing. As with the word, so it is with the 'is.' It belongs no more among the things that are than does the word" (US 193/87). Like the word "word" (*v.* "term"), the "is" *is never at hand.* One might as well say it is *not.*

Now something critical occurs. "Of a sudden," Heidegger says, "we are awakening from the slumber of hastily formed opinions, and are struck by the sight of something or other [*erblicken Anderes:* something *else,* something other or different—Hertz's translation of this as "something or other" is a bit overcautious]" (US 193/87). What is this *Einfall,* this sudden insight or sudden blow from something other or different? Oddly, it turns on the play of an uncanny piece of common speech, the familiar idiomatic expression, *es gibt:*

> What, then, does the poetic experience with the word show as our thinking pursues it? [*das Denken nachdenkt:* thinking doesn't quite pursue anything] . . . It shows what is there [*was es gibt*] and yet "is" not. The word, too, belongs to what is there [*was es gibt, gehört auch das Wort*]—perhaps not merely "too" but first of all, and even in such a way that the word, the nature of the word [*dass im Wort, in dessen Wesen*], conceals within itself that which gives being [*jenes sich verbirgt, was gibt:* the translation, "gives being," is a little premature and over-philosophical]. If our thinking does justice to the matter, then we may never say of the word that it

is [*es ist*], but rather that it gives [*es gibt*]—not in the sense that words are given by an "it," but that the word itself gives. The word itself is the giver [*das Wort: das Gebende*]. What does it give? To go by the poetic experience and by the most ancient tradition of thinking, the word gives Being [*gibt das Wort: das Sein*]. Our thinking, then, would have to seek the word, the giver which itself is never given, in this "there is that which gives" [*Dann hätten wir denkend in jenem "es, das gibt" das Wort zu suchen als das Gebende selbst, aber nie Gegebene*]. [US 193/87–88]

Es gibt: there is. The wonderful thing about idiomatic expressions is their simple, unadorned absurdity. They are never really translatable. Logically, they are the freaks of language. You can't take them literally, nor figuratively. So Heidegger would say that they are of the essence of language, if one can speak of such a thing, and none is more of the "essence" (the *Sprachwesen,* which is not quite a word of the "essence") than *es gibt,* which Heidegger has already highlighted in his "Letter on Humanism" (Wm 165–66/214–15).

One is reminded of Valéry's observation that language is like a fragile hemp and bamboo bridge thrown across a bottomless gorge. We can make our way across this bridge safely enough if we move quickly, scrambling, never slowing or pausing in a way that would allow our dead weight to accumulate upon any one point. Were we to stop and examine any portion of the bridge the whole thing would begin to sway and twist and send us sailing into the abyss. Of course, this looks like another story about the weakness of language. For Valéry, it *is* a story about the weakness of language with respect to meaning, but it is also about its strength with respect to poetry, which allows us to abide with language in a way that makes meaning impossible (which allows us to abide with language *because* meaning, that is, a fixed determination of sense, is impossible). Heidegger would say that the story simply tells the truth about language, which is that it refuses to be objectified. It is ungraspable, like the *es gibt.* When we look for it, at it, it isn't there. *Es gibt:* there is, but not for language, the ungiven giver.

What about this giving? Hertz's translation of "gibt das Wort: das Sein" as "the word gives Being" turns an apposition into a proposition, normalizing the idiomatic expression (fatally) in the direction of a philosophical statement that doubtless has to do with the hoary old concept of "givenness." Pointedly, however, Heidegger inscribes the expression paratactically rather than syntactically—in imitation, evidently, of the ancients, that is, the Pre-Socratics, who did not (Heidegger says) organize their thinking into little totalities of simultaneous gatherings (*syntaxes*) but rather were inclined to leave things open, as if in a space where there are no words—as if in that place into which we are drawn when words fail us or withdraw themselves, leaving us bereft of speech, not knowing what to say, as in the region of *parataxis*. This is how Heidegger thinks of the "word order" of a Parmenidean fragment (for example, "Needful: the saying also thinking too: being: to be [*chre to legein te noein t' eon emmenai*]"; Fr. 6): "We call the word order of the saying paratactic in the widest sense simply because we do not know what else to do. For the saying *speaks* where there are no words, in the field between the words which the colons indicate" (WD 114/186). *Es gibt:* there is—but as Gertrude Stein said of Oakland, "There isn't any there there." Heidegger gives the example of "*Es gibt an der sonnigen Halde Erdbeeren*" (US 194/88)—"There are strawberries on the hillside"—where the "there" isn't anything objective, that is, it is not the subject of the verb "to be," despite its place in the syntactical structure. Syntax here tries to cover up a parataxis. *There*, as such, isn't there, only strawberries are, rather like the "it" in "It is raining," which isn't there, either, only the rain is. So with the word (any word), which isn't there just in this mode of the "it" and the "there" in *es gibt*, although without it nothing is. It gives, but not of itself. Itself it withholds, as in a paratactic tactic, call it a parody of the givenness of the given and of the grounding of the ground.[6]

One might be tempted to say that Heidegger takes *es gibt* literally ("it gives"), and certainly this is one way of putting it, but it would be more accurate to say that he takes it etymologically, against the flow or grain of the idiom—the idiom is never true to its origins. It is by no means clear that the distinction between etymology and idiom parallels or duplicates the distinction between the literal and the figurative. After all, an etymology is, rhetorically, a figure of speech that consists in taking a familiar expression strangely, where the strangeness takes the form of some repressed or forgotten "original sense." But of course there never was such a sense in the sense of a time when etymology determined use. There was never anything but idiom, that is, no time of pristine, undisseminated (fixed) meaning. This isn't what Heidegger means by "originary"; rather, "originary" in Heidegger's lingo is a term of dissemination, that is, a difference from the customary and the fixed, as in obsolete words and repressed senses or expressions no longer in use, or in an unheard-of play upon words. It is that which comes out as the "infelicity" of speech. To imagine a people somewhere actually speaking etymologically is comic theater worthy of Jonathan Swift or James Joyce—or Woody Allen. (Actually, to perform an etymology on a word is to take it as a pun.[7]) One might as well imagine a world where everyone speaks strangely even though there are no outsiders, a community of Babel. Nor is there any rhetorical exegesis that could make *es gibt* come out "there is." The idiomatic character of *es gibt* doesn't consist in taking anything figuratively; if anything, it just means taking *es gibt* as "there is" as a matter of customary (*gewöhnlich*) usage. No one knows why (*es gibt* is "without why," which is perhaps the whole point), but also no one misunderstands "es gibt" except the English schoolboy. (Compare *Was gibt?* In American English, "What gives?" means "What the hell's going on here?" and is not a question.)

If you insist, however, you could say that Heidegger takes *es gibt* metaphorically when he construes "there is" (*es gibt*) as literally having to do with giving. (Got it?) But Heidegger seems to ward off metaphor in his usual fashion by saying, simply, that he means to take the expression oddly, strangely with respect to customary (*gewöhnlich*) usage, without, however, producing anything like a new definition: "In our present reflection," he says, "the expression [*es gibt*] is used differently. We do not mean 'There is the word'—we mean 'by virtue of the gift of the word there is, the word gives . . .' The whole spook about the 'givenness of things,' which many people justly fear, is blown away" (US 194/88). The given in this event is not a logical posit but a parody of it. The point is that the "is" is not something that can be predicated of the word: the word isn't; it gives rather than is, roughly in the way that things thing and worlds world. It is the way language speaks (infelicitiously, endlessly disseminating itself, giving sense but never making it in the sense of making it stick). "This simple ungraspable situation," Heidegger says pointedly—"This simple ungraspable situation [*ungreifbare Sachverhalt*] which we call up with the phrase 'it,' the word, 'gives,' reveals itself as what is properly worthy of thought, but for whose definition all standards [*Masse*] are still lacking in every way" (US 194/88). You may want to ask, What is it that the word gives? The answer is not as easy as it sounds: "*gibt das Wort: das Sein.*" The crucial mark is the colon, the paratactical gap or parody of deep structure that Hertz's translation tries to fill in or correct by way of the proposition, "the word gives Being." But the word does not give Being. The word "gives," but not in the productive sense of being the origin, source, ground, or cause of what is—certainly indeed not in the sense of being a logical foundation (the sublime and mythical Ground of Being). Rather (as in George's poem) "the word gives" means—without the word: nothing. No word: no "there is"; with it, on the other hand, *es gibt*. Think of *es gibt* as the word for word, because there's no getting a fix on it: there is/it gives. Take it as a pun.[8]

The Darkness of Poetry and Thinking

I have been remarking intermittently about the peculiar form of Heidegger's lectures—call it the "woolgathering," "dawdling," or "lingering" form, in which the normal inferential movement of reason toward some conclusion, construction, or final picture is replaced by what seem like endless reflections on a starting point that withholds itself. The Heideggerian mode, his "way," is a going-back-again or a turning-back rather than a going-forth. He is completely reactionary with respect to representational-calculative thinking, which is always thrusting itself forward and overcoming whatever has gone before.

So it is with the end of his second lecture in "The Nature of Language." Heidegger returns to a main question: "What about the neighborhood of poetry and thinking?" (US 195/89). This question has been deliberately left open in a variety of ways. Neighborhood is not the name of any sort of logical relationship between poetry and thinking; it is not a logical or categorical space that can be mapped out in a topographical description. It is the "element" (but this turns out to be the wrong word) of Saying in which both poetry and thinking come into their own. One is still tempted to say that poetry and thinking are two kinds of saying, as if Saying were something for us to perform as speaking subjects, but we know now this isn't right. "We must discard the view," Heidegger says, "that the neighborhood of poetry and thinking is nothing more than a garrulous mixture of two kinds of saying in which each makes clumsy borrowings from the other" (US 196/90). So forget about poetic thinking and thinking poetically. And forget about the idea that Heidegger is a poet at heart. He is not.

Indeed, the hard fact is that poetry and thinking have nothing to do with one another in the sense that they do not communicate anything to each other, do not exchange or carry over anything to one another, do not fuse like horizons or engage in dialogues that one could transcribe if only one could find the common language. They are the downfall of translation and the end of Husserlian ideality. They do not mirror one another except perhaps in a strange *Spiegel-Spiel* of the unpicturable. On the contrary—and here the neighborhood of poetry and thinking undergoes an astonishing transformation—

in truth poetry and thinking are in virtue of their nature held apart by a delicate yet luminous difference, *each one held in its own darkness:* two parallels, in Greek *para allelo,* by one another, against one another, transcending, surpassing [*übertreffend*]. Poetry and thinking are not separated if separation is to mean cut off [*abgeschieden*] into a relational void. The parallels intersect [*schneiden sich*] in the infinite. There they intersect with a section [*in einem Schnitt*] that they themselves do not make. By this section, they are first cut, engraved into the design of their neighboring nature [*Sie werden durch ihn erst in den Aufriss ihres nachbarlichen Wesens geschnitten, d. h. eingezeichnet.* —The next line has been left out of the English translation: *Diese Zeichnung ist der Riss:* This drawing, design, sketch, figure, is the rift]. That cut assigns poetry and thinking to their nearness to one another [*Er reisst Dichten und Denken die Nähe zueinander auf*]. The neighborhood of poetry and thinking is not the result of a process by which poetry and thinking—no one knows from where—first draw near to each other and thus establish a nearness, a neighborhood. The nearness that draws them near is itself the occurrence of appropriation [*Ereignis*] by which poetry and thinking are directed into their proper nature [*in des Eigenes ihres Wesens*]. [US 196/90]

The neighborhood of poetry and thinking is not any sort of framing concept—not a background, common ground, basic ground, context, horizon, environment, or field. Rather, it is formed by, perhaps is nothing less than, the rift (*Riss*). Poetry and thinking come into their own in virtue of this rift, where "coming into their own" means, strangely, that each is now "held in its own darkness" by a "delicate yet luminous difference."

What is this darkness? One would think that coming into one's own means coming into the light or into the open, that is, into (in some sense) *being.* But no. The nearness into which poetry and thinking are drawn (or rifted) is not an accessible place, and indeed it is likely that we are far removed from it, caught up as we are in the productive activities of *poiēsis* and ratiocination. *Dichten* is not *poiēsis* but enigma, and thinking is not explanation and description and the laying-bare of deep structures but inhabits a darkness of its own (a Black Forest?) where it wanders and gropes without method or plot. Consecutive reasoning, the manipulation of clear and distinct ideas, cannot begin until ambiguity has been got rid of and a course has been fixed; but thinking cannot occur except in the realm of ambiguity where one simply takes off, as if there were no formal difference between thinking and wandering. You can hear skepticism licking its chops.

Poetry and thinking are held, each in its own darkness, by "a delicate yet luminous difference": imagine darkness sliced (and therefore doubled or disseminated) by a rift of light. Poetry and thinking are not anything except in virtue of this rift, that is, they do not dwell elsewhere and only subsequently travel or drift into one another's company. On the contrary, neither has priority. They belong together, but at the same time they keep (or are kept) apart, strangers to one another—but theirs is a funny kind of apartness. The translation says that they "intersect in infinity," although the German text reads *schneiden sich* rather than *durchschneiden*, which suggests something ungeometrical about Heidegger's parallel lines. It looks as though we need to imagine an incision within a line (a line sliced lengthwise) rather than an intersection between; that is, "intersection" means a cutting-between the lines, a section-between (inter-section, where the word itself, as elsewhere in Heidegger, is cut in two), rather than the crossing of lines. This section (*Schnitt*) between poetry and thinking draws them (in the sense of engraving, figuring, or cutting-into to make a design)—draws them into their neighborliness. Thus *Schnitt* (incision) gives way to, without being displaced by, *Zeichnung*, drawing in the sense of making a design or sketch—sketch in the further, now familiar sense of *Aufriss*, in which *Riss* sounds, rings, or echoes like a word in a pun. (This whole passage is a cornucopia of puns.) Hence the line that Hertz drops from his translation: *Diese Zeichnung ist der Riss.* It is worth noting that *Zeichnen* is a word for sign, but not of the sort that signifies things. (I'll examine this question of the sign in the later Heidegger in the next chapter, where *Riss* turns out to be a parody of the concept of basic structure.)

Sidenote: recall from the earlier discussion of *Riss* that Heidegger had emphasized the enmity between what the rift brings together (and also holds apart). So earth and world are in a "struggle," and in the lecture on "Language" we are told that "Pain is the rift" (US 27/204). But here the rift seems gentle—"a delicate yet luminous difference [*zarte, aber helle Differenz*]." So the rift between poetry and thinking is not the same as the rift between earth and world or between world and thing. Rift is not a portable concept; it does not travel from context to context but is radically singular, disruptive of every part-and-whole (such as the one that would subsume poetry and thinking as modes of Saying).

What is the difference (*Riss, Dif-ferenz, Unter-Schied*) between poetry and thinking? What is funny about their apartness is that you can't tell them apart. They are different, but not in any logical sense that would allow us to differentiate between them, turning them into categories: it is not possible *to tell the difference*—the difference cannot be put into words—which is why it is a strange difference or dif-ference. It is singular rather than particular. This is what Derrida finds so compelling. The concluding pages of "The *Retrait* of Metaphor" are a sort of commentary on the passage I have just quoted from "The Nature of Language." For Derrida, the rift (Riss: *trait*) reopens the question of metaphor precisely because of its resistance to the categories of the literal and figurative:

> This trait [*Riss*] of recutting relates one to the other but belongs to neither. This is why it is not a common trait or a general concept nor a metaphor any more. We could say of the trait that it is more originary than the two [*Dichten und Denken*] which it splits and recuts/re-intersects, that the trait is their common origin and the seal of their alliance, remaining in this singular and different from them, if a trait could be something, could be properly and fully originary. Now insofar as it frays a differential splitting, a trait is neither fully originary nor autonomous, nor, as fraying, purely derivative. And to the extent that such a trait frays the possibility of naming in language (written or spoken, in the accepted meaning of these words), it is not itself nameable as separation, neither literally, properly, nor metaphorically. *The trait is nothing approximate [approchent] as such.* [27–28]

The French translation (*trait*) adds to the German *Riss* the note of "fraying," as when Derrida says that "the trait frays the possibility of naming in language," which makes fraying sound like another name for the weakness of language. And it is true that Heidegger encourages us to think of language in terms of loose ends rather than as a system that ties everything together, fixes everything in place, excludes all random particles. One can't discriminate between the literal and the metaphorical in a language of loose ends, because what is loose is just the difference/indifference between any two of anything. The space between the two is open, and this is what Heidegger calls the "rift" where dif-ference is not difference but is itself inscribed with a rift that sets it apart as singular and dark, otherwise than difference.

What is at least clear is that it is not the business of poetry or thinking to explicate the *Riss* or to say what things mean. All we can say is that the rift of poetry and thinking "assigns" (*reisst*) the neighborliness in which they are held (gently) apart, each in its own darkness. In this neighborhood, each comes into its own, into its proper *phūsis* or darkness (that which loves to hide), where it has nothing to say, that is, nothing to tell us, no meaning to express, no revelation to bestow. Poetry and thinking, in their nature, are enigmatic: dark sayings like the fragments ("frayings") of Heraclitus or Hölderlin—fragments or texts that linger or bang about like random particles, singular, unsubsumable, uncontainable in any context, resistant to constructions of every sort, inscrutable and dark. What they hold out to us is not a meaning but the possibility of an experience with language as just this withdrawal of the word into darkness, its resistance to the fixed determinations of systematic behavior, its endless proliferation of particles over which we have no control.

Puns

Heidegger's third lecture in "The Nature of Language" begins with a critical (perhaps precritical) reflection on the word "way" (*Weg*). I say "precritical" because, as we have seen, Heidegger wants to turn the word "way" back from its Enlightenment sense of "method" into something else. In the present context the "something else" turns out to be the word *tao*, from the *Tao* of Lao-tzu, which Heidegger picks up on as a way of translating *Weg* into something completely foreign or strange. *Tao* is way, but in what sense?

Naturally Heidegger refuses to determine the sense of "way" which he wants us to follow. This is his "way." Instead of determining a meaning, or determining "way" as a *term*, he allows language to play once more its "gambling game," as in the following passage, parts of which Hertz does not try to translate because of its extraordinary wordplay. Let me quote the passage in its entirety:

> Der Weg ist, hinreichend gedacht, solches, was uns gelangen lässt, und zwar in das, was nach uns langt, indem es uns be-langt [To a thinking so inclined that reaches out sufficiently, the way is that by which we reach—which lets us reach what reaches out for us by touching us, by being our concern]. Wir verstehen freilich das Zeitwort "belangen" nur in einem gewöhnlichen Sinne, der meint: sich jemanden vornehmen zur Vernehmung, zum Verhör. Wir können aber auch das Be-langen in einem hohen Sinne denken: be-langen, be-rufen, be-hüten, be-halten [*Hertz does not*

translate this, but roughly it means that, to be sure, we take the verb "be-langen" *usually in its customary (i. e., legal) sense of being taken in hand or even in custody, summoned to a hearing or to an interrogation or inquest, in other words hauled into court. But we can also think of* Belangen *in another ("higher") sense:* be-langen, *to summon,* berufen, *to call (convene a meeting),* be-hüten, *to guard or protect,* be-halten, *to keep (under guard? in custody? preserve?)*]. Der Be-lang: das, was, nach unserem Wesen auslangend, es verlangt und so gelangen lässt in das, wohin es gehört [*Also left untranslated, it means roughly that the summons* (Be-lang) *is that which reaches out for our being, demands or requests it and thus lets it reach or arrive where it belongs*]. Der weg ist solches, was uns in das gelangen lässt, was uns be-langt [*The way is such, it lets us reach what concerns and summons us*]. Der Anschein drängt sich vor, als verführen wir, das Be-langen also denkend: willkürlich mit der Sprache. Es ist in der Tat Willkür, wenn wir den jetzt gennanten Sinn von Be-langen an dem messen, was man gewöhnlich unter dem Wort versteht. Aber massgebend für den besinnlichen Sprachgebrauch kann nicht das sein, was man gemeinhin gewöhnlich meint, sondern was der verborgene Reichtum der Sprache bereithält, um uns daraus zu be-langen für das Sagen der Sprache [*Now it would seem that by thinking in this fashion of what summons us, we manipulate language willfully. Indeed it is willful to gauge the sense in which we here speak of "summoning" by the usual understanding of the word. But the reflective use of language cannot be guided by the common, usual understanding of meanings; rather, it must be guided by the hidden riches that language holds in store for us, so that these riches may summon for us the Saying of language*]. Die Gegend ergibt als Gegend erst Wege [*The country offers ways only because it is country: i. e., the region as region gives but ways*]. Sie be-wëgt. Wir hören das Wort Be-wëgung im Sinne von: Wege allererst ergeben und stiften. Sonst verstehen wir bewegen im Sinne von: bewirken, dass etwas seinen Ort wechselt, zu- oder abnimmt, überhaupt sich ändert. Be-wëgen aber heisst: die Gegend mit Wegen versehen. Nach altem Sprachgebrauch der schwäbisch-alemannischen Mundart kan "wëgen" besagen: einem Weg bahnen, z. B. durch tief verschneites Land [*Also left untranslated, but Heidegger's point is that we can understand "bewegen," to give or make way, in several senses— bringing things about, letting them happen, letting things change place or size or change overall;* bewëgen *means providing the region with ways (plural); following an old use in the Swabian dialect,* bewëgen *means building a way as if through or across a snowcovered land*].

> Wëgen und Be-wëgen als Weg-bereiten und Weg als das Ge-
> langenlassen gehören in denselben Quell- und Strombereich wie
> die Zeitwörter: wiegen und wagen und wogen [*Also untranslated,
> this means roughly that* "wëgen" *and* "Be-wëgen" *and* "Weg" *as
> letting-reach or letting-arrive belong to the same stream- or river-realm
> as the verbs* "wiegen und wagen und wogen," *that is, to rock (as a
> cradle), to venture (risk), and to sway*]. [US 197–98/91–92]

If one were to try to extract a point from this passage, it would perhaps be that the "way" is multiple, distributed in every direction, and
that the country (*Gegend*) is just this plurality of courses, a dissemination of directions: there is no one way, which is just to say that way
is not method. So also with the way of speaking: one does not follow
customary usage but rather takes a hint and risks a path no one has
followed or which has been forgotten or overgrown or which belongs
to an obsolete or archaic or strange way of speaking, a dialect or *Mundart,* an unheard-of way of the mouth, a deviation from the straight
way, from the tried and true way; in short, a *wandering* way or mode
of ambiguity that allows one to pick up on what remains unsaid or
unthought, what has not been fixed or bounded (the undiscovered or
open country free of itineraries). This is the way as *Gelassenheit.* It is
the way as pun.

Imagine a language in which each word harbors, not just a meaning
(a particularity of sense), but the sounds of every other word in the
language, so that (if one were listening) one could not sound a word
without hearing at the same time an infinitely reverberating vocabulary. Doubtless madfolk hear so. Language in this sense would be a
vast ringing-in-the-ear, an infinite punning in which words turn up
endlessly in one another, ringing the changes on one another, with
new unheard-of words ringing in and out as old ones die away, echoing and re-echoing as they go. Now: imagine this as *our* language,
that is, not some fantastic dream work or runaway *Finnegans Wake*
(although the *Wake* ought to be taken this way as a text close to Heidegger's heart, though he missed it)—in short, not some unheard-of
tongue but *the* language that we speak every day and in which we
make perfectly good sense to one another as we go about our business,
not worrying too much about our words: the same language, in other
words, in which (among other idle things) we gossip and pass the word
along. Heidegger wants us to hear, *in the language that we speak,* the infinite sounding of our language (*wiegen und wagen und wogen*), so that
we can sense the way every familiar word has nevertheless something

uncanny about it, some echoing otherness that belongs to the word, keeps it open, loose, and free, more word than term—and able, therefore, to catch us up, bring us up short, or to get away from us, even fail us (withhold itself), confound and mislead us even in the moment when we think we know unmistakably what we are saying.

We need to be clear about this: there are not two languages, one common and everyday, the other, transcendental, foundational, mythical, purified of every logical weakness—not two languages, only one: one, however, which is not just something that we speak but something more (something other) which makes us aware of itself precisely at those moments when it gets away from us, a language of infelicities. If we always end up saying something more, or different, from what we intend, it is because language itself is always speaking, always sounding, going on in its own way, independently of us, heterogeneous and wild, even as we speak.

What is it, then, to speak? Here we come round again to the inaugural question. "This," Heidegger says, "is the crux of our reflection on the nature of language" (US 201/95).

In the lecture on "Language" this question was construed purely and simply as a question about language in its radical otherness, that is, language taken all by itself and not translated into something not itself (something human). *Die Sprache spricht*, and we have nothing to say about it. Its speaking is not anything human.

Now, however, in the third lecture in "The Nature of Language," the question of speaking becomes one in which we are implicated after all. In the passage just quoted, Heidegger says that his thinking with respect to the word "way," with its echoing *Zeitwörten* (*be-langen, be-rufen, be-hüten, be-halten*), must make him seem "*willkürlich mit der Sprache*"—willful, capricious, frivolous, silly with respect to language. And, indeed, it is hard not to think this about Heidegger's way with words. Nevertheless, Heidegger wants to say that this wordplay is not a style or a rhetoric; it is not a method of freeplay. On the contrary, the point is that "the reflective use of language [*den besinnlichen Sprachgebrauch*] cannot be guided by the common, usual understanding of meanings [*was man gemeinhin gewöhnlich meint*]; rather, it must be guided by the hidden riches that language holds in store for us [*der verborgene Reichtum der Sprache bereithält*], so that these riches may summon for us the Saying of language [*um uns daraus zu be-langen für das Sagen der Sprache*]" (US 197/91). The distinction here is, once more, between the ordinary and the uncanny, but now this distinction is applied to *usage* (*Sprachgebrauch*). What is authoritative (*massgebend*) for usage? When the subject of reflection is language itself, it is not enough to be guided by the rules of the everyday (grammar or correct usage, or indeed logic and the arts of language); one must be guided by something else—by the fact or recognition that *"It is just as much a property of language to sound and ring and vibrate, to hover and tremble, as it is for what is spoken to have a meaning"* [Dass die Sprache lautet und klingt und schwingt, schwebt und bebt, ist ihr im selben Masse eigentümliche, wie dass ihr Gesprochenes einem Sinn hat: *my emphasis*] (US 205/98).

Suppose one were to say that, contrary to what we think of as linguistic experience, not to say linguistic competence, we are connected to language not by way of rules and meanings but by way of sound, where sound, however, is not just what is studied in phonetics. Heideggerian sound is nonempirical, uncanny sound. Even stillness has sound. We must think of sound as something open only to listening, that is, not acoustical responsiveness but being attentive to the sound-ings (*Wëgen und Be-wëgen als Weg-bereiten und Weg als das gelangenlassen gehören in denselben Quell- und Strombereich wie die Zeitwörter: wiegen und wagen und wogen*). Imagine a grammar that tried to characterize linguistic competence as having to do with the hearing of puns rather than with the production of sentences or propositions. The emphasis should fall on hearing. One does not, after all, *make* puns. Punning is not a species of *poiēsis*. Puns, as the Irish will tell you, are already there everywhere in the language ("Lard have mustard on us!"). The punster is the one who is just good at sounding-out or picking-up on what goes on all the time in language. (Heidegger, for example, did not make the pun on *Gestell/Vorstellung*.) The trick is to take the pun as something other than a figure of rhetoric, an artful manipulation of language. The pun belongs to the uncanniness of *Sprachgebrauch*; it turns up of its own accord, a piece of self-dissemination, as every punster knows who cannot help being the nuisance that the pun has made of him or her. Joyce did not write *Finnegans Wake* by thinking up weird words ("quashed quotatoes, messes of mottage" [FW 183]); it were better to say that language, left to itself (let go), will inscribe a *Finnegans Wake*. Punning is a mode of *Erläuterung*, which is itself a pun on sounding. One could say that puns are what language is made of, insofar as it is made of words. Strictly speaking, however, this is only to say (trivially) that words are made of words; "language is language." Language as Saying is not "made of" words or of anything at all. Saying is always unmade, unspoken, unsettling (as puns do) what is already determined. But Heidegger's point seems to be that only the sounding of what is unspoken, the way *Weg* is unspoken but sounding, ringing, vibrating, hovering, or trembling in *be-wegen* and *be-wëgen* (and *wiegen und wagen und wogen*), opens the way to Saying. The pun, or something like it, is close to the essence of language: *Sprachwesen,* which is not quite a word for "the essence of language." It is not "of the essence," since nothing is of the essence of Saying except Saying, but it is close in the sense of near (in the neighborhood). The pun is on the way to language: *be-wegen.* It is the way language sounds. Or, again, puns should be taken as hints given off by language as to its *Sprachwesen.* Puns are not yet *Sagen,* only *Zusagen,* the pun as promise.

It bears repeating with respect to puns that one does not so much speak as hear them; they are a sounding that listening resounds. Puns happen; they are part of what gives with language. We don't cause them; on the contrary, to speak is to prevent them from happening. *Er-eignis* is a happening that Heidegger does not prevent, that is, it is not a word for another word or thing—not an expression or a piece of speech—but a sounding whose limits cannot be determined because we cannot get a fix on where it's coming from, as if it were not just a term in a dictionary, say the German word for happening, but a whole region of language sounding at once in the tiny space of a single word. So *Er-eignis* is not just a way of saying or not saying "Being." There's no saying what the word says or doesn't say. What is this condition of not being able to say what a word says or doesn't say? Whatever it is, it is the condition in which language always places us, that is, the condition of the bewildered translator who knows that a lot is getting left unsaid when she speaks or writes and that the best idea is probably to leave things untranslated (*Gelassenheit* is the motto of the good translator). Language does all it can to keep us from speaking it, the way *Er-eignis* keeps us from translating it. The "weakness of the logos" is *our* weakness with respect to language. The arts of language were invented to help us to get the upper hand so that speaking can become logically possible, or pun-free. In other words, the paradox is that the purpose of grammar and logic is to prevent language from happening, that is, they are part of our effort to bring language under *our* control so that it will only happen when we want it to or when we say it does. Now Heidegger comes along with his uncontrollable language (*Er-eignis, A-lētheia*) to undo centuries—whole metaphysical epochs—of hard work, emancipating grammar from logic. But of course puns and parody and texts like *Tristram Shandy* and *Finnegans Wake* have been undoing this work from the beginning, only we haven't been listening.

Puns belong to (listen to: *gehören*) the earthiness, as against the mere physicality, of words, their *phūsis*. In the long passage that I quoted above, Heidegger calls attention to this earthiness in the way *be-wegen* turns up in the Swabian dialect, namely as *be-wëgen*. A dialect by definition is a different (strange) way of sounding. Heidegger points out that the German word for dialect is *die Mundart,* or mode of mouth. This mode is not method. It is not enunciation. It is not even a physiological mode of making the mouth work this way or that. Heidegger wants to say that in the various *Mundarten* it is the earth that speaks. "The landscape, and that means the earth, speaks in them [*Mundarten*], differently each time. But the mouth is not merely a kind of organ of the body understood as an organism—body and mouth are part of the earth's flow and growth in which we mortals flourish, and from which we receive the soundness of our roots [*das Gediegene einer Bodenständigkeit empfangen*]" (US 205/98).

This recalls for Heidegger Hölderlin's "Germania," with its compelling figure, "*die Blume des Mundes.*" "Language," Heidegger says, "is the flower of the mouth. In language the earth blossoms toward the bloom of the sky" (US 205–206/99). In Hölderlin's "Der Gang aufs Land," the same figure appears:

> So ist der Mensch; wenn da ist das Gut, und es sorget mit
> Gaaben
> Selber ein Gott für ihn, kennet und sieht er es nicht.
> Tragen muss er, zuvor; nun aber nennt er sein Liebstes,
> Nun, nun müssen dafür Worte, wie Blumen, entstehn.

> Such is man; when the wealth is there, and no less than a god in
> Person tends him with gifts, blind he remains, unaware.
> First he must suffer; but now he names his most treasured
> possession,
> Now for it words like flowers leaping alive he must find.
>   [US 206/99–100]

"Words as flowers": but what does it mean to speak this way about words? "It would mean," Heidegger says, "that we stay bogged down in metaphysics if we were to take the name Hölderlin gives here to 'words, like flowers,' as being a metaphor" (US 207/100). But this does not mean that "words, like flowers" is to be taken literally, at least not exactly. Rather, "leave everything open."*Das Metaphorische gibt es nur innherhalb der Metaphysik* (SG 89). Metaphors are for metaphysics, where everything is *exactly* what it is, or is said to be, and not otherwise, except according to the rules of rhetoric that allow us to track the transfer of words from one thing to another, as if words were attached to things, fixed to them as if by nature or assigned by a logic of necessity or system of figural license. Which is evidently only how metaphysics can think of them: taken in any other way (for example, as random particles, or as the endless intersecting of sounds or punning disseminations) words are the enemy of metaphysics, which can leave nothing open. In metaphysics, metaphors are means of closure: the *s* is *p* that cannot be made sense in one context is to be transferred to another in which it makes sense to say, *s* is *p*.

Remember where we have been with Heidegger with respect to words. In part the question here is: How can one speak metaphorically of that which is, strictly (or literally) speaking, *not*, just in the way words are not? *Das Wort: Es gibt.* The word gives, but it is not itself given: it withdraws from metaphysics, and this makes it appear that the word is going out of control, so that (as with puns, or as with idiomatic expressions like *es gibt*) it becomes impossible to determine the difference between what the word says and what it doesn't say (leaves unsaid). Well, of course, the word as word *is* out of control. Language speaks, but the word leaves itself unsaid. Words cannot put themselves into words, not, anyhow, in the sense in which the word is a term of designation in a lexicon of signs. Words put themselves into words only by punning, that is, in disseminations of the word as sound. (The word as Saying is more sound than structure or chain of signifiers: notice that sound here has nothing to do with phonocentrism.) This, at all events, is how they sound in the neighborhood of poetry and thinking:

> When the word is called the mouth's flower and its blossom, we hear the sound of language rising like the earth. From whence? From Saying in which it comes to pass that World is made to appear [*Aus dem Sagen, worin sich das Erscheinenlassen von Welt begibt*: not *made to appear* but *allowed to appear*: Erscheinen*lassen*]. The sound rings out in the resounding assembly call which, open to the Open, makes [*sic*] World appear in all things [*Das Lauten erklingt aus dem Läuten, dem rufenden Versammeln, das, offen dem Offenen, Welt erscheinen lässt in dem dingen*]. The sounding of the voice is then no longer of the order of physical organs. It is released now from the perspective of the physiological-physical explanation in terms of purely phonetic data. The sound of language, its earthiness, is held with the harmony that attunes the regions of the world's structure, playing them in chorus [*Das Lautende,*

Erdige der Sprache wird in das Stimmen einbehalten, das die Gegenden des Weltgefüges, sie einander zuspieland, auf einander einstimmt]. [US 208/101]

And so on: as this paragraph unfolds, Heidegger self-consciously draws away from a discourse his scientific audience can hear toward the unheard-of region (*Gegend*) opened up in the lecture on "Language," where the main question about language (What is it to speak?) was deployed nonhumanly within the nearness of the fourfold where world worlds and things thing in a mirror play, round-dance and ringing radiance. Add to this now, as the Saying in which all of this happens, "the sound of language, its earthiness."

Heidegger concludes his third lecture in "The Nature of Language" with what amounts to a reflection on the strangeness of his own idiom —his talk of nearness, for example, and how silly it must sound to the ear of "the calculative frame of mind [*das rechnende Vorstellen*: pun undeleted]" (US 211/104). Nor is it simply that his own language must sound "obscure and strange" (US 208/101). Nearness itself, and all that dwells with it, including ourselves whether we know it or not, must remain, Heidegger says, "wholly inaccessible to calculative thinking" (US 213/105). At most such thinking can only take the nearness of the fourfold metaphorically as a certain way of describing the space-time continuum. But Heidegger persists in his silly talk, saying that "time times" and "space spaces" and that it isn't metaphorical to talk this way at all, isn't mysticism, isn't regression to a primitive sensibility—isn't *Poesie* (US 214/106).

Where are we, then? I began by saying that the lectures in "The Nature of Language" do not represent an advance of Heidegger's thinking beyond the lecture on "Language" (1950). The point of the lectures, after all, has not been to clarify or develop what had already been thought; the lectures are not part of an ongoing construction. The point instead has been to "open up the possibility of a thinking experience with language." "Have we now," Heidegger asks, "reached such a possibility?" (US 214/107).

Heidegger's response to this question is altogether remarkable and even bewildering. An experience with language as Saying, Heidegger says, would mean "that we enter into something which bowls us over, that is, transmutes our relation to language" (US 214–15/107). Thus our relation to language as Saying is no longer to something that we speak, or rather is no longer by way of speaking. On the contrary, language as Saying is something that holds itself back, holds itself in reserve—and in doing so, Heidegger says, it holds together the regions of the world, the fourfold: "Reserving itself in this way, as Saying of the world's fourfold, language concerns us, us who as mortals belong within this fourfold world, us who can speak only as we respond to language [*als wir der Sprache entsprechen*]" (US 215/107).

At this point we might have expected Heidegger to remark upon poetry and thinking as modes of responding to language as Saying. But Heidegger is nothing if not uncanny. If we ask how language concerns us, those who speak it, the answer, according to Heidegger, is by way of our own mortality. "Mortals are they who can experience death as death. Animals cannot do so. But animals cannot speak either. The essential relation between death and language flashes up before us, but remains still unthought. It can, however, beckon us toward the way in which the nature of language draws us into its concern and so relates us to itself, in case death belongs together with what reaches out for us, touches us [*was uns be-langt*]" (US 215/107–08).

What is "the essential relation between death and language"?

Is death "the way to language"?

Chapter Six
Otherwise than Language

For the god Orpheus, who lives in-finitely in the
Open, song is an easy matter, but not for man.
—"What Are Poets For?"

Do we intend with this reference to shake the
foundations of all philology and philosophy of
language, and to expose them as a sham?
Indeed we do.
—*What is Called Thinking?*

Lingering

What goes on in the writings of the later Heidegger cannot truthfully
be called a reasoning of any sort. From the standpoint of progressive, systematic, calculative thinking, it is certain to appear repetitious,
opaque, pointless or unproductive. It is not (like this book) an attempt
to get straight about anything. It may not even be the sort of thinking
that Heidegger talks about in *What is Called Thinking?* And no one who
had ever given a thought to poetry would call it poetry. One could call
it, loosely, reflection, but Heidegger would probably say that it doesn't
need to be called anything at all. His motto is, "leave everything open."

His writings on language and poetry do not represent the unfolding
of a theory. They are rather a lingering with a subject matter, where
lingering means holding back, not seeking advancement or mastery,
refusing to determine the subject conceptually, acknowledging Plato's
judgment "that everything that lies before us is ambiguous" (WD 123/
201). Which means that it is not just Heidegger who holds back; it is
his subject, which refuses to be put into words. At the beginning of
"The Way to Language" (1959), Heidegger's final lecture on language,
and my present text for study, Heidegger introduces the following
formula (*Wegformel*, he calls it): *"Die Sprache als die Sprache zur Sprache*
bringen" (US 242/112). What would it be to bring language as language

to language? What would it mean, if not a final effort to get language into words?

At the obvious risk of repetition, let me begin by going back (and forth) over where we have been, or where we are, which is what Heidegger would call lingering in the neighborhood. We know, for a start, that for Heidegger truth is not a matter of statements and concepts; it is an event. The German word for event is *Ereignis*, which becomes a crucial (possibly uninterpretable) word in "The Way to Language," where it is translated, for reasons not really clear, as "appropriation." In "The Origin of the Work of Art," Heidegger speaks of the self-divided nature of truth as, on the one hand, *alētheia* or disclosure, and, on the other, as "constant concealment in the double form of refusal and dissembling" (Hw 43/54). *Alētheia* is not unconcealment pure and simple. The word itself is a pun that inscribes a darkness that is "older than truth" (SD 78/71): *a-lētheia*. Truth occurs in the work of art in this self-divided way, epitomized as the rift of earth and world. Thus Heidegger says that the *work* of the work of art, what happens with it, is unconcealment, the opening up of a world, but this is not an opening that occurs in front of us, before our eyes, the way a prospect opens up before the gaze of sightseers; better to say that it is a momentary clearing in the woods, and there we are. The Open cannot be conceptually determined; it is not anything objective that can be represented by (or to) consciousness. It is not a Kantian world. On the contrary, as Heidegger says in the essay, "What Are Poets For?" [*Wozu Dichter?*— Whereto Poets?]" (1946), by putting himself *before* the world, man is excluded from it (Hw 262/107). Our relation to the Open, or for that matter to the work of art, is not one of knowing; it is not just seeing it there in front of us where we can analyze it. And of course this leaves us not knowing where we are, especially if we know no other mode than analysis.

As for the work of art, Heidegger speaks of it as "self-standing," that is, as something reserved unto itself, something that has "cut all ties to human beings" (Hw 54/66). The work of the work is disclosure, but strangely so: call it disclosure as estrangement. This estrangement is not something that occurs in addition to opening or unconcealment; the work does not work dialectically. We must shake the idea that *alētheia* means revelation. Rather, Heidegger says, "the stronger and the more solitary the work becomes . . . , the more simply does it transport us into the open and thus at the same time transport us out of the realm of the ordinary [*Gewöhnlichen*]. To submit to this displacement means: to transform our accustomed ties to world and to earth and henceforth to restrain all usual doing and prizing, knowing and looking, in order to stay within the truth that is happening in the work" (Hw 54/66). The work, the world, breaks free; we must learn to let go, to step back and linger awhile.

Or, in other words, we have to become more like the god, or poet, Orpheus.

In its self-standing, solitary, nonhuman character, the work of art is very like the thing. The thing, as Heidegger speaks of it, is not an object of representation; it is simply that which, against all reason or rules of grammar, *things: Das Ding dingt.* Now it happens that the work *works* just as the thing *things.* The work is not an object of art, not an aesthetic object made up of formal properties, but something whose "createdness" reserves the work to itself. The work is earthly as well as worldly, *phüsis* as well as *logos,* darkening as well as lightening, and in this wise it withholds itself, closes itself up, withdraws into its materials (the poem hiding itself in its words). Of course, in its everyday, familiar, objective character, art is the property of collectors, curators, connoisseurs, critics. For none of these, however, does it make sense to speak of the *truth* (that is, the *work*) of the work of art, just as normal philosophers—empiricists, Kantians, Husserlian phenomenologists, analytic philosophers of language, nonreaders of Heidegger, for short—cannot in any sensible or philosophically serious way speak of the truth (the *thinging*) of things. Philosophically, all of this (all of the later Heidegger) is just silly-talk. Nevertheless, for Heidegger, the work works, the thing things, and in this same event, called *Ereignis,* the world worlds.

Now this event, the worlding of the world, is the event of language. Heidegger calls it the speaking of language. *Die Sprache spricht* is a sentence to be taken in the same spirit (it belongs to the same funny line of locutions) as *Das Ding dingt* and *Die Welt weltet.* Heidegger is relentless in insisting that the speaking of language is not our speech, at least not what we think of as speaking: singing, if we could say what *that* is, might be something else. Language is reserved, withholds itself, solitary and strange, no less than work or thing. It is *not for us,* even though in its everydayness we take it as ready-to-hand and always at our disposal, and we study it, objectify it, take it apart, gerrymander it, reconstruct it according to its logical forms, there is no end to what we can do. Heidegger wants us to understand, however, that language, in the midst of its everydayness, is not familiar and ordinary but *überwältigung und unheimlich,* overwhelming and uncanny. As indeed we know very well in those moments when we try to speak and words fail or run away with us.

Part of this uncanniness is that language, as it speaks, has nothing to say, nothing to express, nothing to do with meaning. Rather, Heidegger says, "*Language speaks as the peal of stillness*" (US 30/207). Moreover, he says, "The peal of stillness is not anything human [*nicht Menschliches*]" (US 30/207). Here uncanniness turns sinister. The phrase, "not anything human," makes Heidegger sound ugly. It is hard not to recoil from the dehumanization of anything, much less of language. Somehow, as the philosophers say, Heidegger is not one of us.

It is certainly true that Heidegger ranges very far from the program of romantic or aesthetic humanism that begins by conceptualizing man as a consciousness on the way to becoming fully itself, fully self-possessed and in command of its processes and productions, its knowledge and its art: consciousness free from falseness or forgetfulness (*lēthē*). The whole emancipatory project of the Enlightenment is designed to get man out from under the forces that seek to repress him and estrange him from himself: call these forces the Unconscious, or the Other, or (on a certain view of language) language, whose grammar is not just syntax and semantics but also culture and ideology. Anyhow there is no mistaking Heidegger as a figure of the counter-Enlightenment, a man of darkness, as when he says: "it is not we who play with words, but the nature of language [*Wesen der Sprache*] plays with us" (WD 83/118). And of poetry and thinking, two undeniably human activities, he has nothing progressive to say. On the contrary, poetry and thinking are remystified in his hands; he shrouds them in darkness, turns them over to enigma and ambiguity. They are no longer operations of the spirit but rather participants, whatever that means, in the event, *Ereignis,* of language. We enter into poetry and thinking, not by acts of the mind, but by relinquishing the will-to-power, that is, the will to speak and to explain. The key word with respect to poetry and thinking is "renunciation" (*Verzichten*), where *Verzichten* is a sort of Saying called *Sichversagen* or self-refusal (US 228/247), which defines the poet's relation to language. *Verzichten* belongs to the same neighborhood as *Gelassenheit,* letting-go, "openness to the mystery" (G 24/55), and it shows itself in listening and in *not* asking questions (in the sense of probing), that is, in thinking. It means keeping still, as if entering into "the peal of stillness." It means stepping-back from the manipulative mode of representational-calculative thinking, the mode of rationality of the *Ge-Stell* or En-framing of technology. It means the end of philosophy, insofar as philosophy since Descartes knows no other mode.

Aesthetic humanism is in many respects the subject of Heidegger's essay on Rilke, "*Wozu Dichter?*"—"What Are Poets For?," although it is not clear how *wozu* is to be translated. For Heidegger, Rilke's poetry shows the dominance of subjectivity that alienates us from the world, excludes us from what is near by enframing us in a state of affairs in which everything—the world, the Open—has been "raised to consciousness." "The higher the consciousness," Heidegger says, "the more the conscious being is excluded from the world" (Hw 264/ 108). This sounds like Owen Barfield or romantic primitivism, and on a certain view it is, as in the following, with its powerful wordplay on Heidegger's keyword for the modern age, *Ge-Stell:*

> Man places [*stellt*] before himself the world as the whole of everything objective, and he places himself before the world. Man sets up [*stellt*] the world toward himself, and delivers nature over to himself. We must think of this placing here, this producing [*Her-stellen*], in its broad and multifarious nature [*Wesen*]. Where Nature [*Natur*] is not satisfactory to man's representation [*Vorstellen*], he reframes or redisposes [*bestellt*] it. Man produces [*stellt*] new things where they are lacking to him. Man transposes things [*stellt die Dinge um*] where they are in his way. Man interposes [*verstellt*] something between himself and things that distract him from his purpose. Man exposes things [*stellt die Dinge aus*] when he boosts them for sale and use. Man exposes [*stellt aus*] when he sets forth [*herausstellt*] his own achievement and plays up his own profession. By multifarious producing [*vielfältigen Herstellen*], the world is brought to stand and in position [*Stand*]. The Open becomes an object [*Gegenstand*], and is thus twisted around toward the human being. Over and against the world as object, man stations himself [*stellt sich*] and sets himself up as the one who deliberately pushes through all this producing [*Herstellen*]. [Hw 265–66/ 220]

Here is man in his assertive mode, or mode of logic. Logic, let us say, is an affair of places (*Stellen*). It is made of posits, positions, propositions, oppositions, suppositions, expositions, impositions, transpositions, and the desire for repose (called certainty); it is a matter of putting questions and settling them; of locating things in their proper categories and knowing their standing relative to the scheme of things (knowing their names); of systems and rules; of grounds and reasons (knowing, for example, what poets are for); it knows only relations, representations, and frames of reference.

What is logic for? Its business appears to be to construct a safe place for (or from) objects of consciousness, or what man knows (what doesn't get away from him). Maybe a good name for such a place is "metaphysics," the place of places, where everything has a foundation and nothing flies in your face—a vast place of noncontradiction and freedom from ambiguity (mere wandering with no place in mind). The famous line in "What Are Poets For?" is: "Only within meta-physics is there logic [*Nur innerhalb der Metaphysik gibt es die Logik*]" (Hw 287/133). Only within metaphysics is everything under control; everything is in order, even language. Logic keeps language from hap-pening on its own, makes it safe to use, puts it into man's hands for safekeeping "as a handle for his representations [*als Handhabe seine Vorstellens*]" (Hw 287/133). Language is for grasping things. This is language as *logos,* which puts everything out in front of us at arm's length where we can keep an eye on it. Language as logos is for making propositions, putting things where they belong and where we won't need to look twice for them; where they won't get away from us, slip-ping away into ambiguity. Language as logos is an affair of foreseeable, and resolvable, predicaments. Even metaphors belong to language as logos; they are part of the rationality of propositions, a way of bring-ing ambiguity under control. Metaphor allows us to say, of what is not, that it is, without getting confused as to what is and what is not the case.

Only, as Heidegger says in the *Introduction to Metaphysics,* "All by itself the logos does not make language" (EM 132/145).

When in "What Are Poets For?" Heidegger speaks of "the conver-sion of consciousness [*die Umkehrung des Bewusstseins:* the turning-round of consciousness]" (Hw 284/129), it sounds like he is counseling the abandonment of logic, and it is true that the theoretical structure of this essay is built upon a traditional opposition between the logi-cal proposition and song, where the one is assertive and productive, whereas the other is, of course, nothing of the sort. The poet noth-ing affirmeth. Two lines from Rilke's *Sonette an Orpheus* summarize for Heidegger the whole point about song:

> In Wahrheit singen ist ein anderer Hauch.
> Ein Hauch um nichts. Ein Wehn im Gott. Ein Wind.

> To sing in truth is another breath.
> A breath for nothing. An afflatus in the god. A wind.
>
> [Hw 292/139]

"A breath for nothing": the poet is the one who gives himself up to language, throws in with it, doesn't try to bring it under control but lets it go, lets it sound itself through him, and so lets himself be drawn into it as into an event or game in which he is the one who is played: drawn, in other words, into the Open, where the open shows itself as something different from logical space or the places of consciousness —different, say, from the Kantian world where everything answers to our concepts. Here the poet is the answerable one: think of him or her in the traditional character as responsive to what is unseen and unheard, who is not under his or her own power but is carried away, frequently bereft of reason (blind, say, or outright mad), the song singing itself through the sounds the poet's voice makes without knowing how or why. Song is not so much the abandonment of logic as the limit of it; it shows us where the limit is, where philosophy is. And at the limit of logic there is, Heidegger says, *risk*. Hence his name for the poets: "the venturesome ones [*die Wagenderen*]," he calls them: they dare, he says, "the venture with language" (Hw 287/133). They play its gambling game.

"The more venturesome ones," Heidegger says, "dare the Saying [*Die Wagenderen wagen das Sagen*]" (Hw 287/133). But what sort of risk is this, exactly? Possibly it is just the usual risk of nonsense, silliness, or madtalk—or just what poetry always sounds like to philosophy, namely something naive and trivial. The poet is a light and winged thing, says Plato, stupid, cheerful, never in touch with reality (*Ion* 534b–c). So what's the risk?

Heidegger's answer to this question is by way of death. Death is of all things human just that which cannot be objectified and brought under control, that which is strangest of all, that which is just where logic, and therefore human knowledge, or say philosophy, ends. At the limits of logic man encounters his own mortality (call this his otherness, or that which is uncontainable in any theory or explanation)—but this is only to say that here man enters into his own, finds himself, or finds where he has always been, where his own place or *ethos* is, his own proper nature (*phūsis*). Mortality is our experience *with* ourselves as that which gets away from us. For the point is that death is always *near;* we are always mortals, dwelling with it, even though in good logic and for serious practical purposes we picture ourselves differently and labor to exempt ourselves, putting mortality at a distance.

Putting mortality at a distance is the whole end of medical technology, which takes us to that limit where it is no longer possible to determine objectively the point at which death occurs. At the limit of technology (at the very frame or border of the *Ge-Stell*), death withdraws itself, withholds itself, so that now we can no longer say, with the sort of certainty philosophy calls for, *now* it has happened ("Ah, the distinguished thing!"). What is it *not* to be able to say this? How came we to this pass? But Heidegger would say that mortality, like stillness, is always sounding, even though we cannot hear it or even cease to listen for it. Somehow we don't acknowledge our mortality quite the way the Greeks did when without blinking, seeing they were not gods, they came right out and called themselves mortals. The word belongs to an archaic or forgotten way of speaking; it's no longer in our vocabulary, no longer part of our self-understanding. Call it a word whose meaning we no longer know, define it as we will. But of course no one is under the illusion that the Greeks got it wrong: "mortal" is our proper name. There is a sense in which it is the *only* thing we know. Death is the limit of skepticism.

Heidegger's effort is to emancipate language from our theories of it, where our theories always picture language as constituting the logical possibility of our discourse. And of course language does avail itself to us in this fashion. We do speak, after all, and we do make sense to one another. Heidegger has never repudiated his earlier idea that we are constituted historically as a conversation (*Gespräch*).[1] But now he wants us to understand language as, nevertheless, *not human*—not in the way speech or conversation is. Language, like death, is the limit of the human. Heidegger wants to disconnect man and language in order to reconnect them in the archaic way in which he reconnects us to our mortality. Thus he asks us to think of language in the same breath as death ("A breath for nothing"), that is, he wants us to think of it as belonging to the same region or neighborhood as death: think of our mortality as the way we connect up with language and, therefore, with the world.

This is how Heidegger ends his third lecture on "The Nature of Language": "The essential relation between death and language flashes up before us, but remains still unthought" (US 215/107). Think of language as belonging to the same neighborhood as our mortality. This is what Heidegger's strange talk about the fourfold (*Geviert*) comes to. Language as Saying is the event (*Ereignis*) in which world and thing are called into the Open. This thinging and worlding of thing and world is the event of the fourfold, the dwelling together, round dance, and ringing of earth and sky, gods and mortals. The fourfold is not some imaginary realm. It is *our* world, and we are nowhere but in it. We are the mortals Heidegger is talking about, dwelling together with earth, sky, and divinities, strange as it is to say so. Entering into this realm means exposing ourselves to our own darkness, which is to say the truth (the dark truth or *a-lētheia*) of our mortality, our being mortal, or that which we cannot bear to think.[2] Or say that we enter this realm when we *are* exposed to the darkness, that is, to the otherness of earth and sky, mortality and divinity. The strangeness of the fourfold, its otherness, its dif-ference from the familiar and the reliable, its singularity, is just that it is irreducible to explanation, ungraspable, outside the laws of intelligibility. "Gods" and "mortals," "earth" and "sky" belong to a forgotten lexicon, say the savage mind from which Plato emancipated us. So we are ashamed to talk of such things. We assign such talk nowadays to poetry, madness, or myth—whatever is on the nether side of logic. It is no longer serious to wonder about gods. The gods withhold themselves from the discourse of modernity, that is, from language as objectifying and analytical logos, the *parole* of the *Ge-Stell*. There are no such beings as gods, just as there are no such beings as words. We can only represent gods as figures of imagination, Hölderlin's mythology. Perhaps they resound in Nietzsche's word, "God is dead." But what sort of talk is Nietzsche's word? Is he speaking literally or metaphorically? For Heidegger, Nietzsche's word has the character of uncanny discourse; it is the cry, or call, of the madman, but the ear of thinking, so under the control of the eye, cannot hear it. "It will refuse to hear it so long as it does not begin to think. Thinking begins only when we have come to know that reason, glorified for centuries, is the most stiffnecked adversary of thought" (Hw 247/112). Nor is the task of thinking to seek the overthrow of reason; it is perhaps no more than it has always been, namely to seek the limits of reason. But for Heidegger this means that thinking must enter into its own darkness and perhaps lose itself in its wandering, as if overtaken by madness; that is, it must expose itself to its other. This means that it must acknowledge the rift that binds it to poetry; that is, it must acknowledge its belongingness to this other—something philosophy could never bring itself to do.

Signs

Heidegger's final text on language, "The Way to Language," was originally a lecture given in 1959 as part of a series of lectures on language by various scholars from different disciplines. Heidegger was
preceded, for example, by C. F. Weizsäcker, who spoke on information
theory. "The Way to Language" has a familiar Heideggerian look: it
does not represent an advance or conceal a change in Heidegger's
thought but is once more a going back and forth along the same
path. It begins with the customary "break" with tradition, where tradition (here figured in the name of Wilhelm von Humboldt) means the
Kantian tradition that wants to know how meaning is possible. In this
tradition, language is the formative, structuring, systematically signifying activity of the spirit. It is that which holds totalities together,
makes totality possible. According to the famous distinction, language
is not a work (*ergon*), that is, not a product of consciousness, but the
activity (*energeia*) of the subject as such. In this tradition, meaning
is form (whatever has form, that is, possesses formal fitness, makes
sense), and consciousness is formative. Meaning is not correspondence
to an object but the way objects hang together in a total composi-
tion (*Gestell*). Nothing is ever of any significance (has any reality) all
by itself; rather, things are for us only insofar as they belong to an
ensemble of relations. The ensemble has been figured in a variety
of structuralisms: (1) epistemologically as a system of symbolic forms
(Cassirer); (2) linguistically or semiotically as a diacritical system of differences (Lévi-Strauss); (3) socially or, say, grammatically as a network
of intersecting language-games (Wittgenstein); (4) logically as a holis-
tic framework of interlocking true sentences, or conceptual schemes
(Quine); (5) politically as an ideological system or as the cultural constitution of the subject (Althusser, Lacan); (6) hermeneutically as a
temporal horizon of presuppositions or world held in common (Heidegger, *Being and Time*, section 32).

In "The Way to Language" Heidegger parodies this structuralist
tradition by speaking of the "web of relations" (*ein Geflecht von Be-
ziehungen*) in which we find ourselves whenever we try to think about
language or speak about it as such (US 242/112–13). Language *is* the
ensemble in which everything hangs together, only of course we are
not outside the web but are enmeshed in it as part of everything else,
woven into the weaving of it, entangled and certainly bewildered as
we listen to so many efforts to unweave the web. The task of thinking,
however, is not to solve the problem of language; it is not to unweave

the intricate latticework or hopeless tangle but just to separate the threads a little, loosen them here and there to create an opening. "Perhaps," Heidegger says, "there is a bond running through the web which, in a way that remains strange, unbinds and delivers language into its own [*in ihr Eigentümliches entbindet*]. The point is to experience the unbinding bond within the web of language [*Es gilt, im Geflecht der Sprache in ihr das entbindende Band zu erfahren*]" (US 243/113). So we are not to think of language as our prisonhouse; emancipation is not our theme. The web is rather something we should enter into, perhaps to wander through, listening as we go (it being too dark to see) for what Heidegger calls "a soundless echo which lets us hear something of the proper character of language [*ein lautloser Anklang, der uns ein Geringes vom Eigentümlichen der Sprache hören lässt*]" (US 243/113).

In the Kantian tradition the concept of concepts is that of the sign or its equivalents (the significant form, the logical term, the element as nexus, gap, place, or difference in the chain, fence, frame, system, or totality of signifiers, signifieds, or conceptual determinations). But instead of speaking of the sign (*Zeichen*), Heidegger, wholly into the spirit of parody, recurs to his mysterious word, *Riss*, that is, the sign as rift, which here takes the form of *Aufriss* or (in its rifted or disseminated version) *Auf-Riss*, the design or de-sign which structures what Heidegger calls the *Sprachwesen*, which is something like a word for the essence or nature of language. "Most of us," he says, "know the word 'sign' ['*Riss*'] only in its debased meaning—lines on a surface [*Riss in der Wand*]. But we make a design also when we cut a furrow into the soil to open it to seed and growth. The de-sign is the whole of the traits of that drawing which structures and prevails throughout the open, unlocked freedom of language [*Der Auf-Riss ist das Ganze der Züge derjenigen Zeichnung, die das Aufgeschlossene, Freie der Sprache durchfügt*]. The design is the drawing of the being of language, the structure of a show in which are joined the speakers and their speaking: what is spoken and what of it is unspoken in all that is given in speaking [*Der Auf-Riss ist die Zeichnung des Sprachwesens, das Gefüge eines Zeigens, darein die Sprechenden und ihr Sprechen, das Gesprochene und sein Ungesprochenes aus dem Zugesprochenen verfugt sind*]" (US 252/121).

Riss: there is probably no coming to terms with this word. First (remember) there was the antagonistic and even violent rift of earth and world ("The Origin of the Work of Art"); then there was the gentler but still painful rift of world and thing ("Language"); and then the still more "delicate and luminous" rift of poetry and thinking ("The Nature of Language"). Now we have the rift *in* language itself—or, more accurately, in the *Sprachwesen,* call it the "being" of language, although now it is otherwise than being, that is, no longer *das Wesen der Sprache* but something else, something more *phūsis* than *logos,* namely the *rift:* say the rift between the spoken and the unspoken, or between language as speaking (saying something, putting something into words) and language as Saying *(Sage),* where, in something less than a manner of speaking, nothing gets said, language withdraws itself, although something happens. In whatever context, the task, or event, of the rift has been roughly to hold things apart, to create a "between" between things without determining the difference between them, as between the literal and the metaphorical. Call rift, therefore, (loosely) a figure of indeterminacy in deference to all those cases in which things don't (or can't) quite get put into words, that is, cases where, for whatever reason, you stop or come up short of conceptualizing things, or saying (exactly) what something means—cases, or say fallings or failings in which the darkness of Saying appropriates our discourse and puts itself, if that is the right way of putting it, into our words. Call this appropriation, or this event, *Dichten.*

In *Being and Time* (section 34), Heidegger speaks of the task of "liberating grammar from logic" (SZ 165–66/209).[3] Parody is the mode of liberation in "The Way of Language," in which we get something like a Heideggerian "grammar," that is, an account (of sorts) of what language is made of, how it is put together, how it works, what its "deep structure" is. *Der Auf-Riss des Sprachwesens* means, roughly, how language, on its own, is, that is, how it is with it, or say how it speaks, even though there's no determining the logic of it. Thus Heidegger the paragrammarian draws or sketches the *Auf-Riss* of language for us in the form of a pun, a little piece of indeterminacy—namely *Zeichen-Zeigen* (sign-show). The rift in language, taken on its own *(Sprachwesen),* can be traced in the difference or dif-ference that this pun inscribes. It is perhaps something like the dif-ference, impossible quite to determine, between word and term that Heidegger talks about in *What is Called Thinking?* (WD 89/130). Or, again, the dif-ference can be traced in a line of puns that the word "sign" sets in motion: *Zeichen—Zeigen—Eigen—Eignen—Ereignis.* In ways that we may never quite grasp, this line of puns shows the way to language.

For now, however, let us trace this line as follows: We speak, let us say, by means of the manipulation of signs, that is, in terms of language, and according to its systematic operations, but what gets said cannot be accounted for simply by a doctrine of signification, since it is always the case that what we say gets away from us and more gets said, something other gets said, than is simply spoken (not to say stated). "The Way to Language" picks this up by stressing what Heidegger calls the "manysidedness" of what is spoken: *Das Gesprochenes bleibt indes vielfältig* (US 251/120). It is this manysidedness that logic is meant to bring under control. This was the whole point about constructing artificial languages obedient to reason—calculi in which the deep structure of language can finally be laid bare. Grasp this structure and you are in command of the secret workings of language, that is, you have the makings of an ideal or logically perfect language, a language of pure syntax and transparent terms. Natural languages, for their part, refuse to do what they are told. They remain opaque, dense (*dicht*), closed to view: it is impossible to give a coherent description of natural language, in which our expressions are always excessive with respect to meaning. Their words resist our efforts to make them transparent. This is the upshot of Heidegger's distinction between words and terms (*Worte* v. *Wörter*): the term means one thing and not another, but not the word, which resonates so as to sound not like one word but many. Words are more like puns than terms. As Gadamer says, besides the Platonic dialectic of the One and the Many that makes possible the fragile unity of predication, "there is another dialectic of the word, which assigns to every word an inner dimension of multiplication [*Vervielfachung*]: every word breaks forth as if from a center and is related to a whole, through which it alone is a word. Every word causes the whole of the language to which it belongs to resonate and the whole view of the world that lies behind it to appear. Thus every word, in its momentariness, carries with it the unsaid, to which it is related by responding and hinting [*winkend*]" (TM 415–16).

Here is structuralism with a difference. For what is it for a word to have "an inner dimension of multiplication"? It is not just that words are polysemantic and capable of being used in radically different contexts; it is that it is hard to tell where one word leaves off and another begins. This is so especially when we take words as sounds rather than by sight. As Heidegger says, "It is just as much a property of language to sound and ring and vibrate, to hover and to tremble, as it is for what is spoken to carry a meaning" (US 205/98). Heidegger asks us to imagine a language whose each word internalizes, not so much its own meaning, its own structural difference from other words in the system, as the sounds of all the other words in the language (perhaps, *Wake*-like, in every language). Sound a word and others answer, as in the pun. Hence the uncanniness of ordinary language where no word is just itself but is always threatening to turn into another, or always carries others clinging to it wherever it goes. In this event it is not enough to characterize words as elements in a signifying system. Language is not a network of implications that differential analysis could explicate. Words are not discrete particles or made of such things but, like puns, they are multiple and dialogical, hetero- rather than polysemous. Imagine language as an infinite conversation in which words talk endlessly back and forth, picking up hints from one another, playing to one another and on one another, internalizing one another, parodying one another, sounding and resounding, echoing and re-echoing so that nothing can ever be said purely and simply but is always in excess of itself, spilling over and spreading in every direction. One could not write a grammar for such a language; that is, one could not say in what the logic of such a language could consist. One would have to say that "in the Nichtian glossary which purveys aprioric roots for aposteriorious tongues this is nat language at any sinse of the world" (*Finnegans Wake*, 183). It is otherwise than language.

Heidegger turns back deliberately from linguistics and philosophy of language toward an antique way of taking language, say before there was a word for language—namely the way of mystery rather than system. "Everything spoken," Heidegger says, "stems in a variety of ways from what is unspoken" (US 251/120). Or, again, "What is unspoken is not merely something that lacks voice, it is what remains unsaid, what is not yet shown, what has not yet reached appearance. That which must remain wholly unspoken is held back in the unsaid, abides in concealment as unshowable, as mystery. That which is spoken to us speaks as saying in the sense of something imparted, something whose speaking does not even require to be sounded [*Das Zugesprochene spricht als Spruch im Sinne des Zugewiesenen, dessen Sprechen nicht einmal des Verlautens bedarf*]" (US 253/122). This is very strange, this talk, but to situate it one could say that before Aristotle, with his *Organon* (that is, before the invention of a logical grammar), there was Heraclitus, whose words we can sound but no longer understand, and whose theory of the sign is like nothing we know because it has nothing to do with meaning, or what we think of as meaning, that is, signifying, determining something as this or that. "The Oracle at Delphi does not speak, it gives a sign [*semainei*]" (Fr. 93). Only this is not the sign of anything, it is nothing logical, nothing semiotic, nothing that can be determined or put into a statement (made to function semantically). The Heraclitean sign is dark, more word than term; it is, as Heidegger emphasizes every time he takes up Heraclitus, something like a hint (*Wink*). What is a *Wink*?

What it is, is close to what "The Way to Language" is about. *"The essential being of language,"* Heidegger says, *"is Saying as Showing [Das Wesende der Sprache ist die Sage als die Zeige]"* (US 254/123). He then adds: "Its showing character [*deren Zeigen*] is not based on signs of any kind" (US 254/123). Signs belong to human speaking, that is, to the making of statements (or of metaphors); they belong to the logos, but not to language. And so it hurts the mind when we try to imagine what it would be like to speak such a language. But speaking, Heidegger says, is finally *not* making statements (or metaphors) or anything at all —not the use of signs. Oh, it is *that* in some sense, anyhow there's no other way (in theory) to figure it.

> But speaking is at the same time also listening [*zugleich Hören*]. It is the custom to put speaking and listening in opposition; one speaks, the other listens. But listening accompanies and surrounds not only speaking such as takes place in conversation. The simultaneousness of speaking and listening has a larger meaning. Speaking is itself a listening. Speaking is listening to the language which we speak. Thus, it is a listening not *while* but *before* we are speaking. This listening to language also comes before all other kinds of listening that we know, in a most inconspicuous manner. We do not merely speak *the* language—we speak *by way of it* [*wir sprechen aus ihr*]. We can do so because we always have already listened to the language. What do we hear there? We hear language speaking [*das Sprechen der Sprache*]. [US 254/123–24]

Die Sprache spricht: language speaks, but nothing gets said, that is, nothing gets signified; rather, in the peal of the stillness of nothing spoken, things make their appearance in the sense of coming into their own (as against coming into view), that is, they *thing* in the manner of self-disclosure or self-showing (*Sichzeigen = Das Ding dingt*). The thinging of things is not a revelation; it is the worlding of the world, the ringing of the fourfold, the round dance of earth and sky, gods and mortals —and *there* we are: that's us moving among them, mortal as we are.

Only here we are getting away from "The Way to Language," which (strangely) doesn't say a word about these things, I mean doesn't so much as hint at earth and world, the near and the remote, thinging things and worlding world, the simple onefold of the fourfold: not a word of it. What is striking about this text is that the idiom of the later Heidegger, put into play as long ago as "The Origin of the Work of Art," and carefully elaborated in the early lectures on language and in the collateral texts on "Building Dwelling Thinking" and "The Thing"—the whole lingo is dropped. Or rather not quite the whole. All that remains is *der Riss,* echoing in the quasi- or para-grammatical notion of *der Auf-Riss des Sprachwesens,* the rift of sign and showing, the spoken and the unspoken, speaking and saying, sounding and stillness. What remains strange, or anyhow unphilosophical, is the priority of listening, and even this Heidegger makes an effort to turn to philosophical account: "Language," he says, "speaks by saying, that is, by showing [*Die Sprache spricht, indem sie sagt, d. h. zeigt*]. . . . We, accordingly, listen to language in this way, that we let it say its Saying to us. No matter in what way we may listen besides, whenever we are listening to something *we are letting something be said to us* [*Sichsagenlassen:* letting Saying happen to us], and all perception and conception are already contained in that act. In our speaking, as a listening to language, we say again the Saying we have heard. We let its soundless voice come to us, and then demand, reach out, and call for the sound that is already kept in store for us [*Wir lassen ihre lautlose Stimme kommen, wobei wir den uns schon aufbehaltenen Laut verlangen, zu ihn hinreichend ihn rufen*]" (US 254–55/124).

What is this *Sichsagenlassen?*

Er-eignis

In the essay, "Logos (Herclitus, Fragment 50)," Heidegger picks up on the pun in *gehören:* "We have *heard* [*gehört*] when we *belong to* [*gehören*] the matter addressed [*Zugesprochenen*] (VS 207/66). In "The Way to Language" he picks up on this again: "We hear Saying," he says, "only because we belong within it [*Wir hören sie nur, weil in sie gehören*]" (US 255/124).

And "all perception and conception," he says, "are contained in that act."

Say that our relationship to the world is not first that of seeing but of listening. Not that we don't (can't) see and conceive how things are, but because of how we are situated (in the mode of hearing) we may not be in a position to get a good look at things; we may not be able to produce the picture we want (for example, an exact likeness). Seeing and conceiving are already contained in listening, not so much in the sense of implied as in the (darker) sense of being situated in an alien mode. For listening is not the spectator's mode. Listening means involvement and entanglement (as in the web of language). It means participation or belonging (*gehören*) for short. The ear's mode is always that of conspiracy, that is, of getting caught up in something (a tangled plot), being overtaken or taken over and put to use. The ear is exposed and vulnerable, at risk, whereas the eye tries to keep itself at a distance and frequently from view (the private eye). The eye is the agent of surveillance. It appropriates what it sees, but the ear is always expropriated, always being taken over by another ("lend me your ears"). The ear gives the other access to us, allows the stranger to enter us, occupy and obsess us, putting us under a claim, driving us mad or something like it, as when we let (cannot do otherwise than let) "a soundless voice come to us, and then demand, reach out and call for the sound that is already kept in store for us." Imagine hearing such a thing! Seeing is objectifying and possessive; hearing means the loss of subjectivity and self-possession, belonging to what we hear, owned by it. Think of the call. The ear puts us in the mode of being summoned (*belangen*), of being answerable and having to appear. It situates us. It brings us into the open, puts us, like the poet, at risk, whereas the eye allows us to stand off and away, not on the way but out of it—seeing but unseen, eminently philosophical.

What is it to be taken over (call it appropriated) in this way? It is usual to think of appropriation (*Aneignung*) as an act of possessive individualism, as one subject appropriating another: I make my own what belongs to someone else, that is, I take ownership of another's property, even take another as property. For Heidegger, however, appropriation is *Ereignis* rather than *Aneignung*. It is the word for event and also a complex pun, as we know from "The Thing": *Das Spiegel-Spiel von Welt ist der Reigen des Ereignens* (VA 173/180), where the round dance is a "figure" of belongingness. Think of *Ereignis* not as a subjective act of appropriation but as an event in which we are caught up—appropriated, if you like, or say expropriated: no longer self-determining but taken out of ourselves and put into play.

Play is a good analogy. As Gadamer has shown, play is like (but not quite the same as) the event of appropriation. Play, he says, "is not to be understood as a kind of activity. . . . The actual subject of play is obviously not the subjectivity of the individual who among other activities also plays, but [is] instead play itself" (TM 99/93). He says, "all playing is a being played. The attraction of the game, the fascination that it exerts, consists precisely in the fact that the game tends to master the players. . . . The game is what holds the player in its spell, draws him into play, and keeps him there" (TM 101–02/95–96). One could explicate listening as a kind of play, as against the seriousness of seeing, which hasn't time for play except as a spectator sport.

Think, however, of the difference between hermeneutical and empirical or psychological experience (*Erfahrung* v. *Empfindung* and *Erlebnis*). This is the distinction Heidegger has in mind when he speaks about "undergoing an experience with language." "To undergo an experience with something . . . means that this something befalls us, strikes us, comes over us, overwhelms and transforms us. When we talk of 'undergoing' an experience, we mean specifically that the experience is not of our own making; to undergo here means that we endure it, suffer it, receive it as it strikes us and submit to it. It is this something itself that comes about, comes to pass, happens" (US 159/57). And naturally one thinks here of "the gambling game of language, where our nature is at stake" (WD 87/128). Hermeneutical experience is not a cognitive event. It does not add to the subject by enlarging its store of knowledge. On the contrary, it is more likely that the subject is bereft of its store, is divested of all that belongs to it, including itself, and left exposed to what happens.[4]

However, this loss of subjectivity does not mean self-annihilation. On the contrary, Gadamer speaks of the buoyancy, the sense of abandonment and freedom from constraint, that is possible when one enters fully into the spirit of the game. Gadamer wants to say: the essence of play is freedom. The game does not so much annihilate the subject as let it go; the game takes us out of ourselves and, putting us into play, brings us out into the open, not in the sense that we are therefore objectified—playing is not self-expression or making inwardness visible. Rather, play puts us at risk. But it is also true that in playing what is in reserve is called upon and brought out. As in the fulfillment of a task or in responding to a challenge, we come into our own (*eigen*).

The loss of subjectivity means self-annihilation only if we hold to the Cartesian outlook of the pure subject—pure in the sense of disembodied and free of all environment and contingency. Descartes's motto, "I think, therefore I am," carries with it the angelic corollary that thinking, and therefore being, can do without the body, has no need for it, cannot, in any case, picture itself that way as having or being in a body; has no language of embodiment in which to sort out the tangle of whether one is "in" or whether one "has" a body —does it belong to us or we to it?—which is just the age-old question of ownership or mastery. How we connect up with the body is just as mysterious as how we connect up with language. The body on the modernist or Neoplatonist view is (like language) a negative entity; it is just that which gets in the way of knowledge—and of being, since the body always lets us down when we want to live, as when it grows old and weak and dies. But of course there is no limit to the ways in which the body can get away from us. The body is a satire upon rationality. The body means historicality and finitude. It means belonging to horizons. One cannot say either that one has or is in a body, as if the body were something objective, an entity apart, a form of containment or prisonhouse. It is true perhaps that in virtue of our bodies we are brought up against otherness, our own temporality, where we are always turning into someone else. But this just means that the body does not seal us off from whatever is other; rather, it is just our mode of being temporal, which is to say mortal. It is in virtue of our bodies that we come into our own, that is, appear as we are —situated, historical, contingent, mortal. The body (the outward and visible sign, not of the soul, but of mortality) catches us up, absorbs us, incarnates us and carries us along, not, however, as its burden or passenger but as its dancer. Think of the dance as a carrying-away, bodily, as by the sheer exuberance and overflowing of embodiment. Dance is the excess of the body. It is no accident that Heidegger figures the belonging-together of earth and sky, gods and mortals (that is, the world) as a dance.[5] The body is our mode of dancing, that is, our mode of belonging to the round dance of the fourfold; it is our mode of belonging to the world, being with it, being appropriate to it, owning up to it, acknowledging it. One could say: the body is our mode of belonging to Saying, whose "soundless voice" calls upon us to speak aloud or sing, as with the body.

This suggests that we should think of the body not Platonically as imprisonment but hermeneutically as releasement in Heidegger's sense of *Gelassenheit* or the letting-go of beings. Heidegger says: "Saying [*Sage*] sets all present beings *free* into their given presence, and brings what is absent into their absence. Saying pervades and structures the openness of the clearing [*das Freie der Lichtung*] which every appearance must seek out and every disappearance leave behind, and in which every present or absent being must show, say, announce itself [*sich hereinzeignen, sich einsagen muss*]" (US 257/126). One should say: the truth of Saying is the event (*Ereignis*) in which everything comes into its own, even that which withdraws itself or conceals itself—*phūsis*, for example, or whatever loves to hide: and there is nothing does not love to do so. Which means that there is nothing that does not belong to Saying, whose essence is withdrawal: Saying, which will not, Heidegger says, "let itself be captured in any statement" (US 161/59). As if Saying were freedom.

Even Being itself is caught up in this play, this song and dance of Saying. This was Heidegger's point in *Identity and Difference* where *Ereignis* is the event in which "Man and Being are appropriated to one another [*Mensch und Sein sind einander übereignet*]" (ID 19/31). The relationship of Man and Being is not to be thought of as a formal connection or a grounding in some primal unity; rather, it is a "*belonging-together* [Zusammen-*gehören*]" in which the notion of ground gives way to the notion of mutual participation in which Being makes a claim upon Man and itself "arrives" only insofar as Man "listens to" the claim, answers to it, belongs to it, as if Man and Being were partners in a dialogue and were nothing apart from it: either in play or nothing. We can, Heidegger says, enter into this mutual appropriation, that is, experience it, but what is required from us is something like the letting-go of the dance—a "spring" away from the ground and into the abyss, where the abyss, however, is no longer a metaphysical void but is now the realm or open place between Man and Being, the region of their mutual belonging [*Der Sprung ist die jähe Einfahrt in den Bereich, aus dem der Mensch und Sein einander je schon in ihrem Wesen erreicht haben, weil beide aus einer Zureichung einander übereignet sind*]" (ID 20–21/33). This region cannot be conceived topologically; it is an event rather than a ground: *Ereignis*. Man and Being are not beings but occurrences in the event of appropriation—but now even *Ereignis* is no longer simply what it names, that is, it is no longer to be taken simply as "event" in the usual sense; rather, the word "is now to be used as a *singulare tantum*" (ID 25/36): the word is no longer a term in a lexicon (*Ereignis*) but is now rifted or dif-ferent, namely *Er-eignis*, a singular, dark, or untranslatable word like the *Tao* of Lao-tzu or the *logos* of Heraclitus (where *logos* and *phūsis*, like Man and Being, belong together as in a dance instead of in a relationship of domination and subjection). *Ereignis* as *Er-eignis*, Heidegger says, "is that realm, vibrating within itself [*in sich schwingende Bereich*], through which Man and Being reach each other in their nature, achieve their nature by losing those qualities [say subjectivity and objectivity, or master and slave] with which metaphysics has endowed them" (ID 26/37). The English translation of *Ereignis* as "event of appropriation" is thus, not wrong, perhaps, but neither is it quite saying what *Er-eignis* is, since that word no longer "means" event or appropriation or anything that can be put into words. Like Saying, *Er-eignis* cannot be captured in a term or statement, that is, there is no other way of putting it. It has the unspeakability, the uncontainability, of the pun.[6]

Basic to *Er-eignis* as pun is *Eignen*, owning, in which, of course, *Zeichen* and *Zeigen* also resound. Heidegger says, "The moving force in Showing of Saying is Owning [*Das Regende im Zeigen der Sage ist das Eignen*]" (US 258/127). It is as if it were the *eigen* in *Zeigen* that gives *Zeigen* its force; or perhaps not "as if," but just so: *Das Eigen*, Heidegger says, "is what brings all present and absent beings each into their own [*in sein jeweilig Eigenes*], from where they show themselves in what they are, and where they abide according to their kind. This owning which brings them there, and which moves Saying as showing in its showing, we call Appropriation [*heisse das Ereignen*]" (US 258/127). And again, echoing *Identity and Difference*: "The appropriating event is not the outcome [*Ergebnis*] (result) of something else, but the giving yield [*Er-gebnis*] whose giving reach alone is what gives us such things as a 'there is' ["*Es gibt*"], a 'there is' of which even Being itself stands in need to come into its own as presence" (US 258/127). Like *Er-eignis*, *Er-gebnis* has been removed, in the Heideggerian manner, from "usual and customary usage." It is as if the meaning of the word were inscribed by the hyphen, the rift of the dif-ference or *mark of the pun* that turns *Ergebnis* into a word (*Er-gebnis*) for the dissemination (*Es gibt*) "of which even Being itself stands in need to come into its own as presence."

And not Being only, but also language: *Die Sprache als die Sprache zur Sprache bringen* (US 242/112). Recall the figure of the web at the outset of "The Way to Language": "Perhaps," Heidegger had said, "there is a bond running through the web which, in a way that remains strange, unbinds and delivers language into its own. The point," he added, "is to experience the unbinding bond within the web of language" (US 243/112). This "unbinding bond" is the rift within the solitary nature of language (*der Auf-Riss des Sprachwesens*) that both divides and joins, brings together and sets free each into its own, Saying and speaking, the unspoken and the spoken, showing and signification, earth and world, world and thing, poetry and thinking. Put it as follows: for us to come into our own means to enter into a dialogue, not with Being, but with Saying. In Saying, nothing gets said, but this does not mean that Saying remains out of hearing. Saying appropriates us in the sense that we now enter into the event of Saying and give voice to it. Saying claims us for its own, and we respond—answer with what is *our* own, namely, as Heidegger says, "the sounding of the word. The encountering saying of mortals is answering. Every word spoken is already an answer: counter-saying, coming to the encounter, listening Saying [*Gegensage, entgegenkommendes, hörendes Sagen*]. When mortals are made appropriate for Saying, human nature is released into that needfulness out of which man is used for bringing soundless Saying to the sound of language [*Die Vereignung der Sterblichen in die Sage enlässt das Menschenwesen in den Brauch, aus dem der Mensch gebraucht ist, die lautlose Sage in das Verlauten der Sprache zu bringen*]" (US 260/129).

Here, however, is the surprise: What Heidegger calls "the way to language" turns out to be, not *our* way, that is, not a way of getting at language, getting the right idea about it or the hang of it—not the "right approach" that might serve us as an alternative to linguistics or philosophy of language. The "way to language" is not anything for us to hold to or follow. The way to language, Heidegger says, "belongs to Saying," not to us. So "way" is not method or theory. Heidegger uses the word idiomatically rather than philosophically. "Way" is the *wëgen* of the Alemmanic-Swabian dialect where it means "way-making [*Be-wëgung*]" (US 261/129–30), which is to say not just moving along a path, making one's way, but breaking open, setting-free, wandering off the straight and narrow.

For Heidegger, *Ereignis* (taken singularly as *Er-eignis*) is to be understood as *Be-wëgung*. It is the "way-making" event that "lets . . . Saying reach speech": "*Das Ereignis lässt in der brauchenden Vereignung die Sage zum Sprechen gelangen. Der Weg zur Sprache gehört zu der aus dem Ereignis bestimmten Sage*" (US 260/129). Letting Saying go this way, letting it reach speech, is the meaning of the formula that Heidegger introduced at the outset of his lecture: *Die Sprache als die Sprache zur Sprache bringen*. *Er-eignis* is the way-making (call it the punning) in which language as language is brought to language. This event has nothing to do with the process of objectifying language, giving a picture of it, framing a theory of it, raising it to consciousness. Language is untheorizable. Indeed, perhaps philosophy of language shows as much in spite of itself with its distinction between natural and formalized or gerrymandered languages: it throws the one away because it is only possible to frame a coherent theory for the other, that is, to produce theories of meaning and truth that will explain how language can be said to hook onto reality. But Heidegger is not to be thought of as intervening in philosophy of language with a counter-theory. On the contrary, in the way-making or punning that brings language as language to language, the being or nature or reality of language, or whatever *Sprachwesen* means—what belongs to language essentially—*conceals itself*: "*In diesem Weg, der zum Sprachwesen gehört, verbirgt sich das*

Eigentümliche der Sprache" (US 260–62/129). As if the philosophical term *Wesen* had now been reenchanted or remystified, returned to its Heraclitean sense of *phūsis,* or that which loves to hide.

So the way to language belongs to Saying. *Er-eignis* is the event in which Saying reaches speech. This setting-free of Saying—this letting-go or releasement—is what bringing language as language (*Sage*) to language (*Sprache*) amounts to. "What looks like a confused tangle," Heidegger says, "becomes untangled when we see it in the light of the way-making movement [*Bewëgung*], and resolves into the release [*Befreiende*] brought about by the way-making movement disclosed in Saying. That movement delivers Saying to speech. Saying keeps the way open along which speaking, as listening, catches from Saying what is to be said, and raises what it has thus caught into the sounding word" (US 263/131). And that word is the lowly pun, the other of the noble concept, the letting-go of language as against the fixing of its sense that bends it to assertiveness.

It is worth emphasizing (once more) that we don't produce puns; they catch us up in an uncanny hermeneutics: we hear them, let them happen to us (*Sichsagenlassen*), pick up on them and sound them out (*er-läutern*—where *erläutern* no longer has to do with explanation). The event, as it catches us up in it, is hermeneutical rather than poetic in the sense of *poiēsis,* and it is bound to bother us that we can't see it this way, can't see ourselves clearly in this event—can't pick ourselves out, identify ourselves at work. Indeed, what is frustrating about Heidegger's thinking is that he doesn't hold up the mirror we're accustomed to, doesn't hold up any mirror, either to language or to ourselves as expressive agents, masters of *poiēsis,* discursive egos, conscious or unconscious subjects in a linguistic process. The "way-making movement . . . delivers Saying to speech": we don't do it. The way-making movement is not a performative activity; it is an event in which we are caught up, to which we belong—in which, let us say, we disappear. We can't picture ourselves in what Heidegger has to say with respect to language, can't recognize ourselves, because that is what it means to belong to language. What belongs to language *essentially conceals itself,* and so it is with us:

> In order to be who we are, we human beings remain committed to and within the being of language [*in das Sprachwesen eingelassen bleiben*], and can never step out of it and look at it from somewhere else. Thus we always see the nature of language [*Sprachwesen*] only to the extent to which language itself has us in view,

has appropriated us to itself. That we cannot know the nature of language [*Sprachwesen*]—know it according to the traditional concept of knowledge defined in terms of cognition as representation—is not a defect, however, but rather an advantage by which we are favored with a special realm, that realm where we, who are needed and used to speak language, dwell as *mortals*. [US 266/ 134]

To belong to language means that we disappear into the event of way-making as consciousness disappears into play, as spectatorship is dissolved by participation, as speaking turns into listening, or as the dancer is carried away by, disappears into, the dance. Or as Orpheus is carried away or appropriated by his song. Or as the thinker disappears into the darkness when consecutive progress gives way to wandering or way-making without why. But of course philosophy was invented to keep this from happening.[7]

Indeed, belonging to language in the way Heidegger speaks of it, with his emphasis on darkness—on withdrawal, on refusal or dissembling, on the disappearance of the subject as a cognitive and vociferous consciousness—is what philosophy has always recognized as the condition of skepticism, or rather the condition that the skeptic always bends our minds to: what Stanley Cavell, distinguishing the skeptic from the nihilist, calls "the truth of skepticism," which is that our belongingness to the other calls upon us to forgo or "disown knowledge."[8] Of course, we do not know the consequences of such disownment, unless perhaps it is the *Eignen*, or perhaps *Er-eignis*, of which Heidegger (darkly) speaks. Anyhow, as Cavell reminds us, tragedy is knowing (too late) the consequences, or limits, of knowing. Comedy is not knowing; comedy is risking it—risking the consequences of exposure to the dark. What remains to be understood—perhaps this is the lesson that remains to be drawn from the later Heidegger—is that skepticism, although far from cheerful, edifying, or even practical—is comic rather than nihilistic, as if the finitude or failure of *theōria* were the releasement of *phronēsis*, or *Gelassenheit:* the letting-go of the ground, the risk of wandering, the uncertainty of listening, the gambling game of language, the venturing of *Dichten*.

Conclusion
The Dark Comic World
of Martin Heidegger

Wann werden Wörter
wieder Wort?
—"Sprache" (1972)

But by writing thithaways end to end and
turning, turning and end to end hithaways and
with lines of litters slittering up and louds of
latters slettering down, the old semetomyplace
and jupetbackagain from tham Let Rise till
Hum Lit. Sleep, where in the waste is the
wisdom?
—*Finnegans Wake*

The folly of trying to follow closely Heidegger's thinking, I mean his later writings, comes out very forcefully when you try to stop, because there is no natural stopping place, no place of arrival where everything falls into place and you can say, "Well now that's done: and I'm glad it's over." Instead, the movement you get into is that of going back over what has been said in order to pick up on what is missing or what has been left out of account. So you are always starting over with something familiar, and then going astray as you try to finish or complete what you think you have in hand. This is why, after a while, repetition and confusion are likely to appear the distinctive features of anything you have to say about Heidegger. Let me illustrate this with a conclusion.

In his Nietzsche lectures Heidegger summarizes a basic principle of Nietzschean aesthetics with the statement that "Art is the most perspicuous and familiar configuration [*Gestalt*] of the will to power" (NI 84/71). One could worry the question of whether Heidegger has got it right about Nietzsche, that is, whether Nietzsche can actually be accused of this view or whether he does not simply lay it bare as one of the fundamental conceptions of the Western view of art, namely the old rhetorical idea of artistry as mastery, where mastery of the materials of discourse develops into the means of social and political control.[1] Conquest of language means conquest of the world. One could take it, for example, that the distinction between Apollo and Dionysius is simply a redescription of the classical struggle between the artist and the genius, where the purpose of art is just to keep genius under control, whereas the thrust of genius is always transgressive, always indeterminately destructive as well as creative since it shows itself most powerfully in the willful breaking of the forms of art and laws of intelligibility; it is the custom of genius to end in noble or sometimes egregious failure. Genius at all events is uncontainable. At the level of sublimity one has the story of Daedalus and Icarus; at the level of banality there is Samuel Johnson's dismay at Shakespeare's obsession with puns: "A quibble is to *Shakespeare,* what luminous vapours are to the traveller; he follows it at all adventures, it is sure to lead him out of his way, and sure to engulf him in the mire. It has some malignant power over his mind, and its fascinations are irresistible. . . . A quibble is the golden apple for which he will always turn aside from his career, or stoop from his elevation. A quibble poor and barren as it is, gave him such delight, that he was content to purchase it by the sacrifice of reason, propriety, and truth. A quibble was to him the fatal *Cleopatra* for which he lost the world, and was content to lose it."[2] Say it is the case that mastery of language means mastery of the world, then Shakespeare's weakness before the pun retells the story of the loss of paradise or empire, all because of weakness for, or of, a woman. This is Plato's story of the weakness of the *logos* owing to the power (or nearness and contagion) of *phūsis.* In Johnson's words, what we are talking about is "the sacrifice of reason, propriety, and truth" —all for a quibble. This is, in so many words, why philosophy tries to close Heidegger's book.

Phūsis is the other (not the opposite) of *logos;* the opposite of *phūsis* is *technē.* In the Nietzsche lectures Heidegger lays it out this way:

> In order to catch [the true significance of *technē,* it is advisable to establish the concept that properly counters it. The latter is named in the word *phūsis.* We translated it "nature," and think little enough about it. For the Greeks, *phūsis* is the first and the essential name for beings themselves and as a whole [*das Seiende selbst und im Ganzen*]. For them the being is what flourishes on its own, in no way compelled, what rises and comes forward, and what goes back into itself and passes away [*sich zurückgeht und*

vergeht]. It is the rule that rises and resides in itself [*das aufgehende und in sich zurückgehende Walten*].

If man tries to win a foothold and establish himself among the beings [*Seienden*] (*phūsis*) to which he is exposed, if he proceeds to master beings in this or that way, then his advance against beings is borne and guided by a knowledge of them. Such *knowledge* is called *technē*. From the very outset the word is not, and never is, the designation of a "making" and a producing; rather, it desig-nates that knowledge which supports and conducts every human irruption into the midst of beings. For that reason *technē* is often the word for human knowledge without qualification. The kind of knowledge that guides and grounds confrontation with and mastery over beings . . . . [NI 96/81]

We may think of *technē* first of all as intervention rather than produc-tion or *poiēsis:* it is knowledge which seeks mastery over that which "flourishes on its own, in no way compelled, what rises and comes for-ward, and what goes back into itself and passes away." *Technē* seeks to rule "the rule that rises and resides in itself." The rule of the *Ge-Stell* is that which seeks to penetrate and lay bare the secret workings of things. What Heidegger calls the "step back" is, in effect, the step back from just such intervention in what is; it is a renunciation of *technē*—call it preservation [*Bewahrung*] as against intervention, in the sense that one refuses to intervene in the reserve of the other (Hw 59/71). This renunciation is what is entailed in poetry as the *Gelassenheit* or the letting-go of language, where language is not something of which we are the master but that which, as *phūsis*, withdraws itself; it is "what flourishes on its own, in no way compelled, what rises and comes for-ward, and what goes back into itself and passes away."

So what Derrida calls the "motif of the proper (*eigen, eigentlich*)" in Heidegger is not what we thought; it has to do with otherness rather than self-sameness or identity.[3] As I showed in the last chapter, Hei-degger takes the *Wegformel* of "The Way to Language," *Die Sprache als die Sprache zur Sprache bringen* (US 242/112), as the event (*Er-eignis*) in which language comes into its own (*eigen*), that is, into its own apart-ness, its darkness and remoteness from the human. "Language," Hei-degger says, "thus delivered into its own freedom [*in ihr eigenes Freie entbunden*], can be concerned solely with itself" (US 262/131). It is this self-concern that language shares with the work of art that cuts its ties with the human; or like the thing, language is self-standing and not for us. It is remote (*abgeschieden*), and this remoteness can never be overcome or disguised by what appears to be the ready availability of language, its equipmental character. Our experience with language cannot be contained in a grammatical description; rather we can enter into this remoteness, belong to it, only by way of keeping silent and listening to the "monologue" of language (US 262/131). This monologue is Saying (*Sage*), in which nothing gets said, that is, in Saying there is nothing put into words. Instead, Heidegger thinks of Saying as being released into song. "Saying," he says, "will not let itself be captured in any statement [*Aussage*]" (US 266/235). Saying reaches speech not in the way of speaking as man's discourse or assertiveness with respect to things; it reaches speech as song: "Saying is the mode in which *Ereignis* speaks: mode not so much in the sense of manner and fashion [*Modus und Art*], but as the melodic mode [*die Weise als das melos*], the song which singing says [*das Lied, das singend sagt*]" (US 266/135). And what singing says is the just the song in which we are taken up and carried away. No secrets are revealed in the bargain.

We belong to this song as the sounding of Saying, not in the sense of *making* sounds or translating what is silent into the empiricism of the voice, giving expression to the inexpressible, but rather as listening that is taken over by Saying as the word that resounds, echoes and re-echoes, rings and vibrates, goes its own way, taking us along (*hörendes Sagen* [US 260/129]).[4] We may think of poetry as this resounding word in which language as Saying is brought to song, where song, however, is not *Poesie* (not what we think of as poetry, namely the poetic product or poem). Song is not a product of any sort; rather it is just that event in which language is out of our control, set free on its own and taking us with it. In this event, our relationship with language can only be understood in terms of appropriation as if in a gambling game in which we lose our stakes (ourselves and all that we possess) to language.

This is the subject that Heidegger takes up in his lecture on "The Word," where he returns to the final couplet of Stefan George's poem, "Das Wort," this time to pick up on the word *verzichten*, that is, renunciation:

> So lernt ich traurig den verzicht:
> Kein ding sei wo das wort gebricht.

Renunciation means giving up language as *logos*, that is, as the power of framing representations. It means giving up signs as "darstellende Worte" that "rule over things" (US 225/144).[5] By means of renunciation, Heidegger says, the poet opens onto "a different rule of the word," one which is not based on signs and has nothing to do with signification. "The poet," he says, "must relinquish claim to the assurance that he will on demand be supplied with the name for that which he has posited as what truly is. This positing and that claim he must now deny himself. The poet must renounce having words under his control as representational names for what is posited. As self-denial [*Sichversagen*], renunciation is a Saying which says to itself: Where word breaks off no thing may be [*Kein ding sei wo das wort gebricht*]" (US 227–28/146–47).

Renunciation means getting out of the mode of worldmaking, giving up the idea of order at Key West. In Heidegger's case, this means rethinking the nature of poetry as he had once figured it. For in "Hölderlin and the Essence of Poetry" the poet was characterized specifically in terms of the foundational power of naming—"Poetry is the establishing of Being by means of the word [*Dichtung ist worthafte Stiftung des Seins*]" (EM 38/281). Here poetry is still being philosophized, that is, assimilated into foundationalism as a condition of possibility, the Kantian *Bedingung*, the act of positing or the objectification of the world. (A place is being found for poetry within philosophy; poetry is being made recognizable in philosophy's terms: this is the upshot of Heidegger's Hölderlin-interpretation.) Thus "when the gods are named originally and the essence of things receives a name, so that things for the first time shine out, human existence is brought into a firm relation and given a basis [*auf einen Grund gestellt*]. The speech of the poet is establishment [*Stiftung*] not only in the sense of the free act of giving, but at the same time in the sense of the firm basing of human existence on its foundation [*im Sinne der festen Gründung des menschlichen Daseins auf seinen Grund*]" (EM 39/28–82). But now Heidegger says that this power is just what the poet must surrender: "The poet must renounce having words under his control as representational names [*darstellende Worte*] for what is posited." In the later Heidegger, poetry is no longer aboriginal naming. Poetry now means letting go of the ground; it means letting language go, which is the same as letting language speak and things thing: "*Das Wort be-dingt das Ding zum Ding*" (US 232/151). Peter Hertz translates this line as "The word makes the thing into a thing," as if to turn Heidegger back into Kant, but the word is not productive or constitutive of things. Poetry is not *poiēsis*, not *Stiftung* and *Gründung*. "Renunciation," Heidegger says, "commits itself to the higher rule of the word which first lets a thing be as thing. The word 'be-things' the thing. We should like to call this rule of the word 'bethinging' [*Bedingnis*]" (US 232/151). Bethinging: the thinging of things, the worlding of the world. It is not too hard to read this as a parody of Kant and the whole idea of foundationalism. The idea now would be to re-read Heidegger's Hölderlin-interpretation in light of later texts like "Das Wort," rather than the other way around.[6]

What is worth knowing about *Bedingnis*, for example, is that it is no longer the sign of anything; it is a word but not a term. Logically, it is a nonentity. "This old word," Heidegger says, "has disappeared from linguistic usage" (US 252/151). Goethe still knew it, he says, but only in the sense in which it would later become a philosophical term of art, namely, as condition. As Heidegger uses it, however, "bethinging says something different from talking about a condition. . . . A condition is the existent ground for something that is. The condition gives reasons, and it grounds. It satisfies the principle of sufficient reason. But the word does not give reasons for the thing. The word allows the thing to presence as thing. We shall call this allowing bethinging. The poet does not explain what this bethinging is. But the poet commits himself, that is, his Saying to this mystery of the word. In such a commitment, he who renounces denies himself to the claim which he formerly willed" (US 232–33/151).

In other words, we no longer know what *Bedingnis* means, what it signifies, and so for us it is a dead word; but precisely for this reason it comes alive for Heidegger. It is a word which has withdrawn itself, secluded itself in darkness—call it a word of self-refusal, as if this dark word could become the word of words, the word for "the higher rule of the word," or, as Heidegger says, the word for "the word's mystery" (US 233/151). Call it a word that language speaks, or a word for what happens when language speaks—but not a word for us. As a word, it leaves us in the dark. But we mustn't be afraid. All this means is that there is no lexicon, no discursive field, no semantic space, no conceptual scheme, no language game, no interpretive community in which this word can be found or where its meaning can be recuperated and fixed, this time not to wander off and become lost. It's what a word looks like, or sounds like, when it has been set free: a *singulare tantum*. Call it (not *logos*) a word for the word.

Now imagine, if you can, a philosophical language made up of such words. Of course, there's no imagining any such thing, but one has the impression that Heidegger would have liked to philosophize in such a language, were such a thing possible. This seems to have been the point of his effort to start up "a dialogue [*Zwiesprache*] with early thinking" (Hw 309/25), that is, with the fragments of Anaximander and

Heraclitus, whose words we can no longer reconceptualize, translate them as we will. These fragments are dark sayings—enigmas, that is, riddles which are not logical puzzles to which answers can be supplied but sayings that do not speak: sayings that have withdrawn from the world back into the earth whence they came. So there is no question of going back to these sayings as if to a starting point that would get the history of philosophy underway anew, this time not to go astray. The idea of starting history over, of revolution, is a Cartesian dream of mastering history; whereas in fact history is ambiguity, wayward-ness, withdrawal, errancy ("Error is the space in which history unfolds" [Hw 310/26]). So it makes a kind of sense that there is nothing pro-grammatic or even purposeful about Heidegger's conversation with the ancients; he isn't recommending this conversation as a new way of doing philosophy (a New Archaism). It isn't clear what this conversa-tion amounts to—other than a trackless reflection, a thinking without why, a wayward musing back and forth upon a handful of overtrans-lated words (*phūsis, lōgos, moira, eris, alētheia, hen*). What Heidegger does, in effect, is "undertranslate" these words, as if to preserve them in their darkness.[7] One could say that he lingers in their company, in their nearness, but instead of trying to remove their strangeness or re-moteness, Heidegger (picking up on these words without the sanction of philology) allows himself to drift away into the dark, leaving us not knowing any longer what to make of him, reading him "without why."

But we should not turn "without why" into a misleading slogan. The fact is that these old words exist in a parodistic relation to the new the way *Bedingnis* lingers as a parody of Kantian *Bedingung*. So the words are not exactly "mute." Heidegger's trackless reflection on archaic words is not a new achievement in philosophy, that is, not a new advancement beyond Kant, but it is hardly idle; rather it exists adjacently to the tradition, playing off of it, turning it back on itself, exposing it to that which it struggles to repress or overcome, namely the weakness of the logos. What happens to philosophy when it is exposed to this weakness? One thing perhaps is that it may encounter its own errancy or historicality, the true waywardness of its thinking. If philosophy were more open to poetry, if it would allow poetry to loosen it a little, it would probably not find Heidegger so weird or unphilosophical—would not think of Heidegger as being incompatible with itself. But possibly if philosophy were more open in this regard, there would have been no (philosophical) need for Heidegger.

In "The Language in the Poem: A Discussion [*Erörterung*] of Georg Trakl's Poetry," Heidegger says that thinking must enter into a dialogue with poetry. As always, dialogue is to be understood in the Heideggerian sense of picking up on the words of another, not in order to *grasp* their meaning, that is, not in the sense of exercising exegetical mastery, but rather to take them in unexpected ways—as hints thrown off and radiating in multiple directions (waywardly). As if the sense in which a word is to be taken were not a meaning—not a context, for example, in which the word fits; not a condition in which it is true to say, *s* is *p*—but rather an opening, a threshold, a line to follow or cross: in short, a *way* of taking it or of being taken by it (as if taken away, expropriated). For the later Heidegger, taking the word this way, being taken across thresholds or lines, is always a movement from the customary into strangeness, a step off the true path (a transgression), a step back from certainty and control to a region where everything is otherwise. In "Language in the Poem" this strangeness is epitomized in the word *Abgeschiedenheit*, which translates as apartness or *remoteness*. *Die Abgeschiedenheit* is called "the place [*Ort*] of Georg Trakl's poetry" (US 52/172); it is the place to which all poetry, all art, transports us. *Die Abgeschiedenheit* is just the place of apartness or strangeness where language abides as language; and when language speaks it speaks the language of *Abgeschiedenheit*. When Heidegger says, in the essay on "Logos (Heraclitus, Fragment 50)," that "It is more salutary for thinking to wander into the strange [*Befremdlichen*] than to establish itself in the understandable [*Verständlichen*]" (Wm 218/76), he is saying, in effect, that thinking must follow the path—the word or language—opened up by poetry. This means speaking in the spirit of apartness or strangeness, taking words (as the later Heidegger repeatedly takes them), in a strange, unheard-of, or forgotten sense, that is, a sense which is different from what is customary or established or used with reason; it is to take them in a sense which is wandering or ambiguous in the manner of the word rather than fixed in the manner of the term. The language of Trakl's poetry, or rather the language *in* Trakl's poetry, the "language in the poem," is, Heidegger says, "essentially ambiguous [*wesenhaft mehrdeutig*]." To which he adds: "We shall hear nothing of what the poem says so long as we bring to it only this or that dull sense of unambiguous meaning [*eindeutigen Meinens*]" (US 74/192). A single meaning is like a single path through the forest: the way is fixed. This is all very well if someone simply wants to know beforehand where one will end up or that one will arrive safely and not get lost. This is the way of method and of consecutive reasoning, of the model and operational character of representational-calculative thinking. But it is no way to think. Entering into a dialogue with poetry means listening to—entering into, belonging to, being open to —the "essential ambiguity" that the poem holds open as its essential darkness. The task of thinking is not to resolve this ambiguity into a concept; it is not to dispel the darkness of poetry. Rather, thinking needs to let go into the weakness (the other) of the *logos*, namely the *phüsis* of language. This way thinking can remain open to what is unthought the way poetry remains open to the unspoken. Thus thinking can, among other things, enter into the conversation that Heidegger speaks of in "The Onto-Theo-Logical Constitution of Metaphysics," where the idea is "to elucidate the otherness of the subject matter of thinking [*der Verschiedenheit der Sache des Denken*]" (ID 36/46). What needs sounding is not the subject but its otherness—its resistance to thinking, its evasiveness, its refusal to be formulated as a topic or question in philosophy.

In a very fine essay Véronique Fóti gives a reading of Georg Trakl's poetry that tries to clarify Heidegger's interpretation of Trakl more or less within the rules of normal exegesis.[8] "Heidegger," she says, "hears Trakl's poetry as the song of the stranger whom Trakl calls 'der Abgeschiedene,' the one who is apart or remote and therefore solitary, or one who has 'departed' into death. But the protagonist of Trakl's poems appears in many guises: as the stranger, the strange woman or, in Trakl's characteristic indefinite neuter construction, as something strange (*ein Fremdes*), something obscure. We also encounter the protagonist as the homeless one, the clairvoyant or madman, the dreamer, or the white magician who, apart in his grave, plays with his snakes. Still more remote is the stranger as dead or unborn" (223–25). I find this very helpful. Fóti's evocation of this many-sided, infinitely variable stranger is superb. The stranger, she shows, is even more heterogeneous and uncontainable than Heidegger makes him out to be. "The wandering of Trakl's stranger," she says, "appears errant and compulsive rather than [as in Heidegger] sustained by any hope of renewal. Sometimes, indeed, he may walk in innocence 'among the creatures of God' or step into the circle of lamplight and share bread and wine; but he soon must leave again into the night and 'gentle madness'" (229). Is this stranger, however, a poet or thinker? Fóti thinks that he is the poet, and that the thinker, by contrast, is one who "seeks a continuing way and an abiding integration which compels pain itself to further the work of the spirit which in turn accomplishes what one might call a sublation of pain. The poet, however, must have the courage of, at best, anarchic multiplicity, and at worst, of disruption and disintegration. Whereas thinking traces its path towards the ungraspable manner which Heidegger frequently describes as a homecoming to a shelter or shrine, Trakl speaks of poetry in metaphors such as a 'golden footbridge' or a dancing boat. Poetry entrusts him [the poet] to the open and to the elements; and it may prove too frail a structure to withstand their uproar" (231).

My thought, however, is that the difference between the poet and the thinker in Heidegger is not so easy to determine—cannot, indeed, be conceptually determined at all, which is what Heidegger means when he speaks of the "rift of poetry and thinking." I think that the "neighborhood of poetry and thinking," which is measured by this rift, this "luminous and delicate difference" that is impossible to fix, is nothing less than the *Abgeschiedenheit* traversed by Trakl's wanderer. Thinking is more wandering than homecoming. Like poetry, it belongs to the wayward. What thinking learns (could learn, has yet to learn) from poetry is just this truth about itself.

Let me try to clarify this by concluding with a question about the relation between wandering and dwelling. We know that a favorite line of Heidegger's is Hölderlin's "Full of merit, yet poetically dwells / Man on the earth," as in "Hölderlin and the Essence of Poetry" where the poet in his orphic character opens a world for man, establishes him in his dwelling place. But the poet is himself the outcast or stranger, a Hermes-figure or creature of the *Between* who agitates the space in which gods and mortals belong together and are held apart (EM 43/ 288–89). The poet is not of the world only but of the sky and earth, the high and the deep, the remote and the near. On my reading of Heidegger the same must be said of the thinker. Repose is not in the nature of thinking. Thinking is not meant for dwelling but for wandering in the between: here is where both poetry and thinking belong. They are not the same, but they belong together, each held apart in its own darkness (US 196/90), moving not just on separate paths but waywardly along many—endlessly disseminated, exposed to "anarchic multiplicity," uncontainable, not to be defined as so many standpoints or positions or avenues of approach, never able to succeed to a final point or ultimate achievement: pointless—but now this word has to be used in a different sense, not according to customary usage, because "without why" does not mean idle nonsense (which is how the philosopher now and always dismisses the poet). The point is to get thinking as well as poetry out from under the question of point.

This means that both poetry and thinking are dangerous things to get into, because both are Cain-like, exposed, unhoused, wandering in the strange, stumbling among fragments, skeptical, vulnerable (perhaps not just vulnerable) to madness, alien to serenity and comfort, abroad without ground, out of control, hopelessly unproductive (there's no saying any more what they are for). Naturally one's next thought is that poetic dwelling on the earth is for us (mere mortals) but not for them—historic figures of exile—and perhaps this is so, but in fact what we learn from poetry and thinking is that poetic dwelling itself is not a restoration of the kingdom, not a return to paradise, the green or golden world where everything is harmonious and safe, a domain of relentless familiar ease.

Possibly one can read "Hölderlin and the Essence of Poetry" and "Remembrance of the Poet" (with its talk of homecoming, the joyous and the serene) in a utopian way, but for such a reading the later Heidegger is nothing but trouble. In the lecture, ". . . Poetically Man Dwells . . ." (1954), Heidegger returns to his earlier idea that poetry is a letting-dwell and even a kind of building that "first brings man onto the earth, making him belong to it, and thus brings him into dwelling" (VA 186/218). Poetry, Heidegger says, takes the measure of this dwelling place—"Poetry is a *measuring* [Messen]" (VA 190/221) —only it is so "with a different stress" that takes measure strangely (*Er-Messen*), turns it, so to speak, against itself so that measuring is no longer a project of familiarization, of making sense of the place, shedding light on it, mapping it out, mastering it, making it safe; rather it is as if measuring were now a reversal of this process of settling or civilizing that brings the earth to order and control. For poetry measures the world not in terms of the familiar but in terms of what is alien and inaccessible—called here, after Hölderlin, "the Unknown One [*Unbekannte*]" (VA 191/222), that is, the god in the archaic sense of that which is absolutely other.

This strange measure-taking, taking the measure of the familiar by the strange, is what makes poetry itself strange, something entirely different from what we take to be the object of study in our schools, where we try to rewrite texts like *Finnegans Wake* in order to be able to reinsert them into the order of signification from which they have withdrawn themselves. Poetic measuring is not representational-calculative, not sense- or worldmaking. It resists the reduction of the Other to the Same. Poetry is itself essentially mysterious, something not our own but set apart so that we finally cannot say what it is (VA 193/224). It is that which opens us to the mystery, exposes us to that which manifests itself *as* alien and inaccessible the way (as we have seen) language speaks *as* that which withholds itself (*worin die Verweigerung des Sprachwesens—spricht* [US 186/80]):

What remains alien to the god, the sight of the sky—this is what is familiar [*Vertraute*] to man. And what is that? Everything that shimmers and blooms in the sky and thus under the sky and thus on earth, everything that sounds and is fragrant, rises and comes —but also everything that goes and stumbles, moans and falls silent, pales and darkens. Into this, which is intimate to man but alien to the god, the unknown imparts himself, in order to remain guarded within it as the unknown. But the poet calls all the brightness of the sights of the sky and every sound of its courses and breezes into the singing word and there makes them shine and ring. Yet the poet, if he is a poet, does not describe the mere appearance of sky and earth. The poet calls, in the sights of the sky, that which in its very self-disclosure causes the appearance of that which conceals itself, and indeed *as* that which conceals itself [*Sichverbergende*]. In the familiar appearance, the poet calls the alien as that to which the invisible imparts itself in order to remain what it is—unknown. [VA 194/225]

I take this passage to mean that, for Heidegger, the poet does not provide man with a clean, well-lighted place in which he is safe from the darkness, but rather that dwelling poetically means living in the open, exposed to "the alien as that to which the invisible imparts itself in order to remain what it is—unknown": exposed, in short, to the absolutely other, not to this or that hidden being, but to self-concealment itself (*Sichverbergende*). Obviously, the "appearance of that which conceals itself . . . *as* that which conceals itself" is just nonsense according to the norms of representational-calculative thinking, whose whole action is the job of worldmaking, that is, the construction of a framework in which everything has a place, where everything connects up with everything else and nothing is excluded except that which cannot be thought. Poetry, however, exposes thinking to what cannot be thought, that is, to the otherness of language, or that which cannot be brought under control. Poetry in this respect is what sets thinking free, turns it loose, emancipates it from philosophy where thinking is shaped into propositions, projects, and programs. The dialogue with poetry is thus not to be thought of as a new way of doing philosophy. Indeed, there is nothing about this dialogue that Plato did not warn us against, for very possibly this way madness lies. Perhaps one could think of the dialogue as what poetic dwelling comes down to, namely an abiding in the company of the other, exposed to the mystery, giving up refuge in the familiar or the same, slipping away into that elsewhere where madfolk are (Hw 320–21/35–36). Poetic dwelling means dwelling with the venturesome ones, the "poets whose song turns our un-protected being into the Open" (Hw 293/140)—turns us loose, lets us go. Poetic dwelling is thus not staying in place; it is wandering. Call it thinking.

So what's the conclusion? One caveat (which I've suggested through-out this book) should finally be registered explicitly. It is widely held, especially among theorists and comparatists, that Heidegger is the phi-losopher of the near and the neighborly, of the home and the hearth, of warmth and shelter, of the folk and the fatherland, of coming-together and belonging and familiarity—all summarized in the slogan, "Language is the House of Being." A single line from Derrida's "The Ends of Man," taken as if it were a final summation, seems responsible in a major way for this common opinion.[9] According to the "meta-phorics of proximity," the poetic is roughly synonymous with "cozy." Readers who have followed me to this point will see that this view is not perhaps *just* a hostile caricature of Heidegger but a caricature that is pretty raw nonetheless—at best a product of loosely reading Heideg-ger against himself, making him say things in a single-minded spirit. Certainly taking Heidegger as a philosopher of home and country, of simple and immediate presence, of unity and totality, is a caricature of Derrida's reading of Heidegger, which is in fact much more compli-cated and unstable than many of Derrida's readers believe. Homecom-ing in Heidegger is at best only another word for lingering; and there is no belonging without apartness, without withdrawal into singularity and darkness. The "metaphorics" of strangeness (just to call it that) seems to me dominant in the later Heidegger *whenever he speaks of lan-guage and poetry,* not to say thinking, that is, whenever he speaks of the truth of these things; it dominates *Unterwegs zur Sprache.* It would not be too much to say that when the later Heidegger speaks of poetry, he undercuts the current ways of reading him; or, to put it another way, when Heidegger speaks of poetry, you have to shut your eyes and strain pretty hard to hear the old story of metaphysics.[10]

All by itself this issue is only mildly interesting, perhaps not very interesting—the incorrigible are incorrigible—but it does help me to explain where my reading of the later Heidegger has left me (for now); or, better, it helps me to explain what I have come round to along the way, which is a picture of the later Heidegger as an essentially comic thinker. This should surprise no one. *Gelassenheit,* after all, is a basic comic principle, older (one is tempted to say) than Being itself, even as the pun is the basic unit of comic discourse, perhaps of every discourse (older than logic). But obviously we are not speaking here of the utopian comedy of wish-fulfillment: Heidegger is not Marx. His is not comedy in the romantic sense of filial unity and social integration, as in the harmony of antagonists emancipated from conflicting desires and settling at last into a warm communal repose; rather it is comic in the darker, more satirical sense of the outsider—the philosophical outcast—who resists "abiding integration" in behalf of scandal and freedom: a nomadic rather than vegetal comedy—a comedy of *eris* rather than *eros,* of rift rather than reconciliation.[11] This means that I take the figure of the wanderer as something other than tragic or pathetic, rather the way I take Hermes, namely as the transgressor or trickster exuberant in release, as Cain freed from the order of things, always leaving worlds behind him—as against the old Oedipus looming ghostlike at every city's gates, carrying his prison with him wherever he goes, brooding upon his failure or success in overcoming metaphysics. The comedy of thinking is its uncontainability, its refusal of control, its lapse from reason (or what we think of as reason), its freedom from the *Ge-Stell,* its nearness to poetry, its ability (which it perhaps shares with poetry) to live with its skepticism. This is the prodigal, nomadic, cold, anarchic comedy from which even Nietzsche pulls up short. I don't think philosophy can make any sense of this. Perhaps it is right for it not to try.

Notes

Preface: From the Orphic to the Hermetic

1 See Victor Hamm, "Roman Ingarden's 'Das Literarische Kunstwerk,'" in *The Critical Matrix*, ed. Paul R. Sullivan (Washington, D. C.: Georgetown Univ. Press, 1961), 171–209.

2 Walter J. Ong, S. J., "Metaphor and the Twinned Vision," in *The Barbarian Within* (New York: Macmillan, 1962), 41–48. But Ong's "twinned vision" is also set against the visualist bias of the New Criticism, since vision for him is a scholastic metaphor for the allegorical power of intellectual judgment —its ability, for example, to grasp in a twinkling the unity of the phoenix and the turtle in the medieval poem of that name. Whereas twinned vision for the rest of us means something like trying to resolve the ambiguity of the duck-rabbit.

3 Not, obviously, the "linguistic turn" of analytic philosophy, or anyhow not just that, but the turn that, most famously, J. Hillis Miller made on his way from *Poets of Reality* (1965) to *The Linguistic Moment: From Wordsworth to Stevens* (Princeton: Princeton Univ. Press, 1985), with its regulating metaphor of the prison-house of language (which is certainly *the* dominant metaphor of the past quarter-century of literary criticism): "Language is an airy and spacious prison (and the prisoners may bend the bars a little), but it remains a prison all the same" (55). Heidegger won't help you to escape this prison, but he might help you escape this metaphor—at least he will help you to understand why you can't have a theory of language without setting up this metaphor as your brand of metaphysics.

4 (Milwaukee: Marquette Univ. Press, 1960).

5 Trans. Ralph Manheim (New Haven and London: Yale Univ. Press, 1953), 1:91.

6 *Modern Poetry and the Idea of Language: A Critical and Historical Study* (New Haven and London: Yale Univ. Press, 1974). See chap. four above on "The Poetic Experience with Language." The categories of the orphic and hermetic have resurfaced in a very interesting and fruitful way in some of Michael Murray's recent essays, especially "The Conflict Between Poetry and Literature," in *Philosophy and Literature* 9 (April 1985): 59–79. The conflict, Murray says, is between a formalist or aesthetic idea of literature and a "hermeneutic" idea of poetry. "Literature is governed by the principle of *aesthetic differentiation,* that is, by the demarcation of literary art as a separate domain cleansed from all practical and theoretical con-

siderations, from all ontology, ethics, politics, and religion, and their texts. This negatively defined rule secures for literature its autonomy and independence as a cultural value, but also denotes its impotency and loss of significant place. By contrast the hermeneutic conception of poetry is framed in inclusionary terms according to which poetry is any creative saying that gathers together and releases into appearance the manifold of reality. Though nondifferentiationist in this regard, such an approach does not debar poetic language from a distinctive nature of its own, namely as being the kind of language that can gather together, juxtapose, and disclose" (68). It is this hermeneutic conception—what Murray calls the "hermeneutics of the world"—that emerges from Heidegger's Hölderlin interpretation. See Murray, "The Signs of the Time: Heidegger's Hermeneutic Reading of Hölderlin," in *The Eighteenth Century* 21 (1980): 41–66, and "The Hermeneutics of the World," in *Hermeneutics and Deconstruction*, ed. Hugh Silverman and Don Idhe (Albany: State Univ. of New York Press, 1985), 91–105. The later Heidegger shows the darker side of this conception—what one might call a "hermeneutics of the earth."

7 If, following Hegel, one thinks of signification as an annihilation of things by means of concepts, then speaking that disrupts signification would be a way of preserving things—or, as the later Heidegger would say, letting them be. For someone like Blanchot, letting-be would not be a way of going beyond skepticism, much less a way of refuting it, but of stepping back into it and living it. See *Modern Poetry and the Idea of Language*, 199–205. I try to work this out a little further in an essay on Blanchot, "Language and Power," in *Chicago Review* 34 (1984): 27–43, and again above, chap. four. As I indicate, *Estrangements* is an attempt to work through this dialectic as it plays itself out in Heidegger's later writings, where the hermetic darkness of poetry, its openness to the otherness of language, its belongingness to the uncanny and the strange, is a way of letting beings be (*Gelassenheit*).

8 I remember being very much influenced by Vincent Vycinas, *Earth and Gods: An Introduction to the Philosophy of Martin Heidegger* (The Hague: Martinus Nijhoff, 1961), which did not, however, have the opportunity to treat the later texts on language. Neither obviously did the older studies by Hölderlin experts like Else Buddeberg, *Heidegger und die Dichtung: Hölderlin, Rilke* (Stuttgart: J. B. Metzlersche, 1953), and Beda Alleman, *Hölderlin und Heidegger* (Zürich: Atlantis, 1954). In many respects Heidegger studies are only now catching up with the later Heidegger. Otto Pöggeler's magisterial study, *Der Denkweg Martin Heideggers* (Pfullingen: Günther Neske, 1963), similarly separates the questions of poetry and language, and *Sage* is discussed only very summarily at the end of the book, of which we now have a translation: *Martin Heidegger's Path of Thinking*, trans. Daniel Magurshak and Sigmund Barber (Atlantic Highlands, N. J.: Humanities Press, 1987). See esp. 167–90: for Pöggeler, poetry and art in Heidegger's thinking belong to the category of "seminality," but I think

this holds mainly for Heidegger's Hölderlin-interpretation, not for Heideggerian aesthetics or for his later reflections on language and poetry. See also Pöggeler's important essay, "Heideggers Begegnung mit Hölderlin," in *Man and World* 10 (1977): 13–61. I find myself preferring Derrida's figure of dissemination. The relation of *Dichten* and *Sage* in Heidegger's later writings is not treated in any substantive way in the essays by Walter Biemel, "Poetry and Language in Heidegger," and Henri Birault, "Thinking and Poetizing in Heidegger," in *On Heidegger and Language*, ed. and trans. Joseph Kockelmans (Evanston: Northwestern Univ. Press, 1972), 65–106, 147–68. The most helpful contribution to this volume is Werner Marx's "Poetic Dwelling and the Role of the Poet," principally 239–43, on the relation of poetry to the double nature of *alētheia;* but Marx's essay seems to me essentially quotation and paraphrase. The later Heidegger is not a factor in Paul de Man's very influential (but very misleading) essay, "Heidegger's Exegesis of Hölderlin," trans. Wlad Godzich *Blindness and Insight*, 2d ed. (Minneapolis: Univ. of Minnesota Press, 1983), 246–66. See below, n. 30. Among the younger commentators, the centrality of the Hölderlin essays is reaffirmed by Michael Murray in the essays cited above (n. 6), and also in his earlier useful discussion of Heidegger in *Modern Critical Theory: A Phenomenological Introduction* (The Hague: Martinus Nijhoff, 1975), 143–202, which makes a strong effort to treat the middle Heidegger's notion of poetry against the background of modern literary criticism and which is very good on the kinship between Heidegger and Wallace Stevens. Murray rightly emphasizes the orphic, antiformalist dimension of Heidegger's thinking (see esp. 176–84), but, as will become clear, I do not follow him when he speaks of the "fundamental semantics of the later Heidegger" (197). The idea of poetry as foundational for the world is also developed by David Haliburton in *Poetic Thinking: An Approach to Heidegger* (Chicago: Univ. of Chicago Press, 1981). Like Murray, Haliburton does not ignore the later writings, but these are incidental to his main concern, which is with Heidegger's Hölderlin-interpretation. This interpretation is also what mainly interests Robert Bernasconi in *The Question of Language in Heidegger's History of Being* (Atlantic Highlands, N. J.: Humanities Press, 1985), 29–47; so also Christopher Fynsk in *Heidegger: Thought and Historicity* (Ithaca: Cornell Univ. Press, 1986), which has an excellent chapter on the Hölderlin-interpretation (174–229). A mildly deconstructive study of Heidegger's appropriation of Hölderlin by Andrzej Warminski, *Readings in Interpretation: Hölderlin, Hegel, Heidegger* (Minneapolis: Univ. of Minnesota Press, 1987), 45–71, situates Heidegger's Hölderlin-interpretation squarely within the categories of *Being and Time* and, more fruitfully, "What is Metaphysics?" A fine but all too brief exception to the rule of Heidegger studies is Véronique Fóti's "The Path of the Stranger: On Heidegger's Interpretation of Georg Trakl," *Review of Existential Psychology & Psychiatry* 17, nos. 2 and 3 (1986): 223–33, which I discuss in the conclusion. Hwa Yol Jung has an interesting essay, "Martin Heidegger and the Homecoming of Oral Poetry," in *Philosophy Today* 26, no. 2 (Summer 1982): 148–70, which emphasizes, in the spirit of Walter Ong, the priority of the oral over *écriture,* and of the hand over the eye, in Heidegger, who needs to be understood (says Hwa Yol Jung) in terms of pre- and postliterate categories of linguistic reflection.

9 I mean this as a theoretical observation rather than as a thesis that criticism should feel necessary to demonstrate. Working out this observation critically might be an interesting dissertation project, but I expect that the critic would shortly find herself demonstrating the obvious. However, I do try my hand at mediating the distance between Joyce and Heidegger in an essay on "The Otherness of Words: Joyce, Bakhtin, Heidegger," in *Continental Philosophy,* vol. 3, ed. Hugh Silverman (London: Routledge & Kegan Paul, forthcoming).

10 See Fred R. Dallmayr, "Heidegger, Hölderlin, and Politics," in *Heidegger Studies* 2 (1986): 81–96; and Bernasconi, *The Question of Language in Heidegger's History of Being,* 29–47. Dallmayr contextualizes Heidegger's Hölderlin-interpretation historically and politically, whereas Bernasconi contextualizes it within what he sees as Heidegger's larger philosophical program—the overcoming of aesthetics, metaphysics, and so forth.

11 Some examples old and new: J. L. Mehta's much-admired *The Philosophy of Martin Heidegger* (New York: Harper & Row, 1971 [rev. ed.]) ignores the subject of poetry completely, as does one of the most interesting books on Heidegger in years, Reiner Schürmann's *Heidegger on Being and Acting: From Principles to Anarchy* [1982], trans. Christine-Marie Gros (Bloomington: Indiana Univ. Press, 1987). Schürmann's neglect of *Dichten* is the more surprising because the subject (as I think my book will incidentally show) is indispensable to his whole project of understanding human practice as "without why." It is the more strange because Schürmann proposes to read Heidegger backward, that is, from the later to the earlier rather than according to customary practice, which is to build the later Heidegger into the categories of *Being and Time.* But in reading backward Schürmann hardly mentions the lectures on language and poetry in *Unterwegs zur Sprache*—he cites them occasionally in footnotes. Unlike most other Heideggerians, however, Schürmann is not ignorant of how *Dichten* is to be taken in Heideigger's thinking (namely, as a pun [12]), but the question of poetry is no less trivial for him—and necessarily so: one can't take this question seriously and then expect to be taken seriously as a philosopher. One of the most valuable readings of the later Heidegger so far (a reading that double-crosses him with Derrida), John Caputo's *Radical Hermeneutics: Repetition, Deconstruction, and the Hermeneutic Project* (Bloomington: Indiana Univ. Press, 1987), ignores the subject almost completely. Poetry is dispatched with two lines from the medieval poet, Angelus Silesius (which,

Caputo will say, tell us all we need to know about poetry—a half-truth at best):

> The rose is without why; it blooms because it blooms;
> It cares not for itself, asks not if it's seen.   [224]

Two recent collections of Heidegger studies tell pretty much the same story. *Heidegger*, ed. Michael Haar (Paris: L'Herne, 1983), contains an interesting essay on Heidegger and the sacred by Jean Greisch, "Hölderlin et le chemin vers de sacré" (403–15), but the place of poetry in the later Heidegger is not an issue. More valuable perhaps is Marc Froment-Meurice's "L'art moderne et la technique" (302–14), which makes an attempt to connect "The Origin of the Work of Art" to the avant-garde. *Martin Heidegger —Unterwegs zur Denken*, ed. Richard Wisser (Freiburg and Munich: Karl Alber, 1987), brings together a number of excellent essays from a symposium commemorating Heidegger's death in 1976—particularly M. Eiho Kawahara's "Heideggers Auslegung der Langeweile" (87–110)—but again poetry is a nonsubject.

12 See Gadamer, *Wer bin ich und wer bist du? Commentar zu Celans "Atemkristall"* (Frankfurt: Suhrkamp, 1973; 2d. ed. 1986); and Pöggeler, *Spur des Worts: zur Lyrik Paul Celans* (Freiburg and Munich: Karl Alber, 1986). See Pöggeler's remarks on Gadamer's *Wer bin ich und wer bist du*, 179–81; and on Celan and Heidegger, 259–68.

13 "Poets and Thinkers: Their Kindred Roles in the Philosophy of Martin Heidegger," in *Phenomenology and Existentialism*, ed. Edward N. Lee and Maurice Mandelbaum (Baltimore: Johns Hopkins Univ. Press, 1967), 109.

14 (Lincoln: Univ. of Nebraska Press, 1978), 77. See my review of White's book, *Canadian Review of Comparative Literature* 9 (1982): 90–96. People scold me for being so hard on White's book, and for failing to sense the philosophical urgency of his argument, for which an independent experience of poetry, much less an interest in it, is not necessary. His book is after all meant for philosophers, not for people like me, which in a sense is my whole point: it's a book A. J. Ayer (whose loathing for Heidegger is notorious) would admire.

15 (Bloomington: Indiana Univ. Press, 1984), 206.

16 The relation of language and poetry enters the discourse of philosophy only in the form of the passing mention. See, for example, Ronald Bruzina, "Heidegger on the Metaphor and Philosophy," in *Heidegger and Modern Philosophy*, ed. Michael Murray (New Haven and London: Yale Univ. Press, 1978), 197–200. Murray's volume excludes the subject of poetry except for these three pages, where Bruzina tries to raise the question of what the relation of poetry and thinking might amount to in Heidegger; but Bruzina does no more than quote without comment Heidegger's own words. The question of what poetry could be that it should bear a funda-

mental relation to *Sage*, and therefore belong together with thinking, has no reality for philosophy. The reason, of course, is that philosophers, after all, are interested in *Denken*, not *Dichten*, so that even in the most thoughtful discussions of Heidegger's notion of language—those, for example, which take up the way "language and reversal belong together"—the question of poetry still gets excluded except perhaps for a nod of courtesy to Hölderlin. See John Sallis's valuable essay, "Language and Reversal," in *Martin Heidegger in America*, ed. Edward G. Ballard and Charles E. Scott (The Hague: Martinus Nijhoff, 1973), 129–45. Sallis, however, has two good paragraphs on "renunciation" as the poet's relation to language in "Towards the Showing of Language," in *Thinking about Being: Aspects of Heidegger's Thought*, ed. Robert W. Shahan and J. N. Mahonty (Norman: Univ. of Oklahoma Press, 1984), 78–89. The poet's renunciation of language is touched on by Bernasconi in *The Question of Language in the History of Being* (53)—a rare discussion of Heidegger's readings of Stefan George's poem, "Das Wort" (which Bernasconi quite properly situates in the context of "Was ist Metaphysik?"). However, with all respect to these intelligent pieces of work, I think that our understanding of the later Heidegger remains quite superficial because poetry is just not a philosophical subject among Heidegger's commentators, who have never put themselves in a position to know what on earth Heidegger could be talking about.

17 *Labyrinths: Selected Stories & Other Writings*, ed. Donald A. Yates and James E. Irby (New York: New Directions, 1964), 149.

18 *Earth and Gods*, 267–77.

19 In *After the New Criticism* (Chicago: Univ. of Chicago Press, 1980), Frank Lentricchia summarizes the general view when he says "Heidegger's romantic exaltation of poetic language places his thought as yet one more, perhaps culminating, repetition of a visionary theory of the poet" (97). I think a careful reading of the later Heidegger will make it difficult to go on holding this view.

20 See Werner Marx, *Is There a Measure on Earth: Foundations for a Non-Metaphysical Ethics* (Chicago: Univ. of Chicago Press, 1987), 154. Marx says quite rightly that for later Heidegger the poets are *die Entsprechenden*, "i.e., those who respond. They respond not only to the 'content,' however, but also to the *alētheia*-structure of saying." I want to press the idea that the *alētheia*-structure is that of the pun. As John Caputo says, truth in the later Heidegger is not Wahrheit nor even *Alētheia* with a capital "A" but *a-lētheia* (*Radical Hermeneutics*, 177).

21 The question of poetry in Heidegger tends to get swallowed up in accounts of his aesthetics, especially those that try to situate him in the history of aesthetics since Kant or, more generally still, within the academic discipline of the philosophy of art, in which the subject of poetry doesn't count for much. See Sandra Lee Bartky, "Heidegger's Philosophy of Art," in *Martin Heidegger: Man and Thinker*, ed. Thomas Sheehan (Chicago: Precedent

Publishing, 1981), 257–74. Bartky examines "The Origin of the Work of Art," she says, "not primarily for the light it sheds upon Heidegger's later ontology, but in its own right as an independent contribution to our understanding of the nature of art" (257). By contrast, I read the essay in light of the later writings for the light it sheds on them.

22 I tried to point out this kinship in "Structuralism, Deconstruction, Hermeneutics," in *Diacritics* 14 (1984): 21–22.

23 *Martin Heidegger's Path of Thinking*, 224: "Sigetics (the name is meant only for those who need titles and classifications everywhere) points toward the essence of language . . . ."

24 Quoted by Pöggeler, *Martin Heidegger's Path of Thinking*, 283.

25 On Heidegger's aestheticism, where aestheticism means withdrawal from social and political reality, see Allan Megill, *Prophets of Extremity: Nietzsche, Heidegger, Foucault, Derrida* (Berkeley and Los Angeles: Univ. of California Press, 1985), 142–80. See Pöggeler, *Philosophie und Politic bei Heidegger* (Freiburg and Munich: Karl Alber, 1972), 121–22. Against the dominant view, John Caputo argues that, despite its "hermetic" character, Heidegger's later philosophy remains distinct from mysticism and poetry. The hermetic is a step back or withdrawal of philosophy from the domain of instrumental reason, but not from social and political reality. "The technical world threatens to consume us, and Heidegger's writings are a summons to find a new possibility in the midst of an all too present and suffocating actuality. Indeed on no point has Heidegger been more unjustly criticized than on the question of his alleged anti-humanism. To my knowledge there is no more eloquent, powerful, and penetrating defense of the humanity of man in the Twentieth Century than is to be found in Heidegger's later writings." *The Mystical Element in Heidegger's Thought* (Athens, Ohio: Ohio Univ. Press, 1978), 263–64. In *After the New Criticism* Frank Lentricchia characterizes Heidegger as an aesthetic humanist—or anyhow says that "Heidegger's existential humanism celebrates as its ultimate category of value the aesthetic" (96)—where "aesthetic" means essentially a romantic mythologizing of art and poetry at the expense of the social and historical. My own account of the "aesthetic" in Heidegger tends to go against this characterization, since I see Heidegger as critical of the outlook of aesthetic humanism and emphasize the way the critique of instrumental reason is developed essentially out of "The Origin of the Work of Art." What remains arguable is whether this critique is adequate according to the standards of critical reason that come down from Marx. There is no doubt that Heidegger's critique of representational-calculative thinking entails a critique of critical theory (a "critique of critique") as well as of scientific, analytic, and managerial reasoning. So it's up for grabs whether Heidegger is radical or reactionary. There will always be endless quarrels over Heidegger and the meaning of historicality in his writings. Foucauldians, for example, see Heidegger's critique as mainly empty because it is

not mediated by a questioning of specific institutions, but I see Foucault as fundamentally Heideggerian with respect to the exclusionary and repressive character of what we take to be normal, institutionally sanctioned exercises of reason.

26 *The Rule of Metaphor: Multidisciplinary Studies in the Creation of Meaning in Language,* trans. Robert Czerny, et al. (Toronto: Univ. of Toronto Press, 1977), 311–14. Ricoeur tries to separate authentic speculative thinking in the later Heidegger from the poetized logic that "leads to a series of erasures and repeals that cast thought into the void, reducing it to hermeticism and affectedness, carrying etymological games back to the mystification of 'primitive sense.'" What Ricoeur deplores specifically is the way Heidegger "sever[s] discourse from its propositional character" (313). I think of my book as an exact counterstatement to Ricoeur's view of the later Heidegger. Ricoeur's philosophical rigidity with respect to Heidegger comes as a surprise to me, since what I have always admired in Ricoeur is the profound sympathy with which he understands thinkers whose outlook differs (sometimes even radically) from his own.

27 Joseph Riddel sticks in my mind as the spokesman of the *consensus gentium* in "From Heidegger to Derrida to Chance: Doubling and (Poetic) Language," in *Martin Heidegger and the Question of Literature: Toward a Postmodern Literary Hermeneutics,* ed. William V. Spanos (Bloomington: Indiana Univ. Press, 1979): "Even for the literary critic, the basic Heidegger text remains *Being and Time*" (235). And again: "Heidegger's later method [!], fully embracing poetic language as originary speech [?], has become increasingly less useful for literary criticism" (239). It's surprising to read through the Spanos volume and to see how marginal the later Heidegger is to the concerns of its contributors, and how consistently the later thinking is translated back into the categories of *Being and Time*. See particularly Albert Hofstadter's contribution, "Enownment," 17–37. For the exception, however, see n. 29 below.

28 In *Inventions: Writing, Textuality, and Understanding in Literary History* (New Haven and London: Yale Univ. Press, 1982), I proposed to try out a sort of criticism that could be called "rhetorical, because it is more concerned with finding than with proving, is more speculative than analytical, more heuristic than polemical, the more so as it requires a discourse that proceeds thoughtfully, even copiously, but not necessarily with great method or system" (1): a criticism, in other words, that withdraws from the marketplace of "approaches" or "methods" of textual analysis into a reflection on subjects or topics (*res*) that need opening up or working out as occasions require.

29 The single, most telling exception to this that I'm aware of is Donald Marshall's essay, "The Ontology of the Literary Sign: Notes Toward a Heideggerian Revision of Semiology," in *Martin Heidegger and the Question of*

Literature, 271–94. This is quite possibly the best study of the later Heidegger by a literary critic to date.

30 In an interview in *The Yale Review* 73 (1984): 602. Almost certainly what de Man wanted to say is the Heidegger was very suspicious about the *concept* of metaphor. But there is no doubt that de Man was very suspicious of the later Heidegger and that he held fast to the picture of Heidegger that he developed in his early essay, "Heidegger's Exegeses of Hölderlin," where he has Heidegger holding the view that language is "the immediate presence of Being" (*Blindness and Insight*, 253). De Man thinks this is self-contradictory, "for as soon as the word is uttered, it destroys the immediate and discovers that instead of stating Being, it can only state mediation" (259). Hölderlin, on de Man's reading, understood this problem, but Heidegger overrides it by misreading Hölderlin ("it is the fact that Hölderlin says exactly the opposite of what Heidegger makes him say" [254–55]), and so "keeps running into the very question he thought he had resolved, but which, for Hölderlin, must remain without answer: if the poet has seen Being immediately, how is he to put it into language?" (261). My own view is that Heidegger never thought of poetry and language in these terms, and that the notion of putting Being into language is very far from Heidegger. De Man also sees hidden theological motives in Heidegger, and has him "identifying" language and the sacred, as if Being were a secret divinity (a Johannine Logos). I think Gadamer is closer to the point when he says that "beings are not correctly defined in their being if they are defined merely as objects of representation. Rather, it belongs just as much to their being that they withhold themselves. As unhidden, truth has in itself an inner tension and ambiguity. Being contains something like a hostility to its own presentations, as Heidegger says" (*Philosophical Hermeneutics*, trans. David E. Linge [Berkeley and Los Angeles: Univ. of California Press, 1976], 226). So there can be no question of "stating Being" or putting Being "into language." The question is rather how language enters into the withholding of things, their withdrawal or self-refusal. De Man's understanding of Heidegger is treated, and also somewhat corrected in light of the later Heidegger, by Jacques Derrida, *Memoires for Paul de Man* (New York: Columbia Univ. Press, 1986), 96–98.

31 See Mikhail Bakhtin, "From the Prehistory of the Novel," trans. Caryl Emerson and Michael Holquist (Austin: Univ. of Texas Press, 1981), 21–26, on the Socratic dialogue as a prefiguration of the novel, where the novel is understood as an essentially parodic, linguistically heterogeneous and unstable genre.

32 See Hans-Georg Gadamer, "Notes on Planning for the Future," in *Daedalus* (Spring 1966): 572–89.

Introduction: Understanding Heidegger

1 "Martin Heidegger: The Great Influence" (1959), *Philosophical-Political Profiles*, trans. Frederick G. Lawrence (Cambridge, Mass., and London: The MIT Press, 1983), 55.

2 What I propose, in other words, is something like a close reading, but (as I try to make clear in this introduction) not of a technically analytical sort—neither old rhetoric or new. For a traditional grammatical and rhetorical analysis of Heidegger's language, see Erasmus Schofer, *Die Sprache Heideggers* (Pfullingen: Günther Neske, 1962), part of which is available in English translation in *On Heidegger and Language*, 281–301. See n. 5 below.

3 David White, *Heidegger and the Language of Poetry*, 215.

4 Here the English language fails us: there is no English equivalent of *dichten,* to poetry, and so some people (mainly philosophers) improvise with the word "poetize." And unfailingly the assumption is that poets "poetize," rather the way they sing or write—but that is not how the later Heidegger (in contrast to the middle Heidegger of the Hölderlin essays) figures it. *Dichten* is not an act of a subject, not a performative, not a process of creativity or imagination or figuration, not the main theme of poetics: not, in other words, *poiēsis.* Better to say that "poetry poetries," silly as it may sound.

5 See *Margins of Philosophy*, trans. Alan Bates (Chicago: Univ. of Chicago Press, 1972), 27. I think that Derrida's reading of Heidegger is more complicated and unfinished (and therefore unpredictable) than many people believe. In "The Anaximander Fragment" Heidegger says: "in order to name the essential nature of Being, language would have to find a single word, the unique word. From this we can gather how daring [*gewagt*] every thoughtful word [*denkende Wort*] addressed to Being is. Nevertheless such daring is not impossible, since Being speaks always and everywhere throughout language. The difficulty lies not so much in finding in thought the word for Being as in retaining purely in genuine thinking the word found" (Hw 337/52). It's a caricature of Heidegger's thinking to say that this primal word is the object of his philosophical quest, his philosopher's stone, the magical word that will make Being show itself at last after the whole history of metaphysics has failed to flush it out of hiding. I think it is Heidegger's point (as it is also Derrida's) that if there is such a word (and it is not clear what it means for this to be the case), that word is just what always withholds itself, refuses itself, remains unspeakable and strange—the word as absolutely other, which explodes every order of signification that we construct in order to subdue it. The task of thinking is not to remove this strangeness but to enter into it, to turn itself loose in the otherness of language, risk itself (its sanity, its ability to do philosophy) by letting go of what is securely grounded. Poetry teaches thinking how to do this; poetry turns the thinker into a wanderer. I see the later Heidegger

as being closer to Derrida, or Derrida closer to the later Heidegger, than perhaps Derrida does, certainly closer than many of Derrida's readers see him. Most readings of Derrida flatten him out by ignoring or understating the close bearing of the later Heidegger on Derrida's texts. This is true even of such superb studies as Rodolphe Gasché's *The Tain of the Mirror: Derrida and the Philosophy of Reflection* (Cambridge, Mass.: Harvard Univ. Press, 1986), where the principal Heidegger text for understanding Derrida remains *Being and Time* (I do not think this would be Derrida's opinion).

At all events, Derrida remains the most brilliant and stimulating reader of Heidegger that we have, and the only one who attends to Heidegger's language in an interesting way. Most people speak as if Derrida has done away with Heidegger—has outstripped him—but I see Derrida as saving the Heideggerian text in Geoffrey Hartman's sense of this phrase (that is, as reading him with a "Conscious Ear" (*Saving the Text: Literature/Derrida/ Philosophy* [Baltimore: Johns Hopkins Univ. Press, 1981], 141). This comes out more forcefully in the later readings, or what, following Heidegger, I would prefer to call "listenings," particularly "*Geschlecht:* sexual difference, ontological difference," in *Research in Phenomenology* 13 (1983): 65–83, and "*Geschlecht II*: Heidegger's Hand," trans. John P. Leavey, Jr., in *Deconstruction and Philosophy: The Texts of Jacques Derrida*, ed. John Sallis (Chicago: Univ. of Chicago Press, 1987), 161–96. One of Derrida's most important readings so far is *De l'esprit: Heidegger et la question* (Paris: Galilée, 1987), esp. 131–59 (on Heidegger's *Gespräch* with Trakl's poetry).

6 This, if I understand, is Richard Rorty's view, as in "Deconstruction and Circumvention," *Critical Inquiry* 11 (1984): 1–23. Heidegger, Rorty says, "had only one theme: the need to overcome metaphysics. Once that theme came to seem self-deceptive, he was left speechless" (10), which is all that the later Heidegger amounts to (with his empty incantations of *Sein, Ereignis,* and *Alêtheia*). For Rorty, Heidegger's withdrawal into poetry and magic, that is, into the mere sound of words, is absurd and self-defeating, since by doing such a thing he simply excludes himself, to no purpose, from the communicative praxis that holds philosophers together. The same criticism applies to Derrida, who simply carries out Heidegger's program of estrangement in a different style, one that emphasizes the differential features of writing rather than the indeterminacy of puns, obsolete words, and untranslatable expressions from antiquity. In effect, Rorty shifts from theoretical to practical grounds (but otherwise holds in place) the judgment that analytic philosophy brought against Heidegger as long ago as Carnap's famous paper, "The Overcoming of Metaphysics through Logical Analysis of Language" (reprinted in Murray's *Heidegger and Modern Philosophy*, 23–34).

7 Theodor Adorno, *The Jargon of Authenticity*, trans. Knut Tarnowski and Frederic Will (Evanston, Ill.: Northwestern Univ. Press, 1973); on Adorno's

reading of Heidegger, see Fred R. Dallmayr, *Critical Encounters* (Notre Dame, Ind.: Univ. of Notre Dame Press, 1987), 57–72. Hermann Mörchen has produced the obligatory massive (716 pages) study of the Heidegger-Adorno relation, *Adorno and Heidegger: Untersuchung einer philosophischen Kommunikationsverweigerung* (Stuttgart: Klett-Cotta, 1981).

8 See Stephen Watson, "Reading Heidegger," in *Research in Phenomenology* 15 (1985): 235–46, who makes roughly this point in reviewing a volume of Heidegger recollections and studies that recently appeared in France, *Heidegger*, ed. Michel Haar (Paris: L'Herne, 1983).

9 I am grateful to Betty Roitman of Hebrew University for pointing out to me the way Heidegger's excessiveness becomes a perfect example of *délire*, which is Jean-Jacques Lecercle's word in *Philosophy Through the Looking-Glass: Language, Nonsense, Desire* (La Salle, Ill.: Open Court, 1985), 6: "*Délire* as I shall now use the word is a form of discourse, which questions our most common conceptions of *language* (whether expressed by linguists or philosophers), where the old philosophical question of the emergence of sense out of *nonsense* receives a new formulation, where the material side of language, its origin in the human body and *desire*, are no longer eclipsed by its abstract aspect (as an instrument of communication or expression)." *Délire* is a word that can be taken very much in a Heideggerian spirit. In addition to being a pun on the word for reading it is a perfect word for the excessiveness or uncontainability of the later Heidegger, who escapes the frameworks, systems, or disciplinary cultures to which he nevertheless belongs.

10 See Cavell, "Politics—As Opposed to What?" in *The Politics of Interpretation*, ed. W. J. T. Mitchell (Chicago: Univ. of Chicago Press, 1983), 197.

11 See Gadamer's discussion of the negativity of hermeneutical experience in *Truth and Method*, 316–20. Much of what I say in the next few pages derives from this analysis, which I have tried to clarify further in a paper on "The Tragedy of Hermeneutical Experience," in *Research in Phenomenology*, 18 (November 1988).

12 See John D. Caputo, "Heidegger and Derrida: Cold Hermeneutics," *Journal of the British Society for Phenomenology* 17 (1986): 252–74; rev. and repr. in *Radical Hermeneutics*, 187–206. I see Gadamer as being closer to the "radical hermeneutics" of Heidegger and Derrida than Caputo does. Radical hermeneutics means exposure to the difficulties, not to say the horror, of existence. The question (which I can't settle here) is whether Gadamer steps back at some point from the horror into the cozy warmth of metaphysics. In any case it is not true that for Gadamer hermeneutics is essentially a "postal service."

13 I try to make something like this point in "Structuralism, Deconstruction, Hermeneutics," *Diacritics* 14 (1984): 12–23. See also Derrida, *Memoires for Paul de Man*, 16: "deconstruction is inseparable from a general questioning

of *tekhnē* and technicist reasoning . . . and . . . is anything *but* a set of technical and systematic procedures."

14 That is, no *modern* philosophy. See the chapter on "Secrecy and Understanding" in *Inventions*, where the category of the secret is what distinguishes philosophy from rhetoric.

15 See *The Fragility of Goodness* (Cambridge: Cambridge Univ. Press, 1986), 195–99.

16 Dallmayr, *Politics and Praxis: Exercises in Contemporary Political Theory* (Cambridge, Mass., and London: The MIT Press, 1984), 104. Cited in the text below as PP. See also Dallmayr's "Heidegger, Hölderlin, and Politics," in *Heidegger Studies* 2 (1986): 81–96. Heidegger's "The Self-Assertion of the German University" and his later reflection, "The Rectorate 1933/34: Facts and Thoughts," have been translated by Karsten Harries in *The Review of Metaphysics* 38 (1985): 467–502. For the idea that after 1933 Heidegger withdrew from politics into the closed world of aestheticism, see Otto Pöggeler, *Philosophie und Politik bei Heidegger* (Freiburg and Munich: Karl Alber, 1972), 15–70. See Graeme Nicholson, "The Politics of Heidegger's Rectoral Address," *Man and World* 20 (1987): 171–81.

17 *Literary Theory: An Introduction* (Minneapolis: Univ. of Minnesota Press, 1983), pp. 63–64.

18 Whereas perhaps the opposite is the case, which is what John Bailiff suggests in "Truth and Power: Martin Heidegger, 'The Essence of Truth,' and 'The Self-Assertion of the German University,'" in *Man and World* 20 (1987): 327–36. The intuition that there is some intrinsic connection between Heidegger's "philosophy" and his political behavior needs to be worked through from many directions. I don't think we have made much of an effort to do this yet, in large part because we don't know how. Victor Farias's *Heidegger et le nazisme*, trans. Myriam Benarroch and Jean-Baptiste Grasset (Paris: Editions Verdier, 1987), esp. 291–301, is provocative but still intuitive. Mainly it persuades us of what no one has much difficulty in imagining, namely that from one end of his life to the other Heidegger was pretty much your basic European anti–Semite. The Holocaust did not touch him, much less make him draw back in horror at his own image.

19 In an essay on Levinas, "Our Clandestine Companion," Maurice Blanchot writes parenthetically: "Nazism and Heidegger, this is a wound in thought itself, and each of us is profoundly wounded—it will not be dealt with by preterition." See *Face to Face with Levinas*, ed. Richard Cohen (Albany: State Univ. of New York Press, 1986), 43.

20 "Words and Wounds," 118–57. See Gerald L. Bruns, "Writing Literary Criticism," *The Iowa Review* 12(4) (Fall 1981): 23–43.

21 "To What Extent Does Language Preform Thought?" (TM 496).

22 Dan Pagis, *Points of Departure*, trans. Stephen Mitchell (Philadelphia: The Jewish Publication Society of America, 5472/1981), 25; cited hereafter as PD.

23 Trans. C. Lenhardt (London and New York: Routledge & Kegan Paul, 1984), 333.

24 *Must We Mean What We Say?* (Cambridge: Cambridge Univ. Press, 1969), 313–14. Cited in the text below as MWM.

25 *Otherwise than Being*, trans. Alphonso Lingis (The Hague: Martinus Nijhoff, 1981), 59.

26 "Martin Heidegger at Eighty," in *Heidegger and Modern Philosophy*, 302n.

27 "Heidegger as a Political Thinker," in *Heidegger and Modern Philosophy*, 304–28.

28 I mean untheorizable here in the sense in which Hubert Dreyfus uses the term in "Holism and Hermeneutics," in *Hermeneutics and Praxis*, ed. Robert Hollinger (Notre Dame, Ind.: Univ. of Notre Dame Press, 1985), 227–47.

29 See *Being and Time*, sect. 31 and 32, where understanding is not a mental act but the condition of belonging to or being in the world. As Gadamer says, "The issue here is not simply that a nonobjectifying consciousnessness always accompanies the process of understanding, but rather that understanding is not suitably conceived at all as a consciousness of something" (*Philosophical Hermeneutics*, 125). See also Gadamer, *Truth and Method*, 419–20: "If we are seeking a right definition of the idea of belongingness between subject and object we are here concerned with, we must take account of the particular dialectic that is contained in hearing."

Chapter One: The Aesthetics of Estrangement

1 Reiner Schürmann, in *Heidegger on Being and Acting*, proposes reading Heidegger backward by situating *Being and Time*, for example, in the context of the later writings, rather than the orthodox method of mapping the later Heidegger onto the projects and frameworks set in place in the twenties and early thirties. On the whole I think that this is a good idea—I think Heidegger studies ought to try to distance itself a little from *Being and Time*—but my choice has been to start out from "The Origin of the Work of Art," because it is here that the uncanniness of truth as *alētheia*, its doubleness as *a-lētheia*, begins to emerge. There is no understanding the relation of language and poetry independently of the strangeness of truth as *a-lētheia*. As I've indicated, however, Schürmann does not really follow very strictly his method of reading Heidegger backward, since he ignores the later texts on language and poetry almost completely, even though (I would have thought) they are central to the question of "action without why" in Heidegger's thinking.

2 "The *Retrait* of Metaphor," trans. F. Gasdner, et al., *Enclitic* 2 (1978): 5–33.

3 *Hermeneutics: Questions and Prospects*, ed. Gary Shapiro and Alan Sica (Amherst: Univ. of Massachusetts Press, 1984), 61.

4 *Modern Poetry and the Idea of Language*, 189–205, on "negative discourse."

Obviously, however, the negative is not just a French appropriation. See, for example, Georg-Michael Schulz, *Negativität in der Dichtung Paul Celans* (Tübingen: Max Niemeyer, 1977), esp. 97–214.

5 However this is to be understood, it is clear that the main purpose of "The Origin of the Work of Art" is to reopen the whole question of the relation of art and truth which the history of aesthetics, not to say of philosophy itself, had shut down (this closing of the question of truth and the work of art is what the first part of Gadamer's *Truth and Method* is all about). It is worth noting that an important part of Heidegger's Nietzsche lectures (volume one on "The Will to Power as Art," sect. 19) carries the title "The Raging Discordance [*erregende Zwiespalt*] between Art and Truth," which is a quotation from one of Nietzsche's notes collected under the title *Will to Power*: "Very early in my life I took the question of the relation of *art* to *truth* seriously: and even now I stand in holy dread in the face of this discordance" [14:368] (NI 166/142). Heidegger does not try to overcome this discordance but to understand it in such a way that discordance no longer means simply antithesis but now requires to be enclosed in quotation marks. "The Origin of the Work of Art" suggests that we can think of "discordance" as that which art "shares" with truth (namely, the *rift*). So Heidegger emancipates himself from (without simply repudiating) the histories of philosophy and criticism, which look in Plato's *Republic*, for example, for the moment of rupture between art and truth. The point is not to close this rupture but to enter into it and abide with it. A fine reading of "The Origin of the Work of Art" from the standpoint of the Nietzsche lectures is given by Christopher Fynsk, *Heidegger: Thought and Historicity*, 131–73—although I would emphasize what Fynsk seems to me to downplay or ignore, namely that Heidegger's aesthetics is a strategic counterstatement to the "Five Statements on Art" that Heidegger uses to summarize Nietzschean aesthetics:

1. Art is the most conspicuous and familiar configuration of will to power.
2. Art must be grasped in terms of the artist.
3. According to the expanded concept of the artist, art is the basic occurrence of all beings; to the extent that they are, beings are self-creating, created.
4. Art is the distinctive countermovement to nihilism.
5. Art is worth more than "truth."

[NI 90/75]

A corresponding (similarly reductive) summary of Heideggerian aesthetics might go like this:

1. Art (as *Dichten*) is *Gelassenheit,* or the renunciation of will to power.
2. Art must be grasped in terms of the work, where *work* is an event rather than a formal object or product of *poiēsis*.

3. Art is not worldmaking but the letting-be of things (*die Gelassenheit zu den Dingen*) or "openness to mystery" (G 23–24/54–55).
4. Art is not anything human. It won't save us.
5. Art is the happening of truth, where truth, however, is not what we think but something otherwise.

It would not be difficult to argue, of course, that these "counterstatements" to Nietzsche are not counterstatements at all but rather belong to what I call Heidegger's "uncanny hermeneutics": the lectures on Nietzsche are not an exegesis of Nietzsche, much less just a misreading of him, but rather a picking-up-on (*Erläuterung*) what Nietzsche says in order to enter into what is not said or is left unthought. But this unthought matter (*Sache*) of aesthetics belongs as much to Nietzsche as to Heidegger. It is not eisegesis, as I try to show in chap. two above. My emphasis on the darkness of the later Heidegger, his otherness or strangeness, could be taken as an effort to bring out what is Nietzschean in his writings on language and poetry, even though nothing of what he says about these subjects can be traced back thematically to Nietzsche, at least not in any interesting way. I think Nietzsche would have found the later Heidegger all but impossible—a Chinese Wall—which is pretty much how he is regarded today. Nietzsche is perhaps more dangerous because easier to get along with, whereas Heidegger seduces nobody, or anyhow few. John D. Caputo seems to me to get the relation of Heidegger to Nietzsche right in "Three Transgressions: Nietzsche, Heidegger, Derrida," in *Research in Phenomenology* 15 (1985): 61–78.

6 See Edward G. Lawry, "The Work-Being of the Work of Art in Heidegger," in *Man and World* 11 (1978): 186–98.

7 *Der Ursprung des Kunstwerkes*, ed. Hans-Georg Gadamer (Stuttgart: Philipp Reclaim, 1960), 102–25.

8 *The Order of Things: An Archeology of the Human Sciences* (New York: Vintage Books, 1973), 300. See *Modern Poetry and the Idea of Language*, 95–100.

9 See Valéry, "Poetry and Abstract Thought" (1939):

Consequently, the perfection of a discourse whose sole aim is comprehension obviously consists in the ease with which the words forming it are transformed into something quite different: the *language* is transformed first into non-language and then, if we wish, into a form of language differing from the original form.

In other terms, in practical or abstract uses of language, the form —that is, the physical, the concrete part, the very act of speech—does not last; it does not outlive understanding; it dissolves in the light; it has acted; it has done its work; it has brought about understanding; it has lived.

But on the other hand, the moment this concrete form takes on, by an effect of its own, such importance that it asserts itself and makes itself, as it were, respected; and not only respected, but desired and therefore repeated—then something new happens: we are insensibly transformed and ready to live, breathe, and think in accordance with a rule and under laws which are no longer of the practical order—that is, nothing that may occur in this state will be resolved, finished, or abolished by a specific act. We are entering the poetic universe.

Trans. Denise Folliot, *The Art of Poetry* (New York: Vintage Books, 1958), 65.

10 See my discussion of Hopkins's "energetic" poetics in *Inventions*, 124–42.

11 Compare Gadamer, *Wer bin ich und wer bist Du?* on the hermetic character of Paul Celan's "Atemkristall": "A poem that withholds itself and does not yield continual clarity always appears to me more meaning-full than any clarity." For a dark poem (this strikes me as a redundancy) is not the same as an empty one, whatever that means.

12 In the first series of Nietzsche lectures Heidegger says that one of the principles of Nietzschean aesthetics is that "Art must be grasped in terms of the Artist" (NI 84/71). In the lecture on "Rapture as Form-Engendering Force" Heidegger writes:

> Nietzsche says (WM 821),—"the effect of artworks is *arousal of the art-creating state, rapture.*" Nietzsche shares this conception with the widely prevalent opinion of aesthetics. On that basis we understand why he demands, logically, that aesthetics conform to the creator, the artist. Observation of works is only a derivative form and offshoot of creation. Therefore what was said of creation corresponds precisely, though derivatively, to observation of art. Enjoyment of the work consists in participation in the creative state of the artist (XIV 136). But because Nietzsche does not unfold the essence of creation from what is to be created, namely, the work; because he develops it from the state of aesthetic behavior; the bringing-forth of the work does not receive an adequately delineated interpretation which would distinguish it from the bringing-forth of utensils by way of handicraft. Not only that. The behavior of observation is not set in relief against creation, and so it remains undefined. The view that the observation of works somehow follows in the wake of creation is so little true that not even the relation of the *artist* to the work as something to be created is one that would be appropriate to the creator. But that could be demonstrated only by way of an inquiry into art that would begin altogether differently, proceeding from the work itself. [NI 137–38/117]

Clearly the account of "createdness" in "The Origin of the Work of Art" can be taken as Heidegger's attempt to produce such a demonstration, if demonstration is the word. "Createdness" is not a formal feature of the work that could be described by an observer; it is not artistry or artificiality or style or any sign of *poiēsis* or show of the artist's hand. Createdness belongs to the work as part of its reserve or self-possession; it concerns the withdrawal of the work, its earthliness or self-refusal.

13 Many will agree with this statement, but there are so many competing historicisms old and new that hardly two people anywhere agree on how the notion of historicality is to be understood. I'm not sure I know of an account of historicality that (1) has not claimed to be the most concrete, and (2) has not been attacked as the most abstract. In "The Origin of the Work of Art," Heidegger characterizes historicality of the work in terms of earth rather than (as in the Hölderlin essays) in terms of world; that is, historicality means here belongingness to the earth, density and resistance; it means refusal of our conceptual designs, our worldly claims and socio-ideological practices. If the work sets up a world, it also withdraws from it and proves uncontainable within the world's horizons. Only a superficial reading of Heidegger would confuse this idea with doctrines of aesthetic purity. On the contrary, the question that is implicit everywhere in the later Heidegger strikes me as central to any notion of historicality that would be of interest to hermeneutics: namely, What are the consequences of our inability to bring the work of art under analytical or interpretive (and therefore socio-ideological) control? What are the consequences of its resistance to appropriation? It would take a good deal of explaining to persuade me that this is not a political question.

14 Nor can one ignore Adorno: "Aesthetics cannot hope to grasp works of art if it treats them as hermeneutical objects. What at present needs to be grasped is their unintelligibility. . . . In negating the spirit of domination, the spirit of art does not manifest itself as spirit *per se* but emerges suddenly in its opposite, i. e. materiality." *Aesthetic Theory*, 173.

15 This is the line that tends to get passed over or indifferently paraphrased in the standard commentaries on Heidegger's essay, because it doesn't fit into the category of "seminality" or orphic origination. See Pöggeler, *Martin Heidegger's Path of Thinking*, 171–74, for a good, brief account, in contrast to the more compendious academic studies by Friedrich-Wilhelm von Herrmann, *Heideggers Philosophie der Kunst: Eine systematische Interpretation der Holzwege-Abhandlung "Der Ursprung des Kunstwerkes"* (Frankfurt: Klostermann, 1980), 317; and Joseph Kockelmans, *Heidegger on Art and Artworks* (Dordrecht: Martinus Nijhoff, 1985), 187. The subject of the estrangement of poetry doesn't come up in Gerhard Faden's *Der Schein der Kunst: Zu Heideggers Kritik der Asthetik* (Würzburg: Königshausen-Neumann, 1986), which is nevertheless an interesting effort to treat the question of aesthetics within the context of Heidegger's whole career. Faden discusses the uncanny (*das Unheimliche*) as this turns up in Heidegger's *Introduction to Metaphysics*. An excellent, provocative study of the earthly in Heidegger's aesthetics is Michel Haar's recent *Le Chant de la Terre* (Paris: L'Herme, 1987), 191–236.

16 I tried to press for this idea in "Stevens without Epistemology," in *Wallace Stevens: The Poetics of Modernism*, ed. Albert Guelpi (Cambridge: Cambridge Univ. Press, 1985), 24–40. There I put the question quite simply: "We know what it is like to read Stevens when we no longer believe in God. What is it to read him when you no longer believe that there is anything like the imagination?" (25). You can imagine the sputter and fury of mainline Stevens critics at such a thought. On the errancy of the history of criticism, see Bruns, "Theory, Practice, and Significance in the Study of Literature," in *Renascence* (forthcoming).

17 See Bernasconi, *The Question of Language in Heidegger's History of Being*, pp. 32–35, on "overcoming aesthetics" in "The Origin of the Work of Art"; and John D. Caputo, "Telling Left from Right: Hermeneutics, Deconstruction, and the Work of Art," in *The Journal of Philosophy* 83 (November 1986): 678–85. Caputo is exactly right when he says that the upshot of Heidegger's aesthetics is to emancipate the work of art—to "let it out of its frame"—and, in the bargain, to set us free, not in the sense of emancipating us from false consciousness, but rather to turn us loose in the world as something other than subjects searching for something fresh and new to experience.

18 So the idea would be that Heidegger's "aestheticism" consists in the way the work of art becomes a "model" for the thing—and not for the thing only, but for language and world as well; except that "model" is not quite the right word, since the thing is obviously not patterned after anything but is, like the work of art, radically singular. See Gadamer's introduction to his edition of *Der Ursprung des Kunstwerkes*, 123–24: "What Heidegger means can be confirmed by everyone: the existing thing does not simply offer us a recognizable and familiar surface contour; it also has an inner depth of self-sufficiency that Heidegger calls 'standing-in-itself.' The complete unhiddenness of all beings, their total objectification (by means of a representation that conceives things in their perfect state) would negate this standing-in-itself of beings and lead to a total leveling of them. A complete objectification of this kind would no longer represent beings that stand in their own being. Rather, it would represent nothing more than our opportunity for using beings, and what would be manifest would be the will that seizes upon and dominates things. In the work of art, we experience an absolute opposition to this will-to-control, not in the sense of a rigid resistance to the presumption of our will, which is bent on utilizing things, but in the sense of the superior and intrusive power of a being reposing in itself. Hence the closedness and concealment of the work of art is the guarantee of the universal thesis of Heidegger's philosophy, namely, that beings hold themselves back by coming forward into the openness of presence. The standing-in-itself of the work of art betokens at the same time the standing-in-itself of beings in general" (*Philosophical Hermeneutics*, 226–27).

19 Or, in other words, poetry is something other than "the most perspicuous and familiar configuration of will to power" that we take art to be (N 84/ 71). Poetry overturns this configuration. This is the notion of poetry that emerges in Heidegger's later essays on language—in contrast to the idea of poetry in the Hölderlin essays, where the poet is a powerful figure of worldmaking whose word names the gods and names all things, establishing them in what they are.

20 So "deconstruction in America," for example, remains reconciled to the *Ge-Stell*. Jacques Derrida's resistance to the technical or methodological appropriation of deconstruction is registered most strongly in *Memoires for Paul de Man*, esp. 16–18.

21 This is the figure of the poet whom the philosophers seems most prepared to acknowledge. Bernasconi's discussion of the "Naming of the Holy" in *The Question of Language in Heidegger's History of Being* is very crisp and to the point (35–47). The idea of the poet as "namer of the holy" does not seem to me to be very pertinent to the notion of poetry in the later Heidegger.

Chapter Two: The Step Back

1 See "Secrecy and Understanding," in *Inventions*, 17–43, which is about the category of the secret in ancient classical, biblical, and Qur'anic traditions. Very roughly, the idea is that the understanding of what is written is to be figured on the model of entering into a recondite teaching, not as a form of exegesis in which one exposes what is hidden or extracts something (say the confession of a text that was composed in such a way as to remain silent). To understand a text is to come under an obligation *not* to say what it means. Luther's radical break with this tradition—his reconceptualization of the Scriptures as lucid and self-interpreting—inaugurated the culture of reading (and writing) that forms the matrix of modern philosophy of language, with its desire to strip away the excess of discourse in order to lay bare its deep semantic structure.

2 According to Bertrand Russell,

> In a logically perfect language the words in a proposition would correspond one by one with the components of the corresponding fact, with the exception of such words as "or," "not," "if," "then," which have a different function. In a logically perfect language, there will be one word and no more for every simple object, and everything that is not simple will be expressed by a combination of words, by a combination derived, of course, from the words for the simple things that enter in, one word for each simple component. A language of that sort will be completely analytic, and will show at a glance the

logical structure of the facts asserted or denied. The language which is set forth in *Principia Mathematica* is intended to be a language of that sort. It is a language which has only syntax and no vocabulary whatsoever. Barring the omission of a vocabulary, I maintain that it is quite a nice language. It aims at being that sort of language that, if you add a vocabulary, would be a logically perfect language.

See "The Philosophy of Logical Atomism," in *Logic and Knowledge: Essays, 1901–1950*, ed. R. C. Marsh (London: Allen & Unwin, 1956), 197.

3 See Michael Dummett, "Frege's Distinction Between Sense and Reference," *Truth and Other Enigmas* (Cambridge, Mass.: Harvard Univ. Press, 1978), 118. For a critique of this idea from within analytic philosophy, see G. P. Baker and P. M. S. Hacker, *Language, Sense & Nonsense* (Oxford: Basil Blackwell, 1984). The upshot of what Baker and Hacker have to say is that modern linguistics and analytic philosophy of language are "nonsense all the way down" (369)—nonsense cloaked in the prose of cool, rigorous, lucid explanation.

4 *The Postmodern Condition: A Report on Knowledge*, trans. Geoff Bennington and Brian Massumi (Minneapolis: Univ. of Minnesota Press, 1984), 5. An important text for study in this context is Geoffrey Hartman's *Criticism in the Wilderness: The Study of Literature Today* (New Haven and London: Yale Univ. Press, 1980), esp. 133–57. Hartman takes the dense, wild, disorienting style of Carlyle's *Sartor Resartus* as a model of the critical text that breaks with the clear, limpid, easily consumable prose of polite literary conversation that comes down to us from the eighteenth century, and which constitutes the canonical style of Anglo-American literary criticism and philosophy. This "transparent and accommodated prose," Hartman says, is in fact a thick reptilian skin designed to protect the sensitive tranquil subject from the shock of reading. Carlyle's *Sartor Resartus*, with its encounter between the polite, urbane, lucid English editor and the wild, transgressive, obviously lunatic German philosopher, is a cautionary tale for every reader of Heidegger.

5 See Jacques Derrida, "Comment ne pas parler: *Dénégations*," in *Psyché: Inventions de l'autre* (Paris: Galilée, 1987), 535–95. This is an essay on "negative theology" in which Derrida asks: "How to avoid speaking, and also not avoid it?" For example, how to keep a secret, when keeping a secret (as I indicate in *Inventions*) is not keeping silent but a mode of discourse proper to that which cannot be spoken or which is beyond language or beyond the thinkable? The unspoken secret belongs to the discourse of "negative theology." It is part of what Derrida, speaking of Dionysius the Areopagite, calls the movement toward "a hyper-essentiality that is beyond Being." To speak of God, one must say nothing, speak and say nothing, in which case one has already spoken of God: language has already been at it, as if in God's (unutterable) name. There is no denying that the later Heidegger

has appropriated the discourse of negative theology, of hyper-essentiality, in order to avoid speaking about language, about which he then speaks, but without appearing to say anything at all—perhaps he says nothing in fact, and it is all mystification, as most people believe. Language occupies that hyper-essential place once reserved for God or whatever is "beyond Being": a place and no place (the elsewhere of estrangement and of the Other). This appropriation has undeniable or at least uncontrollable consequences. As philosophers can claim to have found nothing in Heidegger, so both theologians and deconstructionists can claim to have uncovered onto-theological motives in him. I myself would not be surprised by the existence of these motives; quite possibly they are among Heidegger's dirty secrets. My own choice has been to speak simply of the earthliness of Heidegger's language, its darkness or reserve or self-refusal, without speculating as to what this mystification may be trying to cover up. I have, so to speak, kept my suspicions on this score to myself, even from myself, because, in fact, I cannot speak of my suspicions, since I just do not know what to say about what may be hidden behind Heidegger's obscurity, which opens him to every accusation, perhaps none of which can be denied. Denials in any case, as Derrida says, are always empty. Heidegger's obscurity is the idiom of the sinister. The hermeneutics of suspicion is what comes of speaking darkly. What I stress in this book is that Heidegger's language is always parodic and not simply (pace Habermas) grandiose intimations of the ineffable; that is, his opacity is a satire upon the serious, straightforward word of philosophy. He repeatedly takes perfectly familiar philosophical terms in unheard-of senses or in ways that prove to be untranslatable or uninterpretable in another style. His mystifications have a demystifying power with respect to the discourse of official disciplines: to read Heidegger is to become alienated from one's own disciplinary practices (as I try to suggest above in the introduction). Whether this also entails what Geoffrey Hartman calls a "survival" of visionary or supernatural modes of utterance (which the discourses of sweet reason have repressed) is what remains an open question. See Hartman, *Criticism in the Wilderness*, 33–41. See Hans-Georg Gadamer, "Die religiöse Dimension," in *Heideggers Weg* (Tübingen: J. C. B. Mohr, 1983), 140–51.

Derrida's "Comment ne pas parler" is in part an effort to deny that deconstruction is a negative theology, even though it has appropriated the discourse of not saying anything (essentially); that is, in the manner of negative theology, and also in the manner of the later Heidegger, deconstruction exploits the "weakness of the logos" in order to have its say without metaphysics. Just this exploitation, however, makes it possible for negative theologies to re-appropriate deconstruction in its turn, thus compelling it to confess itself or disclose its deepest (perhaps unthought as well as unspoken) secrets or motives. So Derrida denies that deconstruction is a negative theology, a way of (not) saying Being or God or the Highest, but he knows that these "dénégations" are spoken to the wind. Derrida, too, is caught in this rift (or indeterminacy) of the mystifying and demystifying.

6 *Dialogue and Dialectic,* 110–11, 151–53.

7 See Baker and Hacker, *Language, Sense & Nonsense,* on "The Mythology of Rules," 267–315; Louis Althusser, *Reading Capital,* trans. Ben Brewster (London: NLB, 1970), 182–93; Jacques Lacan, "The Function and Field of Speech and Language in Psychoanalysis," *Ecrits: A Selection,* trans. Alan Sheridan (New York: W. W. Norton, 1977), 64–68.

8 "The Task of the Translator," *Resistance to Theory* (Minneapolis: Univ. of Minnesota Press, 1988), 92.

9 See "Shelley Disfigured," *Deconstruction and Criticism,* ed. Harold Bloom et al. (New York: Seabury Press, 1979), 68.

10 This perhaps holds, as I've indicated earlier, rather more for Paul de Man than for Derrida. See Derrida, *Memoires for Paul de Man,* esp. 13–14.

11 See de Man's "Heidegger's Exegesis of Hölderlin," in *Blindness and Insight,* 2d ed., 246–66.

12 There are many ways in which this renunciation could be described. Andrzej Warminski calls it simply "nonreading" in his dense study of Heidegger's reading of Hegel's "Science of the Experience of Consciousness." See *Readings in Interpretation,* 112–62. See also John Sallis, *Spacings—of Reason and Imagination in the Texts of Kant, Fichte, Hegel* (Chicago: Univ. of Chicago Press, 1987), which contains a very provocative footnote on Heidegger's reading of Kant's text, *Kant und das Problem der Metaphysik* (1929) that brings out beautifully Heidegger's austere/excessive, midrashic way of "reading" philosophical texts:

> What . . . appears distinctive about Heidegger's reading is its marginal character. In contrast to a reading that would confine itself to the text of the *Critique of Pure Reason,* recasting the text in an allegedly equivalent but more transparent form, perhaps, in addition, criticizing that text from some position outside it—in contrast to such a reading, Heidegger links up with the margin of that text, holds in focus certain prearticulating traces that lie outside yet frame the text. More precisely, Heidegger's reading takes up that margin in its engagement with the text—that is, his reading in effect resumes the movement between margin and text, specifically, the movement in which certain developments in the text recoil upon the framing margin, deforming the frame, filling the margin. And yet, in resuming the movement, Heidegger's reading also transforms it. The movement as resumed within the reading is no longer merely the interplay between text and margin, no longer merely something happening on the end of the Kantian text. Rather, Heidegger's reading shifts the edge to the center—that is, it converts the interplay between text and margin into an essentially textual movement . . . that, implicit in Kant, would be

made explicit in the Heideggerian resumption. The frame of pre-articulating traces becomes part of the picture itself. What was outside the Kantian text becomes part of a positive thematic. . . . On the one hand, the reading is to expose the unsaid (*das Ungesagte*) that can be gleaned through what is said (*das Gesagte*). On the other hand, the reading is "to make manifest what Kant brought to light . . . above his express formulations"; it is to make explicit what he wanted to say but did not succeed in saying. It would be possible to distinguish another kind of reading that, while remaining marginal, would forgo making this identification, would forgo assuming that the unsaid is something that belongs, even if only implicitly, to the Kantian thematic. . . . It would be a matter of opening the possibility that the unsaid, Kant's silence, might fall entirely outside the domain of this simple opposition between what he said and what he only virtually intended—that is, the possibility that it might fall outside the thematic of the Kantian text, that it might lie in the margin of the text. The possibility of such a marginal unsaid would broach, then, the possibility of a reading that would preserve the margin as such instead of transforming the play of the margin and text into a new text; such a style of reading . . . would preserve the prearticulative character of the marginal traces and, leaving them outside the text, would follow the lines of movement marked on the edge of the Kantian text. [163–64]

This makes Heidegger sound a bit too much like Derrida, but it is the only thoughtful account I know of that tries to describe a Heideggerian reading. The question is whether what Sallis describes fits as well Heidegger's "reading" of a dark text like a poem or archaic fragment. I think it does, but only in the sense that Heidegger reads the philosophical text—say Kant or Hegel—as if it were dark. So also with a poem like Trakl's whose meaning is plain. That's the whole idea of *das Ungesagte*, which, as I indicate below, is the whole idea of a conversation (*Gespräch*).

13 See Branka Brujić, "'Schritt zurück,'" in *Martin Heidegger—Unterwegs zur Denken*, ed. Richard Wisser (Freiburg and Munich: Karl Alber, 1987), 161–80.

14 This is the first sentence of a famous passage in which Heidegger links *Denken und Dichten* together for the first time:

Only in thoughtful dialogue with what it says can this fragment of thinking be translated. However, thinking is poetizing [*Das Denken jedoch Dichten*], and indeed more than one kind of poetizing [*nicht nur eine Art der Dichtung*], more than poetry and song [*Poesie und des Gesanges*]. Thinking of Being is the original way of poetizing. Language first comes to language, i.e. into its essence, in thinking. Thinking says what the truth of Being dictates; it is the original *dictare*. Thinking is primordial poetry, prior to all poesy, but also prior to the poetics of art [*dem Dichterischen der Kunst*], since art shapes its work within the realm of language. All poetizing, in this broader sense, and also in the narrower sense of the poetic [*Poetischen*], is in its ground a thinking. The poetizing essence of thinking preserves the sway of the truth of Being. Because it poetizes as it thinks, the translation which wishes to let the oldest fragment of thinking itself speak necessarily appears violent.

In the lecture on "The Nature of Language" (1957) Heidegger will revise this conception of the relation of poetry and thinking by replacing metaphors of foundationalism with the notion of the "rift" that holds poetry and thinking together, "each in its own darkness" (US 196/90). It is by no means clear that the later Heidegger holds to the idea that "Language first comes to language, i.e. into its essence, in thinking." See chap. six above.

15 See Rainer Schürmann, *Heidegger on Being and Acting*, 153–81, who acknowledges the muteness of these words but nevertheless finds a place for them in the history of being and construes them as categories of presencing.

Chapter Three: The Abandonment of Philosophical Language

1 See Bakhtin, "Discourse in the Novel," in *The Dialogic Imagination: Four Essays by M. M. Bakhtin*, trans. Caryl Emerson and Michael Holquist (Austin: Univ. of Texas Press, 1981), 270–73.

2 *Enclitic* 2 (1978): 31: provocative, but true. One should say that French is a repressed heteroglossia, in contrast to English, which is wildly disseminated and out of control (threatening even the unitary purity of French with its damnable neologisms and cockeyed expressions). On French as a heteroglossia, see Roland Barthes, "The Division of Languages," in *The Rustle of Language*, trans. Richard Howard (New York: Hill and Wang, 1986), 111–24.

3 See Emil Kettering, "Nähe im Denken Martin Heideggers," in *Martin Heidegger—Unterwegs zur Denken*, 111–30.

4 One could say that there are no things in the world just as there are no words in the dictionary (*Wörterbuch*).

5 For standard accounts of the fourfold, see Vincent Vycinas, *Earth and Gods*, esp. 224–37; and Otto Pöggeler, *Martin Heidegger's Path of Thinking*, 200–16. David White discusses the fourfold at length in *Heidegger and the Language of Poetry* (Part Two), where he regards them as "sectors" in Heidegger's cosmology. But I like Rainer Schürmann's account in *Heidegger on Being and Acting*, 222–29, which situates the fourfold within Heideggerian categories "that articulate thresholds, catastrophes, commotions, breaks in

the history of presencing" (203). My concern is the punning context in which Heidegger unfolds his fourfold in "The Thing."

6 See "Time and Being": "what does this 'It' mean?" Heidegger, stepping back as usual, refuses to answer, that is, he abandons every attempt to determine the "it" by itself. He does say, however, that it "names presence of absence" (SD 19/18).

7 *The Collected Poems of Wallace Stevens* (New York: Alfred A. Knopf, 1964), 129–30.

8 The emphasis should be on belonging (Zusammen*gehören*) rather than on togetherness and unity (*Zusammen*gehören). See Heidegger, "The Principle of Identity":

> If we think of belonging *together* in the customary way, the meaning of belonging is determined by the word together, that is, by its unity. In that case, "to belong" means as much as: to be assigned and placed into the order of a "together," established in the unity of a manifold, combined into the unity of a system, mediated by the unifying center of an authoritative synthesis. Philosophy represents this belonging together as *nexus* and *connexio*, the necessary connection of the one with the other.
>
> However, belonging together can also be thought of as *belonging* together. This means: the "together" is now determined by the belonging. Of course, we must still ask here what "belong" means in that case, and how its peculiar "together" is determined only in its terms. The answer to these questions is closer to us than we imagine, but it is not obvious. Enough for now that this reference makes us note the possibility of no longer representing belonging in terms of the unity of the together, but rather of experiencing this together in terms of belonging. However, does not the reference to this possibility amount to no more than an empty play on words, an artifice without support in verifiable facts?
>
> This is how things look—until we take a closer look and let the matter speak for itself. [ID 16/29]

9 See Derrida, "The Ends of Man," *Margins of Philosophy*, trans. Alan Bass (Chicago: Univ. of Chicago Press, 1982), 129n., on "the motif of the proper (*eigen, eigentlich*) and the several modes of *to propriate* (particularly *Ereignen* and *Ereignis*)." According to such a motif, we must take that which comes into its own as if it were answering to a concept or to a proper name which stands for it. This would be reading Heidegger against himself because for Heidegger answering a call is not filling an assignment or a place in the total scheme of things. That which, like the work of art, stands on its own (*eigen*) cannot be assimilated into the economy of a system. Thus the *eigen* in *Ereignis* is an impropriety that belongs to the speaking of language. On

the punning in *Ereignis*, see chap. six above. Heidegger's puns sound more sinister, or metaphysical, to Derrida's ear than to mine.

10 See "Différance," in *Margins of Philosophy*, 1–27.

11 See *"Ousīa* and *Grammē:* Note on a Note from *Being and Time*," *Margins of Philosophy*, 66–67.

12 Neither does *différance* completely escape the philosophical lexicon, that is, it is not to be thought of as superseding Heidegger's language, succeeding where *Unterschied* fails, although it may sometimes be taken that way. On this question Derrida is as crafty and ambiguous as ever. Near the end of the essay on *"Différance"* Derrida writes:

> For us, *différance* remains a metaphysical name, and all the names that it receives in our language are still, as names, metaphysical. And this is particularly the case when these names state the determination of *différance* as the difference between presence and the present (*An-wesen/Anwesend*), and above all, and is already the case when they state the determination of *différance* as the difference of Being and beings.
>
> "Older" than Being itself, such a *différance* has no name in our language. But we "already know" that if it is unnameable, it is not provisionally so, not because our language has not yet found or received this *name*, or because we would have to seek it in another language, outside the finite system of our own. It is rather because there is no *name* for it at all, not even the name of essence or of Being, not even that of *"différance*," which is not a name, which is not a pure nominal unity, and unceasingly dislocates itself in a chain of differing and deferring substitutions. [26]

13 See Orville Clark, "Heidegger and the Mystery of Pain," in *Man and World*, 10 (1977): 334–50.

14 See Heidegger, *The Basic Problems of Phenomenology*, trans. Albert Hofstadter (Bloomington: Indiana Univ. Press, 1982), 247–48: "nowness, being-now, is always *otherness, being-other*."

15 Spatial rather than temporal, but not in the sense perhaps that Otto Pögeler would take it when he speaks of the later Heidegger's "topology of Being." See *Martin Heidegger's Path of Thinking*, 227–42. The point here is that the whole idea of space-time in the later Heidegger seems to be thrown in the air.

Chapter Four: The Poetic Experience with Language

1 See Robert Bernasconi's discussion of experience in *The Question of Language in Heidegger's History of Being*, 81–85. "'Experience' in Heidegger," he says, "does not have the sense of progressive development as it has in

Hegel. For Heidegger, experience almost always takes place in the face of a lack" (83).

2 See John Sallis, "Towards the Showing of Language," in *Thinking about Being: Aspects of Heidegger's Thought*, 79–83. This is a good discussion of what Heidegger could mean by "experience with language," although I think Sallis would disagree with my reading, which understands the experience in terms of the withdrawal or self-refusal of language, that is, in terms of our bereavement of everything that grammar, rhetoric, and logic seek to bring under conceptual control. For the normal view, see Walter Biemel, "Poetry and Language in Heidegger," in *On Heidegger and Language*, 84–85.

3 The link between poetry (in the wide sense of *écriture*) and the failure or refusal of signification is one of the main subjects of *Modern Poetry and the Idea of Language*, which emphasizes the traditions of Flaubert and Mallarmé; but the idea has now become commonplace in literary criticism. See, for example, J. Hillis Miller, *The Linguistic Moment*, where the "linguistic moment is the moment when a poem, or indeed any text, turns back on itself and puts its own medium in question" (339). The point worth stressing is that this moment of self-refusal is not just a main feature of the modernist tradition that Miller and others study but has always characterized writing and discourse (see chap. 1 of *Modern Poetry and the Idea of Language*, esp. 34–41, on Rabelais and late medieval linguistic skepticism). Mikhail Bakhtin's writings are important in this context, particularly his idea that the discourse of signification—"the straightforward, serious word"—always occurs in an environment of parody and verbal ridicule that calls the word into question. See "From the Prehistory of Novelistic Discourse," in *The Dialogic Imagination*, 41–80. I regard the later Heidegger as a philosopher who has crossed the threshold from the sealed-off world of philosophical discourse into the uncontrollable, sometimes lunatic linguistic world (the world of Aristophanes, of Roman satire and medieval parody, of Rabelais, Cervantes, and Sterne, of Joyce, Beckett, and Thomas Pynchon) that surrounds philosophy and calls it into question.

4 Heidegger returns to George's poem in "The Word" (1958), where he expands considerably on the notion of renunciation. I discuss this in the conclusion.

5 From Beckett's three dialogues with Georges Duthuit, *Transition*, no. 5 (1949): 98.

6 *The Gaze of Orpheus and Other Literary Essays*, trans. Lydia Davis (Barrytown, N.Y.: Station Hill Press, 1981), pp. 42–43. Hereafter cited as GO. "Littérature et le droit à la mort" was published in *La Part du Feu* (Paris: Gallimard, 1949). I discuss this essay in detail in "Language and Power," *The Chicago Review* 34 (1984): 27–43. On my reading it is a profoundly Heideggerian essay, as in the following: "By turning itself into an inability to reveal anything, literature is attempting to become the revelation of

what revelation destroys. This is a tragic endeavor. Literature says: 'I no longer represent, I am; I do not signify, I present.' But this wish to be a thing, this refusal to mean anything, a refusal immersed in words turned to salt; in short, this destiny which literature becomes as it becomes the language of no one, the writing of no writer, the light of a consciousness deprived of self, this insane effort to bury itself in itself, to hide itself behind the fact that it is visible—all this is what literature now manifests, what literature now shows. If it were to become as mute as a stone, as passive as the corpse enclosed behind the stone, its decision to lose the capacity for speech would still be legible on the stone and would be enough to wake that bogus corpse" (GO 47).

7 See Heidegger's "Conversation on a Country Path," where *Gegend* undergoes the same transformation into an event that occurs with the work of art, the world, the thing, and language. As the work works and the thing things and *die Sprache spricht*, so the region regions (*gegnet*) (G 39/66).

8 See Marcel, *Mystery of Being*, trans. G. S. Fraser (South Bend, Ind.: Gateway Editions, 1950), 1:211–15, for the distinction between a problem and a mystery. Naturally we draw back from the word "mystery," which is the sacred word of negative theology. What is Heidegger not saying with this word?

9 *Blindness and Insight*, 2d ed., 257–59.

10 *The Letters of Gerard Manley Hopkins*, ed. Claude Colleer Abbott (London: Oxford Univ. Press, 1935), 90. I discuss Hopkins on this point in *Inventions*, 135–39.

11 Heidegger does not yet picture himself stepping back from the text in order to listen for the unsaid: "If we content ourselves with what the poem directly says, the interpretation is at an end. Actually it has just begun. The actual interpretation must show what does not stand in the words and is nevertheless said. To accomplish this the exegete must use violence. He must seek the essential where nothing more is to be found by the scientific interpretation that brands as unscientific everything that transcends its limits" (EM 124/136). In the later Heidegger, letting-go replaces exegetical violence.

12 See John Sallis, "Meaning Adrift," in *Heidegger Studies* 1 (1985): 98–99. This is a very helpful essay about Heidegger's dismantling (in his 1942/43 Lecture Course on Parmenides) of the whole idea of "fundamental meaning," that is, the idea that "somewhere there is for itself such a thing as fundamental meaning. Somewhere—not only beyond derivative meanings but, more critically, beyond the designating words, beyond in a subsistence for themselves, independent of those words, capable even of drifting away behind the cover of 'derivative' meanings, of having always already begun drifting away, of drifting away just as, according to that history of an error told by Nietzsche, the truth world has drifted away out of sight, beyond recall. Something to be abolished." Fundamental meaning is displaced by,

or taken up by, "what is originary in words, that which, invoked by them, housed in them, lets things originate, come forth into self-showing. The originary in language is nothing other than world, *alētheia*, the open site of self-showing." But, in light of the later Heidegger, one would have to add that the earth, the self-closing, is also what is originary, perhaps even older than world.

13 One could easily develop a Heideggerian account of the origin of the quarrel of philosophy and poetry as just this "breaking apart" of *logos* and *phūsis* (EM 136–37/149–50). For a properly philosophical account of *phūsis*, however, and one very different from the one I give here, see Thomas Sheehan, "On the Way to *Ereignis:* Heidegger's Interpretation of *Physis*," in *Continental Philosophy in America*, ed. Hugh Silverman (Pittsburgh: Duquesne Univ. Press, 1983), 134–64, which is concerned with Heidegger's interpretation of *phūsis* in Aristotle. See Heidegger, "On the Being and Conception of *Phūsis* in Aristotle's *Physics*, B, 1," trans. Thomas Sheehan, in *Man and World* 9 (1976): 219–70.

Chapter Five: Words and Sounds in Heidegger

1 See Ronald Bruzina's valuable essay, "Heidegger on the Metaphor and Philosophy," in *Heidegger and Modern Philosophy*, 184–200. A more analytic approach is taken by Gerald Casenave, "Heidegger and Metaphor," in *Philosophy Today* 26 (1982): 140–47. "Metaphor," Casenave says, echoing Donald Davidson, "opens up a new way of organizing reality" (145). I think Heidegger would probably agree with this statement, adding only that this is why the metaphorical is metaphysical. Metaphor as a power of organizing new views of reality belongs to the discourse of the *Ge-Stell*. When Heidegger speaks of the poet's renunciation, he means giving up metaphor as "a way of organizing reality." But giving up metaphor doesn't mean opting for logical propositions—although, of course, in terms of the *Ge-Stell* it could mean nothing else, there being, analytically, no other options. I think that if we want to understand Heidegger it's more important to think about puns than about metaphors. But, of course, a pun is (loosely) metaphorical. I have already cited Derrida's essay on the question of metaphor in Heidegger, "The *Retrait* of Metaphor," in *Enclitic* 2 (1978): 5–33.

2 "What Metaphors Mean," in *Inquiries into Truth and Interpretation* (Oxford: Clarendon Press, 1984), 259.

3 The idea that any poem naturally resists exegesis is in some respects a New Critical commonplace. But people like Cleanth Brooks thought of this in terms of a resistance to paraphrase, not a resistance to formal analysis that would lay bare the deep structure of stresses and balances and harmonies

that make the poem what it is. Resistance to paraphrase is very different from the hermetic tradition, with its constant allusion to linguistic skepticism, that I try to talk about in *Modern Poetry and the Idea of Language*. Similarly, what Heidegger calls the poetic experience with language is again different from (or anyhow something a good deal more than) what is now called the experience of indeterminacy that is a cornerstone of post-structuralist theory. See Geoffrey Hartman, "Criticism, Indeterminancy, Irony," in *Criticism in the Wilderness* (New Haven and London: Yale Univ. Press, 1980), esp. 269–70: "As a guiding concept, indeterminacy does not merely *delay* the determination of meaning, that is, suspend premature judgments and allow greater thoughtfulness. The delay is not heuristic alone, a device to slow the act of reading till we appreciate (I could think here of Stanley Fish) its complexity. The delay is intrinsic: from a certain point of view, it is thoughtfulness itself, Keats's 'negative capability,' a labor that aims not to overcome the negative or indeterminate but to stay within it as long as is necessary." The question that Heidegger would put to the post-structuralists is: What happens to thinking when it steps back and refuses to overcome the negative? It is not just that thinking grows more thoughtful; on the contrary, terrible things may happen to thinking in this event. It may cease to recognize itself as thoughtful in any usual or customary sense of this word. Hartman gets closer to the Heidegger (without recognizing it) in his book on Derrida, *Saving the Text*, esp. 52: "[Derrida] shows that the more we penetrate a text the more its textual and intertextual weaving appears; and this is not a matter, simply, of coming to know through the chosen book more and more sources. That would be source study and *explication de texte* all over again. What one comes to know is the unintelligibility—the 'abysmation' or 'éschappé de vue ins Unendliche' (F. Schlegel)—of the literary work." Again, the next question is: What happens to thinking once it "knows"—or is exposed to—this unintelligibility? Thinking may no longer know what to call itself in this event. Certainly it can no longer call itself "philosophy."

4 It has always seemed to me that the distinction is in fact even richer than Heidegger himself makes it out to be in his discussion of it in *What is Called Thinking?* (See WD 86–90/126–32). I try to embellish the distinction in "The Otherness of Words: Joyce, Bakhtin, Heidegger," in *Continental Philosophy*, ed. Hugh J. Silvermann (London: Routledge & Kegan Paul, forthcoming).

5 *Die Sage* is, of course, a term in a dictionary, meaning legend or fabulous story, and there's nothing odd about that, unless to a philosopher's ear, but Heidegger's *Sage* is something else besides, which is perhaps why he sometimes, as in the present context, speaks of *das Sagen*, a word for Saying the way *Dichten* and *Denken* are words for poetry and thinking, that is, not —strictly speaking—really words at all: "das Wort, das Sagen, hat kein

Sein" (US 192/87). Moreover, it is not clear that the question *Was heisst Sagen?* makes quite the same sense as *Was heisst Denken?* The question is rather, as in this instance, "*Wohin gehört das Wort, wohin das Sagen?*" (US 192/87). See Werner Marx's response to a question put to him about *Sage* by Wolfgang Zucker in the Kockelmans volume, *On Heidegger and Language*, 250n.

6 See *Being and Time* (212/252): "Of course only as long as Dasein *is* (that is, only as long as an understanding of Being is ontically possible), 'is there' [*es gibt*] Being." The translators add this footnote: "Heidegger insists that the expression 'es gibt' is here used deliberately, and should be taken literally as 'it gives.'" They refer to the *Letter on Humanism*, where Heidegger says that "In *Being and Time* we purposely and cautiously say, *il y a l'Etre:* 'there is / it gives ['es gibt'] Being. *Il y a* translates 'it gives' imprecisely. For the 'it' that here 'gives' is Being itself. The 'gives' names the essence of Being that is giving, granting its truth. The self-giving into the open, along with the open region itself, is Being itself" (Wm 165/214). But in *What is Called Thinking?*, in the lecture on parataxis, Heidegger seems pretty clearly to disconnect *es gibt* from Being—at all events the "it" is no longer identified as Being; "it" is not identifiable. "It" withdraws, withholds itself, is unnamable and ungraspable. If you want to go ahead and call this "Being," you do so without reason ("without why"), that is, you have no call or warrant for speaking this way. When we ask about expressions like "It is raining," Heidegger says, "We are groping in the dark" (WD 115/188).

Heidegger's concern here is with Fragment 6 of Parmenides (*chre to legein te noein t' eon emmenai*). He says: "The key word in Parmenides' saying is *chre*. We now translate it with 'it is useful.' Even on superficial examination the saying speaks of Saying and Thinking, of being, of Being [*vom Sagen und Denken, vom Seienden, vom Sein*]. It speaks of the highest and deepest, the most remote and nearest, the most veiled and the most apparent that mortal Saying can say [*was in sterblicher Sage überhaupt sagbar ist*]. This gives us the occasion and the right to assume that the word *chre*, too, is spoken in the highest sense" (WD 168/191).

What is this "highest sense"? Heidegger doesn't quite say; or, rather, he doesn't specify this higher sense, he simply differentiates it from common usage (*gewöhnlichen Sprachgebrauch*), rather the way words are distinguished from terms:

> A wide range of meaning belongs generally to the nature of every word. This fact, again, arises from the mystery of language. Language admits of two things: One, that it be reduced to a mere system of signs [*Zeichensystem*], uniformly available to everybody, and in this form be enforced as binding; and two, that language at one great moment says one unique thing, for one time only, which remains inexhaustible because it is always originary, and thus beyond the reach of any kind

of leveling. These two possibilities of language are so far removed from each other that we should not be doing justice to their disparity even if we were to call them extreme opposites.

Customary speech vacillates between these two possible ways in which language speaks. It gets caught halfway. Commonness, which looks much like custom, attaches itself to the rule. Common speech puffs itself up as the sole binding rule for everything we say—and now every word at variance with it immediately looks like an arbitrary violation. The translation of the word *chre*, likewise, appears arbitrary if instead of saying "One should" we say "It is useful . . ."

But the time may finally have come to release language from the leash of common speech and allow it to remain attuned to the keynote of the lofty statement it makes—without, however, rating customary speech as a decline, or as low. It will then no longer suffice to speak of a lofty statement, for this, too, is, at least in name, still rated by low standards.

Why this reference to language? In order to stress once again that we are moving within language, which means moving on shifting ground or, still better, on the billowing waters of an ocean. [WD 168–69/192]

Heidegger appears to rehearse here the old Romantic distinction between ordinary, quotidien discourse and a transcendental logos that says everything all at once—"one unique thing, for one time only, which remains inexhaustible because it is always originary": in short, between an empty utterance and a full, or between that which is temporal and discursive and therefore always incomplete and that which is eternal, simultaneous and total. But I think this is a misreading, because the main distinction is between the fixed and the open. Customary usage is ruled, whereas language speaks without constraint. So even the distinctions between high and low, originary and customary, arbitrary and logically determined, mortal utterance and the speaking of language—it appears that all distinctions are called into question or thrown in the air. What Heidegger comes round to is the notion of *Gelassenheit:* "the time may finally have come to release language from the leash of common speech," that is, from fixity and rule. In other words, let go of the ground. "Leave everything open."

7 This is what Heidegger is really doing with his famous etymologies, as in the case of *Denken, Gedachtes,* and *Gedanke* in *What is Called Thinking?*, where Heidegger hears the echo or hint of the Old German *Gedanc,* where thinking and thanking intersect: "We take the hint," he says, "that in the speaking of those words [*Denken*, etc.] the decisively and originally telling word sounds [*das massgebend und ursprünglich sagende Wort lautet*]: der '*Gedanc*'" (WD 91/139–40). What is the "Saying" of this word? Not surprisingly, it is that thinking has more to do with receptivity and openness

than with reasoning in the sense of representational-calculative operations of description and explanation. Thinking is more like listening (to the punning in the words for thinking, for example) than like questioning or probing or proving or building or dismantling, and so on. For more on puns, see the section of this chapter called "Puns".

8 See "Time and Being," where Heidegger reflects (much to the same effect) on the locution "*Es gibt Zeit*," where "Time is *not*" (SD 17–20/16–19).

Chapter Six: Otherwise than Language

1 This is a main theme of "Hölderlin and the Essence of Poetry," which tries to elucidate this fragment:

> Viel erfahren hat der Mensch.
> Der Himmlischen viele genannt,
> Seit ein Gespräch wir sind
> Und hören können voneinander.

> Much has man learnt.
> Many of the heavenly ones has he named,
> Since we have been a conversation
> And have been able to hear from one another.
>   [ED 36/277]

Conversation is what draws us into the orphic event and maintains us there. Heidegger writes: "Since we have been a conversation—man has learnt much and named many of the heavenly ones. Since language really became actual as conversation, the gods have acquired names and a world has appeared. But again it should be noticed: the presence of the gods and the appearance of the world are not merely a consequence of the actualisation of language, they are contemporaneous with it. And this to the extent that it is precisely in the naming of the gods, and in the transmutation of the world into word, that the real conversation, which we ourselves are, consists" (ED 37/279). However, *Gespräch* in this social and historical sense seems to drop out of the later Heidegger's thinking. It appears that for the later Heidegger the crucial conversation is between poetry and thinking, where conversation is not a mutual exchange but a mode of belonging to Saying. At all events the relation of poetry and thinking is not social.

2 See Joseph P. Fell, "Heidegger's Gods and Mortals," in *Research in Phenomenology* 15 (1985): 31: "For one who has walked Heidegger's path from his early thinking forward, the term 'mortals' is richly evocative. It calls up my death, an unsurpassable boundary which throws me right back to my other boundary, my own beginning. Encountering darkness—nothing—as both my 'whence' and my 'whither.' I am thrown right into my own time as my

true place and the place of the only truth I can possibly experience. It is in this time alone, then, that I can ask about the gods. Might, therefore, a necessary step in the question of the role of the gods for Heidegger consist in meditating on death, and so on nothing?"

3 See Michael Murray's discussion of this liberation in *Modern Critical Theory: An Introduction*, 143–202.

4 See Gerald L. Bruns, "On The Tragedy of Hermeneutical Experience," in *Research in Phenomenology* 18 (November 1988).

5 See David Michael Levin on the dance in Heidegger, in *The Body's Recollection of Being: Phenomenological Psychology and the Deconstruction of Nihilism* (London: Routledge & Kegan Paul, 1985), 317–49.

6 Professional Heideggerians are apt to find my account of *Er-eignis* a bit bizarre. Even Jacques Derrida, when he heard me present an earlier version of this chapter at a conference in Jerusalem, questioned my insistence on listening for the pun in Heidegger's words. My impression is that Derrida would prefer to think of Heidegger as being soberly unaware of his puns, which is highly implausible but consistent with the way Derrida once read Heidegger, namely as reinscribing in his metaphors the metaphysics he wants to destroy. As I indicate elsewhere in this book, I see, or hear, Heidegger as being closer to Derrida, or vice versa, than Derrida perhaps does, because I hear more (or something other) than metaphysics in Heidegger's puns. For a proper view of *Ereignis*, see Otto Pöggeler, "Being as Appropriation (1959)," trans. Rüdiger H. Grimm, *Philosophy Today* (Summer 1975): 152–78; reprinted in *Heidegger and Modern Philosophy*, 85–115, and esp. 101–02. "Being as the event of appropriation [*Ereignis*]: with this definition Heidegger's thinking has arrived at its goal." For a more disseminated view, see John Caputo, *Radical Hermeneutics*, 200–201, although even for Caputo *Ereignis* is more term than word. With all respect to the philosophers, I take *Ereignis* as a pun (*Er-eignis*) rather than as a concept, definition, or name (in the sense of designation)—and so, I think, does Heidegger. See, for example, "The Turning" (1950), where, in addition to the puns I've picked up on, Heidegger adds another: *Eräugnis* (TK 44/45). I confess, however, that Heidegger is more philosophically sober on this subject in "Time and Being" (1962; SD 20–25/19–24), but even here he makes it clear that in the phrase "Being as *Ereignis*" the "as" is a term of dissemination like the "hermeneutical 'as'" discussed in section 32 of *Being and Time*. The "as" (like the pun) cannot be contained within propositional discourse. I discuss this "as" in "The Weakness of Language in the Human Sciences," in *The Rhetoric of Inquiry: Language and Argument in Scholarship and Public Affairs*, ed. Allan Megill, Donald McCloskey, and John Nelson (Madison: Univ. of Wisconsin Press, 1988), 239–62. I think that Francis Ambrosio's essay, "Dawn and Dusk: Gadamer and Heidegger on Truth," is very valuable for its discussion of *Ereignis*. See *Man and World* 19 (1986): 21–53.

And even when in Heidegger it appears that "Being *is* Ereignis" after all, it is plain that we are still slip-sliding on drifting or moving ground, as in Heidegger's poem, "Gefährten," with its parodistic archaisms and self-circling, self-cancelling "propositions":

> Einstige kommen
> vom Seyn übernommen
>
> Sie wagen
> Das Sagen
> der Wahrheit des Seyns:
>
> Seyn ist Ereignis
> Ereignis ist Anfang
> Anfang ist Austrag
> Austrag ist Abschied
> Abschied ist Seyn.
>
> [AD 31]

Here the word for Being is no longer (or is in excess of) the word for Being. See the conclusion on the parodistic relation of the archaic to the customary.

7 At the end of "The Way to Language" Heidegger says, in a line that is easy to misinterpret, that "All reflective thinking is poetic, and all poetry in turn is a kind of thinking [*Alles sinnende Denken ist ein Dichten, alle Dichtung aber ein Denken:* not a *kind* of thinking, but a thinking on its own, a singular thinking rather than a particular sort]" (US 267/136). This is not a remark about style or form, or about the resemblance of poetry and thinking. I take it as a statement about letting-go with respect to language, where letting-go means departing, entering into one's apartness or singularity, getting free. I think it would be a mistake to map this line back onto Heidegger's prose in order to figure Heidegger's writing as an exhibition of thinking that has turned to poetry. But his writing does reflect an openness to the pun, a listening, that also belongs to poetry. The question is, Where does this listening take us? The answer is: Elsewhere, where to be always elsewhere is what being on the way comes round to. The vagueness and pointlessness of this answer is repugnant to philosophy. In an essay on "Heidegger and Metaphor" cited earlier (chap. five, n. 1), Gerald Casenave says that "To the end, [Heidegger's] thought remains tentative; he is always on the way and never arriving." Casenave speaks for philosophy when he rejects this state of affairs. "Can fundamental thinking be brought to completion and remain fundamental thinking?" he asks. The answer, he thinks, is yes. "It may be the case that thought can become fully explicit only by becoming representational. That is to say, thinking moves through the break out of metaphor to a more fundamental level of thought, experience, and language, but then it returns to stability with

the achievement of a new order of things. A new break-through to fundamental thought ends with the elaboration and definition of a new realm
of discourse." And so a new "break-through" is required in turn, to be followed by a new elaboration and establishment of a discursive realm; and
so on without end. See *Philosophy Today* 16 (1982): 147. I think Heidegger
would reject this picture of the history of thinking as being nothing more
than a picture of the history of philosophy, with its endless construction
and deconstruction of systems. For Heidegger, thinking, once on its way,
never "returns to stability with the achievement of a new order of things."
Casenave (speaking, as I say, for philosophy) cannot picture thinking except in terms of searching, whereas I think Heidegger figures the thinker
as a wanderer who can never settle anywhere, whose being-on-the-way (to
use that expression) cannot be contained within the romantic concept of
the quest, but is Cain-like in its resemblance to pure exile. There is no
place where the thinker is not a stranger.

8 See Cavell, "Thinking of Emerson," in *The Senses of Walden*, expanded
edition (San Francisco: North Point Press, 1981), 133–34; and *Disowning
Knowledge in Six Plays by Shakespeare* (Cambridge: Cambridge Univ. Press,
1987), 3–5, and esp. 92–97.

Conclusion: The Dark Comic World of Martin Heidegger

1 See Laurence Lampert, "Heidegger's Nietzsche Interpretation," in *Man
and World*, 7, no. 4 (1974): 353–78.

2 "A Preface to Shakespeare," *Selected Writings*, ed. R. T. Davies (Evanston,
Ill.: Northwestern Univ. Press, 1965), 274.

3 See Derrida, "The Ends of Man," *Margins of Philosophy*, 129*n*.

4 Heidegger begins his lecture on "The Way to Language" with a motto
from Novalis's fragment, "Monologue," which is very much a Heideggerian text; or perhaps the truth is that Heidegger is very much the Romantic
Ironist:

> Speaking and writing is a crazy state of affairs really; true conversa-
> tion is just a game with words. It is amazing, the absurd error people
> make of imagining they are speaking for the sake of things; no one
> knows the essential thing about language, that it is concerned only
> with itself. That is why it is such a marvellous and fruitful mystery
> —for if someone merely speaks for the sake of speaking, he utters
> the most splendid, original truths. But if he wants to talk about some-
> thing definite, the whims of language make him say the most ridicu-
> lous false stuff. Hence the hatred that so many serious people have
> for language. They notice its waywardness, but they do not notice
> that the babbling they scorn is the infinitely serious side of language.

[Trans. Joyce Crick, *German Aesthetic and Literary Criticism: The Romantic Ironists and Goethe*, ed. Kathleen Wheeler (Cambridge: Cambridge Univ. Press, 1984), 92–93]

Poetry, however, is where this babbling is free to occur, where its seriousness, if that is the word, can emerge. I prefer to say that poetry enters into the waywardness of language; poetry is what it is to enter into this waywardness. The task of thinking is to follow the opening of poetry, that is, to let itself go into the wayward.

5 Rainer Schürmann gives an account—surely the best we have—of the philosophical implications of renunciation in *Heidegger on Being and Acting*. See esp. 156: "In his abandonment of any origin that commences and commands—of any standard as stander-before, as *thēsis* or position—Heidegger proceeds as in an annulment. His revocation of the titles of rule so generously dispensed by metaphysics follows *criteria*, ways of *krinein*, sorting out and discerning, but not *standards*, postures of measurement. To cancel the juridic instruments of power having passed as legitimate too long is again to bring legal jurisdiction to bear. Two instances or stages (in the juridical sense) of legitimation must therefore be distinguished: the constructive, which establishes the legitimacy of a regulation of obedience, and the deconstructive, repealing the principial representations on which inherited forms of regulation have rested. To pursue the Kantian metaphor of reason as a tribunal: radical phenomenology acts like a deconstructive higher court cancelling the justifications of authority issued by the constructive lower court of metaphysics." The point (which I do not think Schürmann would disagree with) is that this "deconstruction" is always taking place in poetry—it belongs essentially to the event of *Dichten*. But I do not know how an account of *Dichten* could be made intelligible in Schürmann's language (with its Kantian metaphors, its talk of categories and legitimations), which is perhaps why discussion of *Dichten* doesn't figure in Schürmann's (otherwise brilliant and fascinating) book.

6 See Bernasconi's reading of "Das Wort" in *The Question of Language in Heidegger's History of Being*, 49–64. Bernasconi is still trying to clarify the concept of *logos* (61–63), thereby retrieving Heidegger for philosophy. He wants to take *logos* as "the word for the word" (or indeed "the word for the Being of language"), and doesn't believe Heidegger when Heidegger says that there is no such word, and that the traditional word for both Language and Being as the presencing of presence (*logos*) is a sort of catachresis, a word to conceal concealment. What is withheld from us is just the word for what the word is ("*das Wort für das Wesen des Wortes*" [US 236/154]). In this book I've tried not to follow the universal rule of Heidegger commentators, which is to take the locution "*das Wesen des Wortes*" as "the Being of Language," as if *Wesen* as being or essence could be rewritten as *Sein* or the Being of beings. I don't see any warrant in Heidegger's text

for the expression, "the Being of language." Bernasconi complains of Heidegger's ambiguity on this question, but it seems to me that Heidegger is simply being very careful not to say too much—is being careful not to use words to fill the gap left by the withdrawal of language. It is true that *logos,* as "the word for Saying, is also the word for *Being,* that is, for the presencing of beings" (US 237/155), but the whole point of the essay, "Das Wort," is to make us realize how little this tells us. Anyhow one point of my book is that the attempt to clarify the concept of *logos* won't shed any light on what poetry is for the later Heidegger, because poetry belongs to language in its withdrawal from the near into the remote. Poetry is the nearness of this withdrawal; it is what occurs in the experience with language (US 236/254). I want to add that my disagreement with Bernasconi's book doesn't lessen my admiration for it.

7 Rainer Schürmann takes these words as "prospective categories" in the "broken" history of being or presencing. And the idea is that "Past presencing is mute" (158). I found Schürmann's discussion of these "basic words of Greek thinking" some of the most interesting pages in his book (168–81), but it is important to take these pages in the context of Schürmann's whole project (a balancing act between Heidegger and philosophy), especially with a view toward his own proviso (which he puts as a rhetorical question, whereas I take the question as requiring an answer that we act on): "But is it not a monstrosity to draw categories, a system, a table even, from what Heidegger called 'thinking' precisely to oppose it to 'philosophy'? Thinking's 'good and therefore wholesome danger is the nighness of the singing poet.' But its 'bad and therefore muddled danger is philosophizing.' But a monstrosity indeed: the one that I have tried to encapsule in the phrase 'anarchy principle'. It inexorably stamps our age as hyperordered, oversystematized, and yet perhaps as capable of another birth, 'still unnamable, but which announces itself—and cannot but announce itself as is necessary each time a birth is in progress—in the species of a non-species, in the formless, mute, infant and terrifying form of monstrosity'" (162–63). Schürmann's quotations here are (appropriately) from Heidegger's own verse and from Jacques Derrida. Schürmann's effort to mediate the distance between thinking and philosophy is dramatic and compelling for the way in which he is constantly warding off monsters.

8 "The Path of the Stranger: On Heidegger's Interpretation of Georg Trakl," in *Review of Existential Psychology & Psychiatry* 17, nos. 2 and 3 (1986): 223–33.

9 "Whence, in Heidegger's discourse, the dominance of an entire metaphorics of proximity, of simple and immediate presence, a metaphorics associating the proximity of Being with the values of neighboring, shelter, house, service, guard, voice, listening" (MP 130).

10 The question of Derrida's reading of Heidegger, and of what it would be like to read Heidegger back at him, is worked through in a wonderfully

inventive fashion by John Caputo in the middle section of *Radical Herme-neutics*, where his purpose, he says, is "to set the text of Derrida over the text of Heidegger, letting each get entangled in the other—Heidegger in Derrida and Derrida in Heidegger—so that their texts interweave, each intertwined with the other, each showing signs of the other's intervention. In this way I propose a rewriting of Derrida from Heidegger's standpoint, a kind of double repetition, a productive double cross, a palimp-sestuous cross-semination which goes to the heart of what I mean by radical her-meneutics" (155).

11 Like Fred Dallmayr, I take Heidegger to be a philosopher of freedom, where freedom is no longer a property or achievement of the Kantian subject but rather an ontological condition to which we belong. See Dall-mayr, "Ontology of Freedom: Heidegger and Political Philosophy," *Politics and Praxis*, esp. 166–29. But it remains to be seen whether this notion of freedom can be made intelligible within the current possibilities of politi-cal reflection. For the ontological condition of freedom is something from which we are always inclined to withhold ourselves and against which we seek the protection of structures and systems. Reason frequently cannot distinguish it from anarchy. It is the historicality of being that always es-capes our control.

Index